THE EGO

FROM BIRTH
TO REBIRTH

THE NOTEBOOKS OF PAUL BRUNTON

(VOLUME 6)

THE EGO

FROM BIRTH TO REBIRTH

PAUL BRUNTON

(1898–1981)

An in-depth study of
categories eight and nine
from the notebooks

Published for the
PAUL BRUNTON PHILOSOPHIC FOUNDATION
by Larson Publications

International Standard Book Number (cloth) 0-943914-24-8
International Standard Book Number (paper) 0-943914-25-6
International Standard Book Number (series, cloth) 0-943914-17-5
International Standard Book Number (series, paper) 0-943914-23-X
Library of Congress Catalog Card Number: 86-82481

Manufactured in the United States of America

Published for the
Paul Brunton Philosophic Foundation
by
Larson Publications
4936 Route 414
Burdett, New York 14818

Distributed to the trade by
Kampmann and Company
9 East 40 Street
New York, New York 10016

88 90 91 89 87
2 4 6 8 10 9 7 5 3

CONTENTS

EDITORS' INTRODUCTION

This sixth volume in *The Notebooks of Paul Brunton* is an in-depth presentation of the eighth and ninth (of twenty-eight) categories in the personal notebooks Dr. Paul Brunton (1898–1981) reserved for posthumous publication.

Part 1, *The Ego*, is a unique and unprecedented contribution to the literature of self-realization. It goes to the root of the most fundamental and immediate problem facing those who would live with unfailing self-integrity. It confronts this problem at an existential, rather than merely a psychological, level. As such, it is a section the very reading of which can become a profitable spiritual exercise.

To make best use of the opportunity for lasting breakthrough which this section offers, the reader should recognize from the outset that this material abounds in information that the ego does not want its captive to hear. Further, every effort should be made to avoid premature judgements based on associations with other systems, especially psychological systems, where the word "ego" is used differently than here. Relentlessly probing and exploring, this section covers a broad range, and its content is not readily reducible to a neat, tidy structure within which the ego-mind can feel comfortable. From high praise at one extreme to utter denigration at the other, it offers many viewpoints, explores many facets of the complex ego's origin, nature, and destiny. In its entirety, it leads masterfully beyond ordinary intellectualizing and into the intuitive realm of paradox where kernels of deep spiritual realization are lodged.

In structuring the material for publication, we found that any linear structure we were capable of producing had serious limitations. The integrated wholeness of the insight behind this material demands being seen intuitively if it is to be seen clearly at all. The best approach we have seen is the one used by Anthony Damiani, a close and lifelong student of P.B. When first studying this section, he put individual paras on separate cards. He would read each one, then shuffle the "deck" randomly and read them all again. Reading in this way, he said, forced his mind to seek out and dwell in the insight behind the individual paras rather than in the associations his ego would construct between them.

What is true in general for reading *The Notebooks*, then, is especially true for reading the material in *The Ego*. The natural associative activity of the lower mind—its tendency to look for and make connections between paras—should be resisted, even suspended if possible, for the first few readings of the entire material. Individual paras should be *meditated upon* in and of themselves. The reader should *compel* his or her ego to let what is being said be heard.

Only after the entire range of viewpoints, the 360-degree perspective, has been assimilated will the radically transformative truths underlying surface contradictions gradually seep into the psyche and explain themselves. The reader's task for the present should be to savor each para, to take in each one as fully as possible. The inability to see readily how they can all fit together should not become a cause of anxious frustration. Careful study of the material will lead eventually to an integration, through Grace, of understanding at a deeper, now unconscious, level. In the meantime, we hope that the tentative structure we have provided for the purposes of publication in book form will at least not interfere with the working of the reader's intuition.

Part 2, *From Birth to Rebirth*, focuses on two great problems of philosophy—our death and our destiny. These issues are especially relevant to our further understanding of the ego, as it is the ego that recurrently is born and dies, and it is our conscious life in/as the ego which is affected by the laws of recompense and free will.

Chapter one discusses the event of death, in our own lives and in the lives of others. It offers practical advice on helpful attitudes towards death and on how we can approach the experience of dying. It examines after-death states, our limited contact with those already dead, and our permanent connection to the immortal Overself now, and then.

In Chapter two, P.B. reflects on the cycle of life and death, through a consideration of teachings on reincarnation. Here he explores how one's own past reappears in present character, is active in the conditions of birth, and is a significant factor in all subsequent experiences. Many beliefs and superstitions surround this ancient doctrine and its significance in the journey toward wisdom. P.B. sorts through various historical modifications with his usual rational perspective to provide us with a clear, if somewhat complex, treatment of the subject.

Chapter three is a collection of P.B.'s remarks on karma, fate, destiny, and free will. Several paras in its first section indicate that P.B. considered these first three terms as interrelated but distinct forces or cosmic laws involved in the shaping of our lives and egos. The chapter's emphasis is on our experience of these laws: how to recognize their presence, and how our interaction with them may—or may not—change our circumstances. In this context, P.B. introduces a philosophic consideration of astrology, showing what it teaches us, how it can be used to help us understand our destiny, and how it can be misused. The chapter ends with a selection of paras examining free will from the perspective of destiny.

The final chapter deals with the question of free will: its limitations and opportunities, and our responsibility to use it wisely. We see here that death and rebirth, karma, fate, destiny, and limited free will are powers that shape the ego and bind its development to the larger evolution of the World-Idea. The section ends with paras in which P.B. reminds us of our heritage in the Overself, wherein lies freedom, refuge, guidance, and our true home.

Editorial conventions with respect to the quantity of material chosen, as with respect to spelling, capitalization, hyphenation, and other copy-editing considerations, are the same as stated in introductions to earlier volumes. Likewise, (P) at the end of a para indicates that it is one of the relatively few paras we felt should be repeated here from *Perspectives*, the introductory survey volume to this series.

Once again we gratefully acknowledge the continuing dedicated and skilled assistance of many friends at Wisdom's Goldenrod and the Paul Brunton Philosophic Foundation. We are also profoundly grateful for the generosity and support of a growing number of *Notebooks* readers throughout the world. Without this kind of help, these volumes would not be coming into print at their current rate. Further information about publication schedules and related activities may be obtained from the

Paul Brunton Philosophic Foundation
P.O. Box 89
Hector, New York 14841

Part 1:
THE EGO

The danger of most pseudo-spiritual paths is that they stimulate the ego, whereas the authentic path will suffocate it.

The best measuring-stick for progress is, in earlier stages, the degree of disappearance of the ego's rule and, in later ones, the degree of disappearance of the ego itself.

1

WHAT AM I?

Egoself and Overself

That element in his consciousness which enables him to understand that he exists, which causes him to pronounce the words, "I Am," is the spiritual element, here called Overself. It is really his basic self for the three activities of thinking feeling and willing are derived from it, are ripples spreading out of it, are attributes and functions which belong to it. But as we ordinarily think feel and act, these activities do not express the Overself because they are under the control of a different entity, the personal ego.

2

The source of wisdom and power, of love and beauty, is within ourselves, but not within our egos. It is within our consciousness. Indeed, its presence provides us with a conscious contrast which enables us to speak of the ego as if it were something different and apart: it is the true Self whereas the ego is only an illusion of the mind.

3

Is it true that most men suffer from mistaken identity? That they are totally ignorant of the beautiful and virtuous, the aspirational and intuitive nature which is their higher self? The apathy which allows them to accept their lesser nature, their commonplace little self, must be found out for what it is.

4

Since the person a man is most interested in is himself, why not get to know himself as he really is, not merely as he appears to be?

5

Within every human entity there is a silent pull from within toward its centre, the real self. But alongside of this there is a stronger pull from without toward its instruments—the body's senses, the intellect, and the feelings—the false self. The entity is compelled to divide itself, its life and attention, between these two opposites, involuntarily through waking and sleeping, voluntarily through the ego surrendered to the Overself.

6

What is the ego but the Overself surrounded with barriers, conditioned by its instruments—the body, the feelings, and the intellect—and forgetful of its own nature?

7

The ego self is the creature born out of man's own doing and thinking, slowly changing and growing. The Overself is the image of God, perfect, finished, and changeless. What he has to do, if he is to fulfil himself, is to let the one shine through the other.(P)

8

Think! What does the "I" stand for? This single and simple letter is filled with unutterable mystery. For apart from the infinite void in which it is born and to which it must return, it has no meaning. The Eternal is its hidden core and content.

9

The ego is after all only an idea. It derives its seeming actuality from a higher source. If we make the inner effort to search for its origin we shall eventually find the Mind in which this idea originated. That mind is the Overself. This search is the Quest. The self-separation of the idea from the mind which makes its existence possible, is egoism.

10

What he takes to be his true identity is only a dream that separates him from it. He has become a curious creature which eagerly accepts the confining darkness of the ego's life and turns its back on the blazing light of the soul's life.

11

Once this question—*what am I?*—is answered, there are no other questions. In the light of its dazzling answer, he knows how to handle all his problems.

12

The self which gives him a personal consciousness is not his truest self.

13

What does a man regard as himself? It is the conscious centre of all that he thinks and experiences, feels and does.

14

This miserably limited, pathetically finite creature which calls itself man (root: Sanskrit *manas*, mind) knows so little of what it really is *because it does not know its own mind*.

15

This is the amazing contradiction of man's life, that although bearing the divine within himself, he is aware only of, and pursues unabated, its very opposite.

16

This is the paradox of human existence: the ego is yourself and the Overself is yourself, yet the first cannot easily contact the second.

17

A tremendous surprise comes when the Overself shows him to himself—when, for the first time, the ego can see what it is really like by a diviner light.

18

The "I" who looks at this world-spectacle must itself be looked at if we want to know the truth about both.

19

"I am not I." These words are nonsensical to the intellect, which can make nothing of them. But to awakened intuition they are perfectly comprehensible.

20

When, to this question, "What am I?" the full and final answer comes at last as an awakening from sleep, there comes with it a feeling of blessedness.

21

To most Western ears the advice, given as a universal panacea to suffering humanity by monastic hermits, not to trouble about anything except to "know the self" may sound fatuous and irritating. Yet there is deep wisdom in it.

22

It is hard to look upon the reality of one's own personality as a myth. Few are likely even to make the attempt, so undesirable does it seem. And there would be small chance of success if there were not a concurrent attempt at discovering the reality of the Overself, which is to displace the myth.

23

The personal ego derives its own light of consciousness and power of activity from the Overself.

24

The ego is put forth by the Overself.

25

The little ego is the only being he knows: the greater Being of philosophic Consciousness would be, and is, beyond his comprehension.

26

The ego moves through all the three states, but *Turiya* itself is motionless.

27

We must not confuse Atman with ego. The ego is produced, along with the non-ego world, by Atman.

28

The ego borrows its reality, its power of perception, its very capacity to be aware, from its association with the Overself.

29

The ego is a passing thing, but its source is not.

30

The mind has different layers between the outer surface consciousness and the inner fundamental consciousness. Those intermediate layers do not represent the true Self, and are, therefore, to be crossed and passed in the effort to know the true Self. For instance, some of the layers are conscious and others are subconscious; there are layers of memory and layers of desire; there are layers which are storehouses of the results of past experiences in earlier re-incarnations—they contain the habits and trends, complexes and associations which have come down from those earlier times. There are other layers which contain the past of the present reincarnation with its suggestions from heredity, from education, from upbringing, from environment, and from childhood. There are layers which are filled with the desires and hopes, the wishes and aspirations, and ambitions and passions of the ego. All these layers must be penetrated by the mystic and he must go deeper and deeper beneath them for none of them represent the true Self. He is not to permit himself to be detained in any of them. They are all within the confined sphere of the personal ego and in that sense they are part of the false self. Too often they detain the seeker on his path or distract him from his progress: to know the true Self is to know a state of being into which none of them enters.

31

Keep on thinking about the differences between the personal ego and the impersonal Overself until you become thoroughly familiar with them.

32

The true self of man is hidden in a central core of stillness, a central vacuum of silence. This core, this vacuum occupies only a pinpoint in dimension. All around it there is ring of thoughts and desires constituting the imagined self, the ego. This ring is constantly fermenting with fresh thoughts, constantly changing with fresh desires, and alternately bubbling with joy or heaving with grief. Whereas the centre is forever at rest, the ring around it is never at rest; whereas the centre bestows peace, the ring destroys it.(P)

33

The Overself-consciousness is reflected into the ego, which then imagines that it has its own original, and not derived awareness.(P)

34

Each man is three beings: one an animal, another a human entity, the third a spiritual one. Inner conflict is the result where all three are active.

35

It is an excellent question to put before any man—Who am I?—but it will need the accompaniment of another one—What am I?—if the beginner is to get an easier and fuller working of his mind's attempt to procure a less puzzling answer.

36

Why I chose "*What Am I*": (1) Because I wanted to start with the idea of a non-"I" consciousness instead of their own "I" with which they are continuously occupied; (2) Because the word Brahman is of neuter gender, neither masculine nor feminine. Brahman in us is Atman, the Self—but utterly impersonal. "What" lends itself more easily to this impersonality than "Who"; (3) The answer to "*What Am I?*" is multiple but it begins with "a part of the world!" and is followed by another question, "What is my relation to this world?" The answer requires the discovery of Mentalism, leading back through the thought of the world, thinker, and consciousness, to Brahman.

37

We have to distinguish constantly between the universal integrity of undivided being and the finite, individual ego with which that being is associated and for which it is consequently mistaken.

38

The answer to the question "What am I?" is "A divine Soul." This soul is related to, and rooted in, God. But that does not make us equivalent to God. Those who say so are using language carelessly.

39

The ego must be there, for it is needed to be active in this world; but it need not take sole charge of the man. There is this other, this higher Self too.

40

There are other forces at work in us besides those which everyone recognizes. Some are higher and nobler than our ordinary self, others lower and unworthier.

41

Ordinarily the ego is the agent of action. This is apparent. But if an enquiry is set going and its source and nature penetrated successfully, a surprising discovery about the "I" will be made. Its true energy is derived from non-I, pure being.

42

This unusual interrogation of himself, this demand to know *what he is*, may take a full lifetime of the deepest examination to satisfy.

43

Man is a point in the universal mind. As such he is alone, so that in the world he lives with others—quite near to them, yet quite apart.

44

Ramana Maharshi's frequent reference to the "I-I" simply means the Unchanging Self (as contrasted with the ever-changing ego).

45

The ego does not possess the final answer to our deepest questions, nor can it. We must look elsewhere.

46

Man is like an actor who has become so involved in the interpretation of his role that he has forgotten his original identity. It effectively prevents him from remembering who and what he is.

47

Not Descartes' formula "I think, therefore I am" but the mystic's "The Soul is within me, therefore I am." For Descartes' "I" is relative and changeful, whereas the mystic's is absolute and permanent.

48

If there were not something within a man higher than his little ego, he would never be brought to abnegate it as, on occasions, he does abnegate it.

49

The "I" knows itself as the Overself when it ceases to limit itself to the individual entity, thereby liberating its will to the full extent at last. Schrödinger's idea of the self is pure consciousness, or "ground stuff" upon which our personal experiences merely collect.

50

The essence of man is perfect, but the ego of man is not.

51

One's adventures in self-discovery will only fulfil themselves when he discovers that which is beyond the ego.

52

What is man's permanent identity? Is it not logical that when a man's mind is full of his "I" to overflowing, there can be no room for that which transcends it, the Overself?

53

Who is this being in the mirror? The reflected image of your body, comes the reply. So there I am! No, it continues, the body is only a part of you, that part which is the object receiving your attention. What about your awareness of it? *You* are having the experience of it. So who is this entity which is you? To get the further answer I found it necessary to engage in a twofold enterprise. First I had to think my way very carefully and deeply through a little piece of psychological philosophy which was hidden in the core of an Arabic tale which may have been the forerunner of our own English Robinson Crusoe, but which rose to a higher level of understanding and intuition. It was Ibn Tufail's *Awakening of the Soul*. Second I had to practise something quite opposed to thinking, something I came to call the Stillness.

54

There is the personal self within me. There is the impersonal Self or Overself also within me. We can react wrongly through the ego's limited outlook—or recognize the Overself.

55

Our real Self is not in movement or change or form. We have to identify with this unseen Self.

56

"Knowledge proceeds from 'What am I?' to 'I am.'"—Abu Hassan el-Shadhili the Sufi

57

Just as the Divine Being is both Mind-in-itself and Mind-in-activity, according to which aspect we look at, as well as Power-static and Power-dynamic, so its ray in man is Pure Being-Consciousness appearing as the mentally-active ego, as well as Life-Force appearing as physically-active body.

Body and consciousness

58

Neither the body with its senses nor the mind with its thoughts is the ultimate being that I am. The body acts and the mind moves, but behind them is the thought-free Awareness, the Knowing Principle.

59

The first great error to be thrown away is a common one—acceptance of the physical body as the real self when it is only an expression and channel, instrument and vehicle of the self.

60

Our every thought and mood suffers from body reference.

61

You have a body but the real *you* is not physical. You have an intellect but the real you is not intellectual. You have emotions but the real you is not emotional. What then are you? You are the infinite consciousness of the Overself.

62

The ego expresses desires and preferences, the intellect thinks and remembers, the body's sense organs experience and perceive the world outside. None of these three is the real "I"-ness of a man.

63

Too often we say that we are what we are by nature and heredity, but too often we leave out the more important ingredient of selfhood, the one most hidden and most elusive yet the very source of the personal life. That this omission is caused by ignorance, or by lack of any enlightening experience, is true, but does not pardon our inertia and apathy. For Consciousness gives us the "I," gives us the world, gives us wakefulness and sleep. It is the stuff of what we really are. Yet all we can say about it is to confuse it with a *thing*, the fleshly brain, and let it go at that dismissal.

64

As he understands himself to be, so will he understand the world to be. If he understands that he is only a material body, the world will appear to him likewise. If he finds no spiritual content in himself, he will not find it in the world either.

65

The body in which he dwells is not himself. The intellect with which he thinks is not himself. The consciousness by which he utters "I" *is* himself.

66

This ability to utter the pronoun "I"—to comprehend that he is himself and no one else—vouches for a consciousness which transcends "I" and supports himself.

67

It is a one-sided view which sees man as only a physical being or only a mental being. Nor is it even quite correct to see him as having these two as separate aspects. He is both at once, a psycho-physical being.

68

The body is a thought-complex which I have, and as a thought it is certainly part of myself. But that does not make it properly me.

69

There is something in each man which says "I." Is it the body? Usually he thinks so. But if he could set up a deeper analysis, he would find that consciousness would carry him away from the body-thought into itself. There, in its own pure existence, he would find the answer to his question, "Who am I?"

70

This sense, force, or feeling within him, which calls itself *I*, has its innermost part in that which observes it, the Overself.

71

Everyone can give his assent to the statement that his physical environment is not himself, but it requires great penetration to give his assent to the equally true statement that his thoughts are not himself.

72

The "I" is *not* a thought at all. It is the very principle of Consciousness itself, pure Being. It is neither personal mind nor physical body, neither ego nor little self. Without it they could not exist or function. It is their witness.

73

We all think, experience, feel, and identify with the "I." But who really knows what it is? To do this we need to look inside the mind, not at what it contains, as psychologists do, but at what it is in itself. If we persevere, we may find the "I" behind the "I."(P)

74

It would be wrong to believe that there are two separate minds, two independent consciousnesses within us—one the lower ego-mind, and the other, the higher Overself-mind—with one, itself unwatched, watching the other. There is but one independent illuminating mind and everything else is only a limited and reflected image within it. The ego is a thought-series dependent on it.(P)

75

The mystery of personality can be solved if we will first grant that there can be but one real self. Once this is granted, it will be seen that anything else claiming to be the personality can only be a false self.

76

The ego has no totally separate existence because its thoughts and flesh come to it as much from outside as from inside itself.

77

The Overself abides in the void within the heart. From it springs the ego's sense of "I." Only, the ego misconceives its own nature and misplaces the "I" as the body.

78

There is only a single light of consciousness in the mind's camera. Without it the world could not be photographed upon the film of our ego-mind. Without it, the ego-mind itself would be just as blank. That light is the Overself.

79

If only he could become aware of his own awareness!

80

How could anyone say he experienced the world unless he were separate from it and could interact with it? But this truth must be extended to include his body which, although less obviously so, is something likewise experienced and felt. In his error he identifies himself with his body when there must be an experiencing Principle, something that feels the world and the body as being there and that must therefore be other and apart from them. This Principle is, and can only be, the stable Self, the real and permanent of a man.

81

The person is simply the totalized collection of all the thought-forms of experience throughout the day. That element in all these ever-altering thought-forms which does not alter but remains fixed throughout is the pure awareness of them.

82

We must indeed make a distinction between the conscious self which is so tied to the body and the superconscious self which is not got at or grasped by the bodily senses.

83

Psychoanalysts who have looked into man's deeper nature and found only sexual impulses or racial complexes need to look deeper still.

84

In my capacity as an author, when sitting at the desk using a pen, the term "I" identifies me with the body; but in my capacity as a creator of the thoughts expressed in the writing, it identifies me with the mind. It is quite proper to use the term in both cases, but which of the references is *I* myself? Moreover, when I sleep and dream recurringly of living in France during the Revolutionary period, the term "I" is still appropriated to the figure saved from the guillotine, for who is the dreamer but myself? My sense of the *I* changes with each of these situations. But looking more closely into them, one thing emerges as being common to all the "I"s—consciousness!

85

Consciousness ordinarily believes itself to be limited to the physical body. This belief it calls "I," it claims to be the "I." That they are associated together is unquestionable. But further enquiry will yield a further and startling result: it functions *through* the body and to that extent the connection gives life to the body, thus creating the belief that it is the body when in reality it only permeates it. What happens is that a part (the body) is imposing itself upon the whole (the consciousness).

86

Normal experience leads a man to identify with his body but he fails to go farther and deeper to ask himself: "Who is present in the body?"

87

Much depends on what meaning we put to this word "self." We can put a lesser or a larger one, a shallow or a deeper one, a false or a true one.

88

With his thoughts and feelings centered in the body, a man's self is still not complete nor even as real as it seems to be.

89

He is but a member of the human ant-colony lodged on a tiny speck in the solar system, which is itself a microscopic dot in the galaxy of the Milky Way. This would be perfectly true if he were nothing more than his physical body.

90

Is man nothing more than a little animal made perverse and corrupt by the growth of intellect? This is a shallow concept of the human entity.

91

The final "I" is not the "I" of the senses nor of the desires but a deeper entity, free and unattached, serene and self-sufficient.

92

Nineteenth-century materialistic science gave birth to materialistic doctrines that man is governed by physical forces alone and that his history is shaped only by physical events, his destiny determined by physical surroundings. This is only partly true and confines man to animal interests. Ideas and ideals, beliefs, also contribute to his making.

93

This same religious or occult materialism is often carried into so-called spiritual thinking when it is propounded and believed that the soul is an immaterial duplicate of the body.

94

He is no more to be identified with his body than Dr. Samuel Johnson was with his soup-stained coat. But the coat was still part of the scholar's personality.

95

Mental attitude is all-important. He may respond to either suggestion—that he is the feeble ego or that he is the divine Overself; it is a matter of where he puts his faith.

96

The ultimate goal is to regard oneself as *primarily* a mental being and not a physical one, to cease this idolatrous identification of self with flesh, blood, and bone.

I-sense and memory

97

How is it that I am—and know that I am—substantially the same man today as yesterday, that I remember the happenings of a year ago? The answer must be that there is a continuous self, or being, or mind, in me, distinct from its thoughts or experiences.

98

Neither deep sleep nor brain concussion prevents us from recovering the sense of "I" when they end.

99

If we look for the self in this jumble of contradictory instincts and changing tendencies, we find only a jumble. These things are the *content* of awareness, not the *faculty* of awareness.

100

Even the shell-shocked soldier who suffers from an almost total amnesia, forgetting his personal identity and personal history, does not suffer from any loss of the consciousness that *he exists*. Its old ideas and images may have temporarily or even permanently vanished, but the mind itself carries on.

101

The senses may trick us with a physical illusion, but can the self trick us with a mental one? Is not the one certain fact which does not depend upon the sense's experience the fact that we exist as individuals and consciously exist? Is not the right to say "I am" the one certainty which cannot be dispelled, the one truth which cannot be denied?

Ego as limitation

102

The personal ego of man forms itself out of the impersonal life of the universe like a wave forming itself out of the ocean. It constricts, confines, restricts, and limits that infinite life to a small finite area. The wave does just the same to the water of the ocean. The ego shuts out so much of the power and intelligence contained in the universal being that it seems to belong to an entirely different and utterly inferior order of existence. The wave, too, since it forms itself only on the surface of the water gives no indication in its tiny stature of the tremendous depth and breadth and volume of water beneath it.

Consider that no wave exists by itself or for itself, that all waves are inescapably parts of the visible ocean. In the same way, no individual life can separate itself from the All-Life but is always a part of it in some way or other. Yet the idea of separateness is held by millions. This idea is an illusion. From it springs their direct troubles. The work of the quest is simply this: to free the ego from its self-imposed limitations, to let the wave of conscious being subside and straighten itself out into the waters whence it came. The little wave is thus reconverted into the infinite Overself.

103

It is ludicrous if that part of the mind which is only within the personal consciousness, the ego, sets itself up to deny the Mind-in-itself—its own very Source. For the ego is shut in what it experiences and knows—a much limited area.

104

Advaita Vedanta's tenet that the divine spirit has been overpowered by ignorance is unacceptable to philosophy. What the latter would say is that something has come out of or emanated from the divine spirit and it is this that has been overpowered by ignorance. But the divine spirit itself remains quite untouched. That "something" is the ego and it is like the image in a mirror. Although the image is not the object itself, yet it draws its existence from the object. But whatever happens to it does not affect the object.

105

Yes, we *are* that Consciousness. But we restrict it to the forms it takes, while we constrict ourselves in the ideas it produces; we shorten and narrow them down to the ego's thoughts.

106

The supreme quality and august immensity of Mind cannot be cramped into the little ego, nor its truth into the latter's falsity.

107

When it is said that separateness is the great sin, this does not refer to one's relation with other human beings. It refers to having separated oneself in thought from one's higher self.

108

The mind must be freed from its false beliefs. The illusion which darkens it most is that the *I* which is most familiar is real. A lifetime of wrong thinking and deluded faith has brought it to enslavement by error, conjecture, and opinion. The way out demands courage to tread new paths and sharp intelligence to comprehend true identity. The personal *I* separates itself from the real *I*, misinterprets Reality, ignorant that it is itself but a thought in the ALL-MIND.

109

Even irreproachable conduct and impeccable manners belong to the ego and not to the enlightenment.(P)

110

We draw the very capacity to live from the Overself, the very power to think from the same source. But we confine both the capacity and the power to a small, fragmentary, and mostly physical sphere. Within this confinement the ego sits enthroned, served by our senses and pandered by our thoughts.(P)

111

This narrow fragment of consciousness which is the person that I am hides the great secret of life at its core.

112

The Infinite Mind refuses to be personalized, and we shut it down to the ego only by shutting it out altogether.

113

Whoever enters into the philosophic experience for the first time and thus penetrates into the real nature of the ego, discovers to his surprise that instead of being a centre of life as it pretends to be it is really a centre of death—for it immensely minimizes, obstructs, and shuts out the undisclosed life-current in man.

114

Thoughts rise and fall on the surface of consciousness just like waves on the ocean. Both thoughts and waves disappear again into their source. The ego is a totality of strongly held thoughts with a long ancestry behind them. So it too dissolves eventually into the universal mind. Its supporting consciousness is not lost, is this same permanent Mind. The personal self is an individualization of this mind. It did not emerge from nothing and therefore cannot go back into nothing when it dies; it dies into this living Universal Mind, is absorbed by it.

115

Being cannot cease; this immortality is possible because of its universality. But its projection, the little personal ego, *can* cease.

116

We take part of the human being for the whole being, and then wonder why human happiness is so elusive and human wisdom so rare.

117

The lower part of man's mind which calculates, analyses, criticizes, blames, and organizes is the part which has no understanding of divine principles, and therefore its plannings are frequently futile. Man has no business to limit himself to the lower mind, and when he understands this he will leave his future in the hands of God, and then his real needs will be met.

118

What anyone sees of other persons is neither their essential being, their most important part, nor their best part, but only something which is being used for self-expression under greatly limited, deceptive, and obscuring conditions.

119

It is an irony of life that a man can plainly see the physical ego, but that on which it depends for existence, the Overself, he does not see. Therefore he neglects or ignores the attention it needs and misses much of the opportunity that a reincarnation offers to further his inner unfoldment.

120

The egocentric view of ordinary men is not final. One day they will evolve to the cosmic view.

121

In one sense, the ego is a corruption of divine consciousness, as well as a diminution of it.

122

The ordinary human consciousness has been imposed on a diviner one and hides it, covers it by monopolizing all the attention of thought and feeling.

123 ✓

Whatever imperfections or blemishes we find in the universe, we must always remember that we are making a judgement, a human judgement—and therefore one from a limited point of view.

124

Beneath the little "I" stretches the universal Consciousness.

Ego as presence of higher

125

There is no need to lament our situation as an ego confronted by a world, as a duality, as a self aspiring—often vainly—to its Overself.

126 ✓

Only by looking deeper, on another level, in another dimension, can we see that this pitiful creature, this feeble-willed flesh-subservient ego-limited human is not less a showing forth of the Divine Mind, a fragment of the World-Idea, than any other of Its expressions.

127

The ego to which he is so attached turns out on enquiry to be none other than the presence of World-Mind within his own heart. If identification is then shifted by constant practice from one to the other, he has achieved the purpose of life.

128

What we find as the attributes of the ego are a reflected image, limited and changing, of what we find in the Overself. They ultimately depend on the Overself both for their own existence and their own nature.

129

However badly we all reflect the Overself in the personality, however tiny broken and distorted the reflected image usually is, still it *is* a reflection. It is within the capacity of all to make it a better one, and within the capacity of a few to make it a perfect one.

130

Let them not waste so many words about or against this little ego of ours, decrying its character or denying its existence, but try to understand what is really happening in its short life. Let them find out what is actually being wrought out within and around it. Let them recognize that the Governor of the World is related to it and that we are steeped in the Divinity whether we are aware of it or not.

131

It is not quite correct to assume that we are the manifested forms of the perfection from which we emanate. More precisely, we are projections of a denser medium from the universal mind, appearing by some catalytic process in natural sequence within that medium. The cosmic activity provides each such entity-projection with an individual life and intelligence centre through an evolutionary process, whereby its own volitional directive energies are, ultimately, merged with the cosmic will in perfect unity and harmony.

132

The importance which he gives his own ego is not baseless. It derives, if traced to the deepest ground, from the Overself. He has misplaced his true identity but the false one is not entirely so.

133

Here, in the miserably limited ego, we have a "sign" of the gloriously unlimited Overself, an indication that it is present as the very source.

134 ✓

If we could pin down this sense of "I"-ness which is behind all we think, say, and do, and if we could part it from the thoughts, feelings, and physical body by doing so, we would find it to be rooted in and linked with the higher Power behind the whole world.(P)

135

The ego's consciousness is a vastly reduced, immeasurably weakened echo of the Overself-Consciousness. It is always changing and dissipates in the end whereas the Other is ever the same and undying. But the ego is drawn out of the Other and must return to it, so the link is there. What is more, the possibility of returning voluntarily and deliberately is also there.

136 ✓

Unless the human ego were itself an emanation of the Overself it would be quite unable to identify itself with the sensation of severance from the body during the process we call dying.

137

This thing which the Overself has projected in space-time has not lost all link with its source, whatever outward appearances suggest to the contrary.

138

Just as a shadow bespeaks a light, so the ego bespeaks its source in the Overself.

139

The personality is rooted in the Overself. Hence its own power and movement do reflect, albeit minutely, slightly, and distortedly, some of the Overself's own attributes.

140

Expressed in more familiar religious language, it may be said that God has put something of Himself into each one of us. But it is there only as a potential; we must make the necessary effort to make ourselves more and more conscious of it.

Two views of individuality

141

The essence of his human personality is a divine individuality.

142

The "I" of the ego is supported by the "I" of the spiritual being, the spiritual self. Indeed the first derives its reality from the second and the second survives when the first passes away.

143

The personal ego has its singularities and particularities, its present aims and past memories, its life within time, its own temperament and special characteristics. All this amounts to this: it is unique. The individuality is the highest, subtlest, and finest, even divinest part of being. It is out of time. It is pure essence, the other is a compounded entity. For it the hours do not pass; for the other there is a constant sequence, a moment-to-moment existence. Sometimes men catch a glimpse of it, this other self which is really their own best self and which is not something to be attained by a progression since it is forever present. It does not have or need thoughts. Every moment which they give to identifying themselves with it is their salvation. If this takes one far from kith and kin, from all speech with all persons, it also carries him into a diviner relationship and communication with them.

144

As egos they are certainly individual lives and beings. Their separateness is unquestionable. But as manifestations of the One Infinite Life-Power, their separateness from It is a great illusion.

145

It is what stands behind the individual, and not the individual himself, that really matters.

146

The whirling dervish who revolves on his own axis while, at the same time, revolving in a larger circle with his fellow dervishes, is symbolic of the ego's own centricity side by side with its unconscious evolutionary movement.

147

Whether I look within or without, the "I" is found to be my centre. This statement keeps true whether I descend into the narrowest limits of selfish personality or ascend to the widest freedom of will; from the lesser nature to the highest and noblest, the ego changes its nature but not its centrality.

148 ✓

Losing the ego is to surrender it to a higher Power, but to lose the individuality is not the same.

149

The ego is the centre of human individuality.

150

That which separates a man from others, which makes him a person, an individual being, is his ego.

151

Could he be minutely examined it would be found that each human being was uniquely individual, with his own intrinsic essential character, his own inborn ways, compulsions, and tendencies. The human species is infinitely varied.

152 ✓

No one ego is exactly the same in characteristics and outlook as any other ego in the whole world. Each is unique, stamped with its own individuality. But all egos are exactly the same in this, that their attachment to the "I" and their consciousness of self are overpowering.

153

The conscious thinker, the "I," the ego.

154

One's ego, oneself, "I," lies behind and beneath thoughts and acts, feelings and passions.

155

The individual man, the person that he is, is unique: he is distinct from others in form and character, separate from others in existence. He is himself, his own self with his own aura.

156

His individuality must be noted if he is a separate human being. Outwardly all differ but in the deepest root of consciousness all are the same.

157

A student said, "How can anyone—however much he is spiritually self-realized—say that he has no ego? For without it how could he function in this world? It is the ego which tells the body what do do—raise a hand, walk, and so on." What he could properly say is that it has become a channel. But to avoid confusion it would be better to call this channel, "the individuality."

Perfection through surrender

158 ✓

How can man fully express himself unless he fully develops himself? The spiritual evolution which requires him to abandon the ego runs parallel to the mental evolution which requires him to perfect it.

159 ✓

Despite all the talk disparaging the ego, it is not wrong but praiseworthy to develop the best personality one can and then use it. Its character can be purified, its passions controlled, its weaknesses overcome, its ignorance dispelled. New virtues can be introduced and new power developed. One can then make better use of such a personality—for one's own advantage and for service of others—and one should.

160

He must learn to transcend his own ego, and yet demand his place and keep his balance in the world; to transcend his family's egoism, and yet respect their dues and rights.

161

All experiences play their part in developing the whole consciousness of the ego. In the earlier stages this development is limited to seeing, hearing, smelling, tasting, and feeling things; but in the later stages it expands to understanding them. Still later, the ego's attention is turned to its own self and, through the intuitive faculty, learns to recognize the hidden creative principle which brought it forth.

162 ✓

We came to this earth to understand ourselves, bit by bit.

163

This very egocentricity has prepared the way for its own collapse, and thence for the spiritual mentality which transcends it and which is next to be developed.

164

If, on the one side, philosophy bids him follow the line of Nature in building up the ego and developing all these four elements of his personality—will, thought, feeling, and intuition—on the other side it paradoxically bids him to negate all personality. If the ego is to be accepted because it cannot be destroyed, it is still to be mastered and its hold destroyed.

165

The ego is a part of the divine order of existence. It must emerge, grow, enslave, and finally be enslaved.

166

This is the paradox, or irony, of evolution: that first the ego grows into full being through plant, animal, and human form; then it reverses the objective and assents to its own alteration and death.

167✓

The paradox of the human situation is a tremendous one. He has to give up the self-life and yet to develop the self-nature. He has to crush the ego's desires and yet permit its fullness to unfold.

168

If the teaching minifies the importance of the human ego in certain ways, nevertheless it magnifies the sense of human worth in other ways.

169 ✓

If he will stop looking at his own life from the shut-in standpoint of his little ego and instead look at it from the wide-angle standpoint of its place in the reincarnationary cycle of development, it will become filled with new meanings, rich with higher significances. To bring his personal idea into alignment with the World-Idea will then become both his duty and his happiness.

170

Is it not ironical that the Overself projects the ego so far that it denies its source, and then waits indefinitely for the ego to give itself back?

171

It is time to talk of impoverishing the ego—let alone of annihilating it—when the ego has become developed and enriched enough to have something to offer or to lose. It is also time to talk of renouncing the world when there are enough worldly possessions or personal attachments, or enough position, to make renunciation a real sacrifice.

172 ✓

After the physical, intellectual, aesthetic, and spiritual capacities of the ego have been developed, then it is the correct time to renounce, not before. But the selfishness and indiscipline of the ego may and should be renounced at any time.

173

When the ego discovers that it is a part of the whole, it will naturally cease to live only for its own good and begin to live for the general good also.

174

If the earlier experiences of life are intended to develop the ego from the primitive animalistic to the fully humanistic stage, the later experiences are intended to induce the man to give the ego as an offering to the Overself.

175

The ego is not in itself evil, but what seems to make it so is its refusal to recognize and then take its subordinate place to the Overself, which it ought to serve.

176

If it is true, the human equipment has to be sufficiently developed and sensitive to be capable of recognizing it as such. Not only that, but the human willingness to accept self-discipline in thought and deed must also be present if it is to be a *lived* truth, that is, Egohood. Without these conditions, it is still possible to find a fraction if the whole is rejected. There is a risk here in that case of distortion and adulteration to suit the ego's desires, but a full and frank sincerity may avoid it.

177

Although Nature's unfoldment of the ego first blinds it with ignorance, her further unfoldment enlightens it with knowledge.

Ego subordinated, not destroyed

178

When the consciousness of true and real primary being is finally discovered, thought out, and felt as himself, the secondary being need not be disowned, denied existence and suppressed, as so often taught. But because of its tyranny, its usurpation certainly must be stopped and its proper secondary place imposed upon it; and because of its ignorance a re-education into mentalism must also be imposed upon it.

179

It is not so much a matter of destroying the ego as of balancing it with the Overself, for its need of development must be recognized. Such an act will not give it equal power but put it in its proper place, as a child's individuality needs to be balanced with its parents'.

180

(1) How, why, and to what extent is ego real? (2) It is absurd to dismiss ego as non-existent when without it no individual experience would be

possible, since it includes the physical body. (3) Semantic confusion is here when Advaitic statements dismiss it and deny the world. "Who denies his own existence is a fool." —The Dalai Lama

181

Every individual life from the mighty elephant down to the microscopic cell is a self-evolving entity moving through time and space. It has meaning, a purpose, and eventually, a fulfilment here. Why then talk of destroying the one with which you are most intimate—your own ego?

182

Is the ego to be built up through so many lives only that it may be destroyed in the end?

183

To free himself, for however short a period, from the consciousness of self may seem an impossible achievement. But the statement of it often leads to a confused understanding and needs to be more narrowly confined. It applies to the surrender of personal consciousness to the impersonal Overself consciousness. There is some kind of self in both.

184

The ego will not end its existence but it will end its dominance.

185

Nothing can annihilate the ego during the body's lifetime, but its function can be reduced to one of mere subservience to the Overself.

186

The ego must live in the world, must satisfy its needs out of its environment. It is therefore entitled to its point of view. The mistake lies in tyrannically making that the only point of view.

187

This widely held concept that the ego is (a) man's biggest enemy, and (b) a non-existent non-thing, vanishes with his newer insight. "A" is an idea which arises with the beginner's glimpse. "B" arises when an attempt to communicate with others is made, for it ends in a miscommunication; no words can be fully accurate when describing what is a paradox, a bafflement for human intellect. Silence alone holds truth. "A" can be corrected later but is a useful stage if not allowed to become a stop. "B" is a concept expressed in words and reaching someone else who tries to turn it into his own thoughts. But just as consciousness seems non-existent after entering deep sleep, so ego can be lulled and lost; but, like consciousness, it returns later. What happens, then, if the man really is absorbed into the Overself? The ego is put into its place, the little circle finds itself held in, and surrounded by, the larger seemingly measureless one. It is no longer the despotic ruler. Its tyranny is gone. It sees the game being played out, the scene being enacted, yet the initiative no longer comes from itself but henceforth from the World-Mind. If the Great Teachers preach its denial, that is their way of persuading others into self-control morally and self-detachment intellectually.

188 ✓

At every point of his progress the ego still functions—except in deep, thought-free contemplation, when it is suppressed—but it becomes by well-defined stages a better and finer character, more and more in harmony with the Overself. But total relinquishment of the ego can happen only with total relinquishment of the body, that is, at death.

189 ✓

The highest goal of the quest is not illumination gained by destruction of the ego but rather by perfection of the ego. It is the function of egoism which is to be destroyed, not that which functions. The ego's rulership is to go, not the ego itself.(P)

190

In all human activity the ego plays its role, and so long as this activity continues the ego continues. There is much confusion and much misunderstanding about this point. We are told to kill out the ego; we are also told that the ego does not exist. The fact is it must exist if activity exists. What then is to be done by the spiritual aspirant? He can bring and eventually must bring the ego into subjection to the higher Power. It is still there, but it is put in its proper place. Now why are we told to kill out the ego if it is not possible? The answer is that it is possible, but only in what is the deepest point of meditation, called *nirvikalpa* in Sanskrit, where all thoughts are blotted out, all sense reports cease to exist, and a kind of trancelike condition comes into being. In this condition, the ego is unable to exist; it becomes inoperative, but it is certainly not killed or it would not return again after the condition ends as it must end. It does not really help to assert that the ego does not exist or if it does exist that it must be killed. The fact is it must be taken into account by everybody who seeks the higher life; whatever theories he entertains about the ego, it is there, must be reckoned with, must be confronted. Some of the confusion is due to the fact that the ego is a changing thing; it changes with time and experience, whereas the Infinite Being, the Ultimate, is changeless. In that sense reality cannot be ascribed to the ego, but only in that ultimate sense. We however are living down here, in time and in space, and to ignore that fact is to cultivate intellectual deaf and dumbness.(P)

191

An ego we have, we are; its existence is inescapable if the cosmic thought is to be activated and the human evolution in it is to develop. Why has it become, then, a source of evil, friction, suffering, and horror? The energy and instinct, the intelligence and desire which are contained in each individualized fragment of consciousness, each compounded "I," are not originally evil in themselves; but when the clinging to them becomes extreme, selfishness becomes strong. There is a failure in equilibrium and the gentler virtues are squeezed out, the understanding that others have rights, the feeling of goodwill and sympathy, accommodation for the common welfare—all depart. The natural and right attention to one's needs becomes enlarged to the point of tyranny. The ego then exists only to serve itself at all costs, aggressive to, and exploitive of, all others. It must be repeated: an ego there must be if there is to be a World-Idea. But it has to be put, and kept, in its place (which is not a hardened selfishness). It must adjust to two things: to the common welfare and to the source of its own being. Conscience tells him of the first duty, whether heeded or not; Intuition tells him of the second one, whether ignored or not. For, overlooked or misconstrued, the relation between evil and man must not hide the fact that the energies and intelligence used for evil derive in the beginning from the divine in man. They are Godgiven but turned to the service of ungodliness. This is the tragedy, that the powers, talents, and consciousness of man are spent so often in hatred and war when they could work harmoniously for the World-Idea, that his own disharmony brings his own suffering and involves others. But each wave of development must take its course, and each ego must submit in the end. He who hardens himself within gross selfishness and rejects his gentler spiritual side becomes his own Satan, tempting himself. Through ambition or greed, through dislike or hate which is instilled in others, he must fall in the end, by the Karma he makes, into destruction by his own negative side.(P)

192

This does not mean destroy the ego—as if anyone could!—but destroy its tyranny, harmonize its personal will with that of the World-Idea.

193

The ego may be suppressed but not eradicated, as when a person is used by the higher power to give a message, a guidance, or a revelation.

194

At every stage of this quest, from that of the veriest postulant who has just entered upon it to that of the well-advanced proficient, the need of subduing the ego is ever-present.

195

The separateness of the person is denounced as illusory by the Hindu *Upanishads* and most Buddhist texts; but as an illusion it is still there, still experienced, still lived. This is the peculiar predicament of the human being. Let us not make it more complicated, more enigmatic, by denying this experience which all of us have, rishees and unenlightened alike. Let us see things as they are: this will not diminish our higher nature or lessen our spiritual dignity. Why not accept it for what it is, but put it in its lowly place?

196

The loose talk about detachment from the ego coming from modern expounders or propagandists, both Eastern and Western, of the ancient "philosophy" is sometimes delusory, sometimes derisory, too often illusory, and too seldom practised or practicable. These persons are theoreticians, dreamers, who use their own egos to tell others to get rid of theirs! As if anyone could! But what one can do—and ought to—with the ego is beyond their wisdom. For, being based on the philosophy of truth, it is the only practicable way. When examined, the ego is found to be a complex of body and thought, physical senses and mental tendencies. Preaching to men that they should detach themselves from all these things is usually wasted energy, for the consciousness is so linked with them that it cannot be taken away from them. How could anyone be active in the world without them! Detachment—if full and real—would mean having no awareness of the world: the ego is a necessary part of existence. If a man were utterly freed from his ego, he would become utterly unable to attend to the ordinary affairs of his own existence! But let us turn aside from this nonsense and look at the body and the world in the light of the philosophy of truth. We learn that they are only appearances within the personal experience, that at the end this is mental despite its solidity and intensity, that the "I" is reducible to a single thought, that its relation to, and dependence on, its real being and essence can be brought to light, that the mind can then be re-educated and controlled so that the ego falls back into its proper place, no longer tyrannizing over him. This may happen by itself in a sudden sunburst or, more likely, slowly, imperceptibly, and subtly. This process can be called detachment and his work is to co-operate with it. But remember: the understanding gained from reflection upon the philosophy of truth, combined with the meditations prescribed by it, detaches him naturally. There is no forced, artificial, and false effort.

197

There is much confusion about this matter of the ego and much looseness in the use of words concerning it. We are told to eliminate the ego and to eradicate the personal self. But the fact is that so long as he is upon this earth he is using a body and a mind and inheriting a whole combination of factors, tendencies, characteristics which have come down from former lives and together now constitute his personality. They will still be present so long as he is alive. To destroy the ego completely would necessarily mean to destroy the physical body, which is a part of it, and to remove his particular individuality which sets him apart from others. This cannot be done, but what can be done is to render the ego subservient to the higher self, an obedient instrument of the higher will.

198

Perhaps one day some bright mind will write a book entitled *Inspired Egoism* to bring people into the understanding that the ego too has its place in the scheme of things. It is the little circle within the larger one of the Overself, and if it remains conscious of its true relationship to the Overself, it may still rest there and carry on with its functions.

199

Despite all religious preachments and moralizing arguments, all intellectual analytical dissertations, does not the ego seem an irreducible and irresistible element in human nature? Despite all the tall talk which has issued from the institutions or glibly flowed from the mouths of those concerned with religion, mysticism, and metaphysics, the ego still remains as the very foundation of their own existence, their own activity. The very person who denies its reality must use an ego to make his denial!

200

For a man to deny himself may seem to be the denial of all that is human. But this is not necessarily so, except where imbalance or fanaticism reigns. No one in fact escapes his humanity: he only ennobles, debases, twists, or shrivels it.

201 ✓

Philosophy denies to the ego the final rulership of man but allows to the ego the necessary activities of man. How else can he live in this world? The ego may stay in its proper place attending to the needs and sustenance of his body and intellect, but always as a subordinate to the higher self and obeisant to the higher will.

202

From a long-range view, individual consciousness is not lost. There are times when it is attenuated temporarily and even plunged into complete oblivion for a while. This happens both during life in the body and out of it. When, as through a blow or through being gassed, it vanishes, it has merely gone into a latent state and will be revived again.

203

Jung believed that the meditational effort to transcend the personal ego would end in utter oblivion because without it all awareness would vanish. In this he erred and, I believe, in the last years of his life changed his view.

204

Without the ego how could we live and act our role in this world? It is a tool which we use. A man whose ego has broken down and collapsed is usually considered insane and is segregated.

205 ✓

What is wrong with the idea of personality if it is correctly understood, if its signs and patterns are kept down to inferior status? Let it be accepted as a changing passing thing, if you like; let it always be subservient to the ever-present reality of Overself: but why fear its expression?

206

It is both true and untrue that we cannot take up the ego with us into the life of mystical illumination. The ego is after all only a reflection, extremely limited and often distorted, of the Higher Self . . . but still it *is* a reflection. If we could bring it into correct alignment with, and submission to, the Higher Self, it would then be no hindrance to the illumined life. The ego cannot, indeed, be destroyed so long as we need its services while in the flesh; but it can be subjugated and turned into a servant instead of permitting it to remain a master. When this is understood, the philosophical ideal of a fully developed, mastered, and richly rounded ego acting as a channel for the inspiration and guidance of the Higher Self will be better appreciated. A poverty-stricken ego will naturally form a more limited channel for the expression of the Higher Self than would a more evolved one. The real enemy to be overcome is not the entity ego, but the function of egoism. (P)

Ego after illumination

207

Is the ego totally lost, utterly obliterated in this attainment? I can only say that none of our usual concepts fit the actual result, that it is hard to describe, and that suggestion must here replace description. For the ego and the Overself fuse and unite, yet the union does not destroy the ego's capacity to express itself or to be active in the world. Its own annihilation is a transient experience during the contemplative state. Its resumption of worldly life while permanently established in perfect harmony with, and obedience to, the divine Overself is the further and final goal.

208

If a man could withdraw sufficiently from his ego to stop letting its interests and desires overpower him, he would thereby let peace come to triumph in his heart. The true paradise, the real heavenly kingdom, which has been postponed by an ignorant clergy to the post-mortem world, thus becoming far-off and elusive, is in fact as near to us as our own selves, and as present as today. If we are to enter it, we can and must enter while yet in the flesh. It is not a time or place but a state of life and a stage of development. It is the ego-free life. The ego is not asked to destroy itself but to discipline itself. The personal in a man must live, but only as a slave to the impersonal. These two identities make up his self.

209

If the ego continues to perform its functions, as it needs must even after Fulfilment, it no longer does so as his master, no longer as his very self. For henceforth it obeys the Overself.

210

For the man in that high consciousness and identified with it, the ego is simply an open channel through which his being may flow into the world of time and space. It is not himself, as it is for the unenlightened man, but an adjunct to himself, obeying and expressing his will.

211

At such a stage the ego becomes a mere instrument, put down or picked up at any and every moment by the Overself. No longer are its own thoughts, emotions, desires, or lusts in control; instead, they are fully controlled by the higher power.

212

He will possess the power to dismiss his ego at will.

213

The ego totally ceases to exist and is fully absorbed into the Overself only in special, temporary, and trance-like states. At all other times, and certainly at all ordinary active and everyday times, it continues to exist. The failure to learn and understand this important point always causes much confusion in mystical circles. The state arrived at in deep meditation is one thing; the state returned to after such meditation is another. The ego vanishes in one but reappears in the other. But there are certain after-effects of this experience upon it which bring about by degrees a shift in its relation to the Overself. It submits, obeys, expresses, and reflects the Overself.

214

When he clearly realizes and intensely feels that his ego is non-existent, unreal, and fictitious, how can he assert that he has found God, Truth, or

Illumination? For he will then just as clearly see that there is no one to make the assertion. The others who do so, thereby show that they still have an ego; consequently they still remain outside the Truth. Their claim to enlightenment is, by their own words, stamped as false.

215

If he loses his ego utterly and completely so that no trace of it exists at all, he would have to die, for his body is part of the ego. But he lives on. This shows that what he really loses is not the *ego-nature* but the *ego-will*. It is replaced by the higher will.

216

The ego lives entrenched in the seeker's inner world. If he becomes a saint, it is lost from time to time in meditation but it is found again whenever he emerges from it. If he becomes a sage, it is lost forever. That is one difference.

217

Yes, the ego as individuality, a separate identity remains. But it becomes reborn, purified, humbled before the higher power, no longer narrow in interests, no longer tyrannizing over the man, no longer selfish in the sense of the word. For as an enlightened being it may remain, harmless to all beings, benevolent to all creatures, respondent to a timeless consciousness enfolding its ordinary personality. The smaller circle can continue to exist within the larger one until the liberation of death. It is no longer the source of ignorance and evil; *that* ego is dissolved and obliterated. The new being is simply separate in body, thought, feeling from others but not from the universal, mass being behind them. There all are one.

218

In this mysterious new relationship he is not stopped from being aware of the ego, even though the Overself now directs him. But there is a unity between them which was absent before.

219

The ego fades away into a kind of non-entity, subsides like a wave into the ocean of universal life.

220

If the individual merges into pure Being, what is the ego which ceases to exist? For the physical body still remains and must be included in a man's consideration. This is one reason why even the highest mystical attainment must be naturalized, integrated even with his normal life as householder, professional, or intellectual. He then functions on three levels—animal, human, and angelic—but they fit together in harmony like a mosaic tiled wall. Whoever thinks otherwise is confusing two different situations, is superimposing the seeker upon the fulfilled man. If, for instance, he grants the possibility to monks alone, then he puts a limit on the Limitless and narrows the area of its presence. For the man who is established in the Light will act from within and by it, no matter whether he be engaged in the world's work, no matter whether married or not.

221

The proof that most mystics contribute something from their own personal self to their mystical experience, something from their own ego, lies in the fact that the vast majority of Christian mystics do not generally have inner experience concerning any spiritual leader other than Jesus Christ. Similarly, the vast majority of Indian mystics do not have such experiences except concerning Indian spiritual leaders, such as Krishna. This is because the religion which they hold, the faith in which they believe, the ideal saviour or guru to whom they direct their prayers or worship, is constantly held in their mind; he becomes the dominant thought, since it is by his Grace, they believe, that the experience has come to them. If they get a mystic experience they expect it to be associated with their own particular faith and so this is what has happened. But the interesting point here, psychologically, is that the ego is present in some way, either just before the experience or just after it—before in expectancy and after in interpretation. Then what happened between these two moments when the experience actually occurred? Well, if thoughts went into abeyance at the time, if all thoughts were lulled, then the thought of the saviour or guru was lulled too; but it was lying there on the very fringe of the experience at the beginning and at the end and it was the very first thing they picked up when they began to think again. It is however a rare occurrence for thought to be utterly stopped, for that state is equivalent to what the Hindus call *nirvikalpa samadhi*. They have another state, not so far gone, which they call *savikalpa samadhi*, where thoughts subsist inside the mystic experience and the thinking goes on but is held, so to speak, by the higher experience. This is what usually happens in the majority of cases of the mystics. The traits of character, the tendencies of the mind, may vanish during the experience and he emerges from it as if he is a new being, utterly changed; but then the effect of the experience gradually fades and with it he discovers he is still the old being. The ego has not vanished in his normal life because he is using it in order to attend to his affairs of waking consciousness. If in addition to the practice of meditation he has undergone the training in philosophy, then real changes take place in the man's character and the negative side of the ego gets less and less, the higher and positive side gets more and more until his character reaches a point where he is called selfless and egoless; but such terms are mis-nomers. They are correct perhaps if used in the moral sense, but not in the psychological sense. He is an individual and an individual he remains throughout life.

222

Yes the ego is there and must be there if we are to live on this plane. But it can undergo a spiritual rebirth and no longer be a tyrant who denies us our spiritual birthright and our spiritual consciousness but rather a chan-nel serving that consciousness.

223

The ego will always have its problems. By always, one means from birth all through the years until death. This is true of every human being, although a superior human being will deal with them in a superior way.

224

If the ego is not there, something else is; some agent which does what it is presumed to be doing.

225

The differences between persons are differences of bodily and mental tendencies. In their totality these belong to the ego. Even the spiritually enlightened man has them still although they no longer tyrannize over him. It is not correct to say to an aspirant that they must be gotten rid of, killed, and destroyed. Rather they have to be transcended. For even the enlightened person still uses the ego to direct his body's activities, whether simple ones such as taking a meal or complicated ones such as solving a problem. His ego, having become a channel because it is transcended, does not get in the way. The ordinary man and his activities are ruled by it.

226 ✓

Body is part of ego; the vital body (etheric double) and astral emotional body are also a part of it; the mental body of thoughts is part of ego, too. *All these bodies continue to exist even after realization since they are necessary to human life; to say there is then no ego is NONSENSE.* These bodies are to be purified and surrendered.

227

The illumined man is still conscious of his individuality but it is a different, a transformed individuality.

228 ✓

The "I" is still here, not the old familiar petty uncertain creature but another "I," a gloriously transformed one.

229

The ego, the person, is there still; whoever denies its existence, must deny the body's existence, and with it all his physical experience. Would it not be better, less muddled, to admit the ego to its proper place, and deny it any reality above that of an idea?

Reincarnation

230 ✓

That part of man which is within the physical world, the ego, must in the end come to recognize and revere his higher individuality, unseen and unknown though it may be. This requires a growth through time, through many rebirths.

231

What he calls the "I" does not get reborn in further bodies, as he believes, nor did it do so in the past. But it does appear to do so. Only deep analytical thought associated with mystical meditation can de-mesmerize him from his self-made idea.

232

It would be an error to believe that it is the Overself which reincarnates. It does not. But its offspring—the ego—does.(P)

233

This is the ego that we falsely think of as being our real self. This is the ego to which memory ties us. This is the illusive part of our dual personality; this is the known part of our being, a mere shadow thrown by the unknown part which is infinitely greater. This moves from one earthly body to another, from one dream to another through the phantasmagoria of existence without awakening to reality.

234

Immortality of the kind for which most human beings yearn can be found in one aspect of the Overself, which retains a sort of individuality because of its historical and psychological relation with its offspring. Hence, when it was written that the immortality of the True Self is relatively permanent, the term "relative" was used from the highest possible standpoint and not from the human standpoint. It is sufficient and quite true from the human outlook to accept the statement that the immortality of the Overself is true immortality, if not the ultimate, because the former must be attained first.

235

"My Emanation far within/ Weeps incessantly for my sin." How wrong
was William Blake when he wrote these lines!

236

The entity which lives in the spirit world after death is the same ego that
dwelt on earth, emanating from and sustained by the same Overself. In
this relationship, they are still distinct and separate entities, even though as
intimately connected as parent and offspring.

237

How senseless it is to demand permanency and immortality for an ego
which has already undergone countless changes of inner nature and outer
form, only the resolute truth-seeker, unwilling to live by illusions, can
perceive.

238

A perpetual survival of the little personal ego throughout endless time is
impossible, undesirable, and ridiculous. But heaven as a temporary state is
both a need and a fact.

239

Immortality in its truest sense is, and can only be, the total surrender of
individuality and ultimate merging of the little mind with Absolute,
Undifferentiated Mind.

2

I-THOUGHT

I-sense and I-thought

What we commonly think of as constituting the "I" is an idea which changes from year to year. This is the personal "I." But what we feel most intimately as being always present in all these different ideas of the "I," that is, the sense of being, of existence, never changes at all. It is this which is our true enduring "I."

2 ✓

If past and future are now only ideas, the present must be idea, too. So runs the mentalist explanation. But this can and should be carried still farther. If the experiencer of past and future is (because he is part of them) now an idea, then the experiencer of the present (and in the present) must be idea, too. As anything else than idea, he was (and is) only a supposition, which is the same as saying that the ego is only an apparent entity and has no more reality (or less) than any thought has.

3

Everything remembered is a thought in consciousness. This not only applies to objects, events, and places. It also applies to persons, including oneself, he who is remembered, the "I" that I was. This means that my own personality, what I call myself, was a thought in the past, however strong and however persistent. But the past was once the present. Therefore I am not less a thought *now*. The question arises what did I have then which I still have now, unchanged, exactly the same. It cannot be "I" as the person, for that is different in some way each time. It is, and can only be, "I" as Consciousness.

4 ✓

All that a man really owns is his "I." Everything else can be taken from him in a moment—by death or destiny, by his own foolishness or other people's malice. But no event and no person can rob him of his capacity to think the "I."

5

The "I"-consciousness is the essence of the "Me," the seeming self.

6

With the body, the thoughts, and the emotions, the ego seems to complete itself as an entity. But where do we get this feeling of "I" from? There is only one way to know the answer to this question: the way of meditation. This burrows beneath the three mentioned components and penetrates into the residue, which is found to be nothing in particular, only the sense of Be-ing. And this is the real source of the "I" notion, the self-feeling. Alas! the source does not ordinarily reveal itself, so we live in its projection, the ego, alone. We are content to be little, when we could be great.

7

That which claims to be the "I" turns out to be only a part of it, the lesser part, and not the real "I" at all. It is a complex of thoughts.

8

When the "I" is thought to be the body, appearance has replaced reality.

9

This feeling of I-ness may be associated with the body, emotions, and thoughts—whose totality is the personal ego—or shifted in deep meditation to the rootless root of being, which is the Overself; or, it may be associated with both, when one will be the reality and the other a shadow of reality.

10

The idea of a self first enters consciousness when a child identifies itself with bodily feelings, and later when it adds emotional feelings. The idea extends itself still later, with logical thoughts and, lastly, completes itself with the discovery of individuality.

11

Descartes' reference in his statement, "I think therefore I am," is simply to himself as a person, a self limited to body emotion and thought, that is, to ordinary experience and nothing higher or deeper than that, a being whose consciousness is unexamined and unexplored.

12

Ego means the consciousness of self.

13

We are but fragments of mind thrown into momentary consciousness.

14

If we analyse the ego, we find it to be a collection of past memories retained from experience and future hopes or fears which anticipate experience. If we try to seize it, to separate it out by itself, we do not find it to exist in the present moment, only in what has gone and what is to come. In fact, it never really exists in the *NOW* but only seems to. This means that it is a phantom without substance, a false *idea*.(P)

15

His first mental act is to think himself into being. He is the maker of his own "I." This does not mean that the ego is his own personal invention alone. The whole world-process brings everything about, including the ego and the ego's own self-making.(P)

16

Philosophy does not ask us to attempt the impossible task of casting the body-thought entirely out of our consciousness at all times and in all places—which doctrines like Advaita Vedanta and Christian Science ask us to do—but to cease confining the I-thought to the body alone—which is quite a different matter.

17

Whoever wants the "I" to yield up its mysterious and tremendous secret must stop it from looking perpetually in the mirror, must stop the little ego's fascination with its own image.

18

Our attachment to the ego is natural. It arises because we are unconsciously attached to that which is behind it, to the Overself. Only, we are misled by ignorance wholly to concentrate on the apparent "I" and wholly to ignore the unseen, enduring self of which it is but a transient shadow. The "I" which trembles or enjoys in the time-series is not the real "I."

19

All thoughts can be traced back to a single thought which rests at the very base of their operations. Can you not see now that the thought of personality, the sense of "I," is such a basic thought?

20

The "I" which says, "I think so and so" or "I feel so and so" or "I do so and so" is the first thought to arise, as well as the last one to die. This "I" is the personal ego. There can be no thinking or feeling or willing without a prior sense of identity as to the person in whom these functions manifest. The ego-thought is always the prior thought, but its activity follows so swiftly as to seem simultaneous. Indeed, the mental emotional and volitional activities flow out of the ego's own activity—hence, there can be no real conquest or control of mind, feeling, or body without the conquest of ego itself. This done, victory over them follows automatically. This not done, their subjugation oppresses their manifestation but leaves their root unharmed. The way to attack this root is to concentrate attention on the source whence the ego-thought arises.

21

The ego is simply that idea of himself which man forms.

22

The body, the emotional feelings, and the intellect, are all placed on the *circle*-line. That which is at the *centre* of being is consciousness-in-itself.

23

The "I" of a person has several different faces, each belonging to the different activities, roles, relationships, and segments of his human nature.

24

What is the most immediate of all experiences? It is the "I." For all others are experiences of an object, be it a thing or a thought—the body, the world, or the mind; but this is their subject, the first identity in life, the last before death.

25

What other experience is there than my experience? All of it centres around an *I*. What is this *I* other than a series of states of consciousness, a stream of thoughts and an accumulation of feelings? What is that but to declare the ego to be entirely mentalistic in origin and nature?

26

The subject which is of most interest to every man is himself. The object of all his thoughts is likewise himself, or if they refer to some other person it is in connection with that person's relationship to himself. Thus we see that the idea of the ego, the I am, is strongly implanted by Nature in everyone.

Ego exists, as series of thoughts

27

The teaching that the ego does not exist—repeated so often in so parrot-like a way—can help no one, can only create intellectual confusion and thus harm the search for truth. But the teaching that the ego is only an idea—however strongly held by the mind—and as such does exist, can help everyone in the struggle for self-mastery and can throw intellectual light on the search for truth.

28

Our thoughts follow each other so swiftly that they keep up in us the feeling of a particular personality which the body gives us.

29

The ego is nothing more than a shadow. Its stuff and reality are merely that transient ever-changing play of light and colour. It exists—a word whose very meaning, "to be placed outside," is also metaphysically true. For he who immerses himself in its consciousness places himself outside the consciousness of Overself.

30

When we think we see a single smoothly moving cinema picture of a running man we are really seeing thousands of separate stationary pictures of the man. The experience of smoothly convincing personality is an illusion which arises in the same manner out of our mental fusion of a series of separate ideas into a single human being. The term "illusion" here used must not be read as meaning that the human being does not exist. On the contrary, this sentence would not be written or read if it were not so. It means that he exists, yes, but that he does not exist as other than a transient appearance. He is not fundamentally *real*.

31

There is no real ego but only a quick succession of thoughts which constitutes the "I" process. There is no separate entity forming the personal consciousness but only a series of impressions, ideas, images revolving round a common centre. The latter is completely empty; the feeling of something being there derives from a totally different plane—that of the Overself.

32

When it is declared that the ego is a fictitious entity, what is meant is that it does not exist as a real entity. Nevertheless, it does exist as a thought.

33

If he identifies with the ego as a real entity by itself, and not as the complex of thoughts and tendencies which it is, he is caught in the net of illusion and cannot get out of it.

34

The practice of the impersonal point of view under the guidance of mentalism leads in time to the discovery that the ego is an image formed in the mind, mind-made, an image with which we have got inextricably intertwined. But this practice begins to untie us and set us free.(P)

35

The ego may be a transient phenomenon and a metaphysical fiction. Nevertheless, complains someone, it is all that I know. I am hemmed in all around by its "I" and utterly limited to its "mine."

36

The ego is only a field of force, not a real entity in its own right. Or, it is a composite of thoughts assembled together, not a real individual.

37

The ego is a collection of thoughts circulating around a fixed but empty centre. If the habits of many, many reincarnations had not given them such strength and persistence, they could be voided. The reality—MIND—could then reveal Itself.

38

The "ego" is all that you know as yourself.

39

It is not only that man does not know his spiritual nature but, which is worse, that he holds a false idea of his own nature. He takes the shadow—ego—for the substance—Overself. He takes the effect—body—for the cause—Spirit.

40

The idea of a permanent ego which common experience imposes on us is shattered by philosophic analysis and philosophic experience.

41

Everyone's outlook is conditioned by several factors: by family upbringing and surrounding, by evolutionary level, by traditional religion and prevailing culture, by personal circumstances and reincarnated tendencies. His reactions are shaped for him and make up his "I." This is a very limited entity, pursued by the consequences of its own limitations.

42

Descartes would not trust the truth of the thoughts which his mind gave him. Yet he was quite willing incautiously to trust the mind itself! For what is this everyday mind which he took to be his "I" but a persisting series of recurring thoughts? What is this "I" but an entity created by habit and convenience out of their totality?

43

The personal ego is not a metaphysically permanent thing. But it is a practical working tool which serves the convenient purpose of personal identification. It need not be denied. Why call it non-existent, a fictitious entity, while making full use of it?

44

The ego is a structure which has been built up in former lives from tendencies, habits, and experiences in a particular pattern. But in the end the whole thing is nothing but a thought, albeit a strong and continuing thought.

45

When he is conscious of himself he is conscious only of his idea of himself, the fantasy which the ego has made for him.

46

If we have written of the ego as if it were a separate and special entity, a fixed thing, a reality in its own right, this is only because of the inescapable necessities of logical human thinking and the inexorable limitations of traditional human language. For in FACT the "I" cannot be separated from its thoughts since it is composed of them, and them alone. The ego is, in short, only an idea, or a trick that the thought process plays on itself.(P)

47

Because this emanated consciousness of the Overself ties itself so completely and so continuously to the thought-series, which after all are its own creations, it identifies itself with the illusory ego produced by their activity and forgets its own larger, less limited origin.

48

There is *no* entity called intellect or ego or personal "I" or individual mind apart or separate from thoughts themselves, existing alone. People give it such a supposed existence by their habitual attitude, lifelong belief. This shows the power of auto-suggestion and memory to create a purely fictional being. The sustenance, reality, life it has is false, illusory. Mind as such is devoid of all thoughts.

49

All our thoughts necessarily exist in the successiveness of time, but the thought of the ego is a more complicated affair and exists also in time and space, because the body is part of the ego. Whatever we do, the ego as such will continue its existence. But we need not identify ourselves with it; we can put some distance between us and it. The more we do so, the more impersonal we shall become, and vice versa.

50

Of what use is it to delude a man into imagining himself to be unaware of the ego or into believing that he is without one?

51

All the time that he talks of there being no ego, no entity at all, he is feeling the pressure of its sensations, hearing the sound of its words.

52

Every human institution, every human value, gets worn threadbare by use and has to make way for a new one. Even the most sacred and religious authorities lose their sway with the flow of time. When the whole universe around us is so uncertain and unsettled we need not be surprised to discover that the very *I* of man is transient too. Our centre of gravity is a shifting one.

53 ✓

Descartes, who has been called the father of philosophy in the Occident, began his thinking with the certainty of the personal self. Two thousand years earlier, Buddha ended his own thinking with the certainty of the illusoriness of the personal self!

54 ✓

From childhood through adulthood, man passes from one change to another in himself—his body, feelings, and thoughts. The idea of himself, his personality, changes with it. Where and what is the "I" if it has no unbroken integrity?

55 ✓

May not his present self alter or even vanish as much as his former self altered or vanished?

56 ✓

The tendencies and habits, the physical and mental activities which we have brought over from our own past, settle down and congeal themselves into what we call our personal self, our individuality, our ego. Yet life will not permit this combination to be more than a temporary one, and we go on changing with time. We identify ourselves with each of these changes, in turn, yet always think that is really ourself. Only when we still these activities and withdraw from these habits for a brief period in meditation, do we discover for the first time that they do not constitute our real self, after all. Indeed, they are then seen to be our false self, for it is only then that we discover the inner being that is the real self which they hide and cover up. Alas! so strong is their age-old power that we soon allow them to resume their tyrannous ways over us, and we soon become victims again of the great illusion of the ego.

57

When all thoughts vanish into the Stillness, the ego-personality vanishes too. This is Buddha's meaning that there is no self, also Ramana Maharshi's meaning that ego is only a collection of thoughts.

58

We dwell in a universe of illusion, for the effects and forms we perceive possess a stability which is not there and a reality which is imagined. Even its time space and motion depend upon the perceptions which announce them or the mind which is aware of them. The mystic seer's flashing enlightenment reveals this to him, but science's own reflections about its atomic discoveries are pointing to the same idea. All this has been told and taught in *The Hidden Teaching Beyond Yoga* and *The Wisdom of the Overself*. But the seer's enlightenment did not stop there. He saw that the perceiver himself was not less illusory than the universe of his experience, not less unstable, not less unreal. He saw that the human ego was but a human idea. It had to be transcended if truth and reality were to be experienced.

Subject-object

59

The sense of egoic existence precedes, and gives rise to, the sense of the world's existence.

60

The ego appears in Mind, the universe appears to the ego: together they form that subject-object duality which characterizes the thoughts.

61

The ego-thought is behind every activity of a man. It is always coupled with the object-thought.

62

The "me" is the knower of the world outside (things) and inside (thoughts). But only relatively is it a knower, for it is itself an object, known to a higher power.

63

The "I" thinks: this is the subject. But the "I" it thinks of is "me," which is an object. Ordinarily, consciousness must have an object of consciousness. This coupling is an essential of our mental life.

64

Just as in grammar there is, upon analysis, a sentence's subject and object, so in ordinary thinking there is a division between the thinker and the thought held, the thing or person receiving attention, between "I" and the other.

65

The ego of which we are conscious is not the same as the mind *by* which we are conscious. He who perseveres until he can understand this, opens the first door of the soul's house.

66

All your thinking about the ego is necessarily incomplete, for it does not include the ego-thought itself. Try to do so, and it slips from your hold. Only something that transcends the ego can grasp it.(P)

67

The body is in reality an object for the mind, which is its subject; and not only the body, but also whatever the ego thinks or feels becomes an object, too. It is less easy to see and even more necessary to understand that this ego, this subject, is itself an object to a higher part of the mind.

68

We understand correctly our relation to external possessions like chairs and carpets, but not to possessions like hands and thoughts. Here our understanding becomes confused. Our habitual speech betrays this. We say, "I am hurt" when it is really the *body* that is hurt, or "I am pleased" when a *thought* of pleasure arises within us. In the first case the body still remains an object of our experience, despite its closeness. In the second case, thinking is a function performed by us. Both are to be distinguished from our *being*, however interwoven with our *activity*.

69

The ego becomes the observed object, when it is finally and completely analysed in terms of awareness. It is no longer the observing subject.

70

The ego is as transient an idea as the so-called physical objects which it perceives. Both the ego and the objects appear together as thoughts within the Universal Mind and collapse together.

71

To the real person, the consciousness, body, nerve, and sense organs are only objects being used as mediums and channels.

72

Wherever human consciousness exists, wherever there is a thinker, there are also his thoughts. Subject and object join to make conscious existence of an ego, an "I," possible, both in waking and dream states.

73

The world-thought is an object to the ego-mind, which is the subject to it. But the ego-mind is itself an object: the awareness of it is simply the awareness of the ego-thought.

74

The ego is an object. The mind knows only objects. Therefore man does not know himself when he knows only ego.

3

PSYCHE

Ego as knot in psyche

The ego is a knot tied in the psyche of our inner being, itself being compounded from a number of smaller knots. There is nothing fresh to be gathered in, for b-e-i-n-g is always there, but something is to be undone, untied.

2

The ego is like a repression which must be dug out of the subconscious mind, seen and understood for what it is, and then let go until it vanishes, losing all its secret power thereby.

3

Most neuroticisms come from refusing to let go of the personal ego. How the ego makes its own anxieties and sufferings is depicted in the famous Buddhist picture called "The Wheel of Life," supposed to be six realms of existence, but which really represents six kinds of psychological conditioning from the beast to the human and the gods.

4

The ego, although itself a projection, draws from its creative source enough power to project in turn its own small world.

5

The ego's sphere of activity is fivefold—thought, imagination, memory, feeling, and action.

6

The ego has two sides to its nature: a dark and a bright one, an animal and a human one.

7

The character which a man reveals openly to the world is not at all the same as the one hidden in himself. This is not the result of hypocrisy, but of the polarity which divides nature, and hence man.

8

The place where he was born or lives, the time of day or epoch when he was born, and the parental heritage—all make their contribution to his personality.

9

We may distinguish the ego by certain signs: it is not stable, for its characteristics fluctuate; it is not sinless, for somewhere in its nature there will be one or more flaws, no matter what the judging test may be; it does not feel totally secure for a fear, a doubt, an uncertainty about the future there will be.

10

What is the ego but a load of mixed memories?

11

Thoughts form themselves, emotions rise up, moods come and go in a rhythm; the ego lives and moves behind them all.

12

He is a pathetic creature, split off from awareness of his Overself and split into two hostile sides in his ego-self.

13

The network of interests, attachments, desires, ideas, and identifications is the ego.

14

The body's sense-organs demand satisfactions, but at the root of their desires is the ego, a whorl of emotional-mental tendencies.

15

The ego is the shadow-self accompanying the light-self, or Overself. The ego holds all that is dark in the man's character.

16

We talk of the ego, but which ego do we mean? For each of us has several egos within him.

17

The persona, the mask which he presents to the world, is only one part of his ego. The conscious nature, composed of thoughts and feelings, is the second part. The hidden store of tendencies, impulses, memories, and ideas—formerly expressed and then reburied, or brought over from earlier lives, and all latent—is the third part.(P)

18

Inside ourselves there is not one ego but several. We live in a condition of recurring feelings that successively contradict one another, deny each other, or shame each other. The "I" is really torn into pieces, each claiming ascendency but none holding it permanently. The animal, the human, and the angel jostle elbows in our hearts. We are degraded today, elevated tomorrow. The quest seeks to integrate all these different egos.

19

When we talk of the ego we mean the mind, the body, the senses, and the memory. For take them away and we are as nothing.

20

The many voices within, which beckon for attention, are evidence of the many selves which the ego jubilantly and misinformedly proclaims itself to be.

21

A man is made up of several different factors: what he has inherited from his parents; what he has picked up from his surroundings; what he has brought over from previous reincarnations; what he thinks, feels, and does; what his reactions are to other people. It is the combination of all these elements which make one man.

22

This split in his ego will be recognized by every man who is honest with himself.

23

The sum total of our past actions and thoughts, and especially of our tendencies, constitutes our character and makes us what we are today.

24

The ego moves from childhood to old age, from waking to dreaming, but it moves round in a circle. It does not move toward freedom, reality, or peace.

25

Each consciousness of the personal self not only includes thoughts, but also feelings and volitions.

26

We are strange creatures, as remote from the real human ideal as we are from the selfish animal type.

The "subconscious"

27

There are forces active below the level of consciousness which belong to two widely different poles of human character—the savage and the spiritual.

28

There is really no subconscious mind. There is only the thinking mind and the still centre behind the mind.

29

Jung thought he had found, in what he called the unconscious, the source which twisted, negated, or opposed the ego's ideals. This source was the shadow. He needed to go farther and deeper for then he would have known the shadow to be the ego itself.

30

What we think touches the surface of consciousness and sinks below to be stored and hidden away.

31

What is upon the surface of the mind comes more easily to his attention, for it is, in a sense, openly displayed. But what is at the root and the cause of the surface things is hidden within and less easily found. It is there in the so-called subconscious level of the ego, but still a part of the ego—not in that far greater depth or height where the Overself is met.

32

Men suffer from various illnesses, for which they flock to physicians, clinics, and hospitals to find a cure. But they ignore the only illness which is more deeply rooted than all the others and which never leaves them. It is the ego's octopus-like hold upon every atom of their being.

33

The ego explorations of psychoanalysis are not directly concerned with securing a liberation from the ego itself, but only with improving, adjusting, or altering its mental attitudes and emotional stresses.

34

The So-called Liberation of Psychoanalytic and Dianetic Therapy

The Infinite is a wonderful machine which remembers, compares, and recalls experience. It does this in words or pictures.

But it holds so many recordings of the past that matter of its present living is unconsciously a response of memory stirring up the past.

Psychoanalytic and dianetic therapies try to eradicate these past patterns by using the reaction to impulse or the recall of the subconscious with particular reference to childhood. But to say, as psychoanalysis says, that the mind which is successful in retreat is free, or, as dianetics says, clear, is to make an unwarrantable claim and to overlook the tremendous size of its task. For all that such therapy has really done is to liberate the patient from a few of his known compulsions. But what about the enormous number of the unknown ones? What about the most terrifying compulsion of all—

the ego itself? How can an analyst who is still governed by so many complexes himself, of which he is not even aware, completely liberate other persons? He himself is the victim of an illusion-making mechanism that is incredibly ingenious.

In every mind there is an unconscious conflict which he is ordinarily powerless to deal with—the conflict between the line of evolution which the Overself has marked out for the person, and the line of blind desire which the ego is trying to pursue.

Again, what is the use of taking a few small sections of the past, such as childhood or adolescence, and attempting to deal with them only, when the true past of the ego contains innumerable subconscious memories of former lives on earth and numerous tendencies which arise from episodes belonging to that vanished history? The only thorough and complete way to deal with the ego is not only to deal with its surface manifestation, but to get at its own hidden existence on the one hand, and to work by aspiration, meditation, and reflection upon the Overself on the other hand.

35

Egoistic motive notwithstanding, it forever feigns its absence, hides in our deeds all the time. Freud demonstrated the strength of the unconscious motives, and without accepting his view of the human personality, which is as erroneous in some respects as it is correct in others, we may honour him for this restatement. He was certainly right in pointing it out.

36 ✓

The prejudices and the biases in favour of one's own ego play mostly an unconscious part.

Trickery, cunning of ego

37

At every chance of a forward step he will be tricked, deceived, misguided, or even driven back by the ego—if he will not be alert enough to recognize the endeavour.

38

To say that the ego keeps us captive is only one way of stating the problem. That we are infatuated with it, is another way.

39

The ego simulates some of the Overself's qualities and reflects some of its consciousness. But the image which is thus created is a false one.

40

The "I" gets angry when someone provokes it, then remembers it must gain self-control, and thus forms a higher and calmer state for itself but one which is still within the personal ego-sphere. It has not escaped from itself but only replaced a negative emotion by a positive feeling.

41

Men not only permit themselves to be deluded by their ego-bred illusions, but even welcome them.

42

It is natural for the ego to react negatively to its experiences when these bring loss or opposition. But this is so only when, as is most common, man is still unawakened, untaught, uncontrolled, and unable to enter into higher states of being.

43

The ego is forced to ape the non-ego, is compelled to hide the narrowness of its attitude behind a mantle of supposed justice, truth, or even altruism.

44

If the ego can keep your energies entangled in its psychical doings, or your time absorbed in developing its occult powers, it will keep you from devoting them to seeking the Overself and thus preserve its own existence.

45

The ego finds every kind of pretext to resist the practice required of it.

46

It requires a subtler intelligence or a simpler heart to realize that a man's best course is to put his forces at the service of a worthier cause than the mere perpetuation of his faulty ego. The parable of the Prodigal Son then assumes an intimate meaning for him. While reading it again, he may derive an astringent wisdom from remembering all the unpleasant consequences of the lower ego's activities. These are too often like a blind man tremblingly feeling his way and moving from one mishap to another and making one false step after another.

47

How few are willing to suspect their own motives until the flash of light from the Overself shows them the truth by enabling them to stand away from themselves and benefit by the new perspective!

48

The ego lays its crafty plans to catch him through his better side where it cannot do so through his worse one.

49

Let him examine himself and see how his ego leads the whole troop of other faculties or hides among them for refuge, asserts itself or deludes him. If it can perpetuate its hold through grandiose vanity, it will parade his highly magnified virtues and make him sticky with smugness; if through humility, it will over-emphasize his sad crew of faults, and make him neurotically self-centered and morbid.

50

Few beginners have either the will or the perception, the knowledge or the guidance to get past their ego's tricks to circumvent their aspirations, and so few arrive where they set out to go.

51

There is no limit to the ego's pretensions. It will pose as the humble pupil today but as the pontifical master tomorrow.

52

The ego hides from them the ugly motives which prompt their actions.

53

The ego knows that it will be in deadly danger if it allows him to penetrate to its lair and look it straight in the eyes.

54

The ego knows well enough how to protect itself, how to prevent the seeker from straying away from its power over him.

55

The ego is just as powerful whether it is condoned or condemned, for in both cases it keeps the man engaged on a self-centered quest.

56

Every move made by the ego has as its basis the desire of its own survival, its own self-perpetuation.

57

The ego is perfectly capable of making all sorts of compromises or truces with itself—moral ones with its conscience, logical ones with its intellect, spiritual ones with its aspirations—and perfectly capable of all sorts of dodges, quibbles, evasions, and disguises, whether dealing with matters on the highest or lowest level of reference.

58

How much do these declamations of serving mankind really point in the opposite direction—serving the ego? How much does even the babble about sacrificing the ego really give it excessive attention and end by making it stronger? And how often does it really mask the desire for greater power?

59

If the ego cannot assert itself openly, it will insert itself insidiously.

60

The ego poses as being the only self, the real self, the whole self.

61

The ego has many hiding places. Exposed in one of them, it soon occupies another.

62

The ego seems to have a colossal capacity for trickery and deception concerning its own motives.

63

The ego will accept discipline and even suffering rather than let itself be killed.

64

The ego may be dormant and not really dead. Or it may seem inanimate and yet be biding its chance.

65

The ego can find many dodges and give many pretexts to prevent him from making the first humiliating gesture of mental surrender. They are intended to protect its own life or power and to keep him, through pride, from making any space for the Overself's entry.

66

The ego has set up for itself, which it could do only by turning a fiction into reality, by supposing that it is what in fact it never has been.

67

If this truth sounds too cold to some hearers, too cruel to others, the emotional reaction is understandable and pardonable. But does that make it less true?

68

There are various ways in which the ego wriggles out of his grasp when he tries to catch it.

69

No aspirant knows how much the ego can do to deceive his mind with fantasy and to mislead his steps with vanity.

70

All those types, encased in the ego and its desires as they are, are kept out of the kingdom by no other hands than their own.

71

The ego uses all the cunning of its logical intellect and all the seduction of its pleasure-loving nature to keep a man away from the quest.

72

The ego may warp his mind with feelings of unwarranted despair and imaginations of unjustified defeatism or with feelings of exaggerated achievement and imaginations of unjustified optimism.

73

If he tries to set up opposition to the ego, he may by that very act simply shift its area of activity, yet be deluded into thinking that he has weakened its activity!

74

The ego naturally resents and is implacably opposed to the only course that will lead to its final overthrow.

75

The ego can mask its desire for power and prominence with a concern for the service of humanity.

76

Is the ego ever really happy? At best it is only for the occasional moments when it forgets or loses itself in something higher, but ordinarily how could it be? It is never fully satisfied with its lot, always craving for something needed or desired. Oh yes! It may hide its unhappiness, even from itself, but the trick must have an end.

77

In trying not to look at the real image of themselves, they look at the more comfortable one—the ego. In refusing to come to the full consciousness of themselves, they come under the sway of passions and desires, tendencies and feelings which smugly but deceitfully replace it.

78

The ego is defiant, cunning, and resistant to the end.(P)

79

The ego is by nature a deceiver and in its operations a liar. For if it revealed things as they really are, or told what is profoundly true, it would have to expose its own self as the arch-trickster pretending to be the man himself and proffering the illusion of happiness.(P)

80

Everyone is crucified by his own ego.(P)

81

The ego is arrogant, haughty, conceited, and self-deceived.(P)

82

If the ego can trick him into deviating from the central issue of its own destruction to some less important side issue, it will certainly do so. Its success in this effort is much more common than its failure. Few escape being tricked. The ego uses the subtlest ways to insert itself into the thinking and life of an aspirant. It cheats, tricks, exalts, and abases him by turns, if he lets it. Anatole France wrote that it is in the ability to deceive oneself that the greatest talent is shown. It is a constant habit and an instinctive reaction to defend his ego against the testimony of its own activity's unfortunate results. He will need to guard against this again and again, for its own powers are pathetically inadequate, its own foresight conspicuously absent.(P)

83

The ego lies to itself, lies to the man who identifies himself with it, and lies to other men.(P)

84

So long as the ego's rule is preserved, so long will the karmic tendencies which come with it be preserved. But when its rule is weakened they too will automatically be starved and weakened. To start this process, start trying to take an impersonal detached view.

85

True altruism of a philosophic kind is not done by the self but through the self, not by the ego but by the Overself using the ego. Few make this grade. Most practise their altruism by blending it with selfish motive or, in other cases, by masking that motive entirely so as not to upset their own or other people's illusion.

86

Words which sting by their truth usually tell the ego what it prefers not to hear.

87

That the Neo-Vedantist refuses to recognize the sinful nature of man hardly helps him. What he is in his inmost being must certainly be declared, but what he is in his outer and everyday being must not be ignored. The philosophic view of man, being a properly balanced one, puts together both appraisals at the same time. It says man is essentially divine but immediately sinful. Hence it proclaims the need of self-purification.

88

The ego does not have to struggle for supremacy; it *is* supreme.

89

To retain its hold, the ego will devise subterfuges in his action and insinuate concealed evasions into his thinking.

90

Where reason serves vanity, and imagination moves only at the ego's behest, a man makes his own pitfalls.

91

The ego makes every concession to its own weakness, and finds every support for its bad habits.

92

The Overself is there but the ego intercepts its communication.

93

Without understanding either themselves or the workings of the World-Mind, men arrogantly deliver judgements upon other men, upon life in general, and upon God.

94

Such is the strength of the ego that it can soon efface the idea of a new moral reform that a time of inner silence revealed as necessary.

95

The rationalizations by which the ego can persuade him that he is loftily motivated when he is not, are many and subtle.

96

The ego is soon appeased by flattery, soon bruised by criticism; but the man who transcends its tyranny is able justly to evaluate both.

97

The ego's point of view is too often a distorted one, a prejudiced one, and so a wrong one. In a more advanced person it may be a mixed one and therefore confused.

98

The ego's posturing can take various forms: high as well as low, so-called spiritual as well as outright materialist.

99

Outwardly he may seem to be working solely for the sake of the cause, the movement, the party, or the institution. He may profess and even believe this to be so. But inwardly he may really be working for his own ego, that is, for himself.

100

One of the ego's chief delusions takes the form of believing that its advance planning, its reasoned management, and its apparent solutions of problems are more important than they really are.

101

Deceived by their strong personal self-interest, their perspicacity is often non-existent when it is believed to be most active!

102

The ego plays up his emotions through all their wide range, using the most opposite and conflicting ones at different times to suit its purpose.

103

A man may be the biggest fool in town yet his ego may be still bigger and not allow him to see what he is.

Defense mechanisms

104

The ego, which is so quick to complain about other people's bad treatment of it and so slow to confess its own bad conduct, is his first and worst enemy.

105

The ego has very powerful defenses, mostly emotional ones, to which it turns instantaneously.

106

The ego will always seek, and find, ways to excuse itself. It will do anything else it can rather than honestly confess its own vileness or weakness or erroneousness. It will cling stubbornly to them rather than admit the need for a thorough change.

107

The ego has an infinite capacity for putting a favourable construction or justification on all its actions, however wrong or foolish.

108

When the ego sees a danger to its own continued existence in any proposed move or decision, it creates fears, invents false hopes, and exaggerates difficulties in order to prevent it.

109

The ego's self-justifications are a match for all its follies and sins. Its self-contradictions are a display of lofty aspirations mocked by lower acts.

110

When the ego is hurt, feelings of pride arise.

111

All are ready to justify self and judge others; few are ready to judge self and justify others.

112

If the ego were as prone to condemn itself as it is to justify itself, or to justify others as it is to condemn them, how quick and easy would the quest be.

113

So strong and deep is the hold which the ego has over him, that the flattery which condones that hold is accepted smilingly, whereas the criticism which weakens it is rejected irritably.

114

The ego's cunning endeavour will be to persuade him to ascribe his irritating troubles to anything but the correct primal cause—within himself—and to anyone but the correct primal person—he himself.

115

There is opposition from the ego, threatened for its life. It seeks to cajole, tempt, or terrify us at different times.

116

The ego knows well how to cover up its ugliest activities with the noblest self-justifications.

117

The personal ego is surrounded by defense mechanisms which make difficult the operation of penetrating to its lair.

118

The more he advances intuitively, the more will the ego's sophistries seek to lure him astray.

119

The ego automatically assumes the posture of rectitude, spontaneously comes to its own defense, rather than to examine whether it really is right.

120

Freud gave out much that in the end has wreaked more harm than good. But his positive contributions include the unmasking of defense mechanisms.

121

The ego's lower nature becomes fearful of being dislodged at last. To avoid this fate it goes into battle with every weapon from open resistance to smooth deception.

122

Alas! the ego pursues him wherever he goes. This is bad enough but when he fails to recognize it and blames other egos only for his troubles it is pathetic and even saddening.

123

The ego is full of subterfuges to keep him from getting away. These go all the way from sheer megalomania to the suggestion that it does not exist. It resents criticism, however truthful, but accepts praise, however undeserved.

124

The ego always looks for, and finds, excuses for its indiscipline, justifications for its misdemeanour, defenses against accusations written by its own personal history.

125

The ego may carefully suppress its more obvious manifestations, both from other people and from himself.

126

The ego can be depended on to give every reason for his troubles but the right one. In that way, it secures self-protection and prevents aggression against itself.

127

The ego will persistently lead him to indulge in wishful efforts to rationalize his past mistakes. He must choose between such pleasant deception and the unpleasant truth.

128

The ego's ingenuity shows itself in many different phases through which he may have to pass. In all these phases, it will seek to perpetuate its own rule by fostering misleading illusions and stimulating wrong impulses.

129

To claim that the familiar and the habitual are the right and proper is a semantic deception whereby the ego diverts attention from its own failures.

130

The ego senses the peril in which it is placed and resorts to tricks, deceptions, and subterfuges to save itself.

131

The ego uses the most specious arguments to keep him from attaining truth, appealing to his subconscious selfishness or his intellectual gluttony or his occult-power-seeking vanity.

132

When his conduct is indefensible, the ego will prompt him to defend it.

Self-idolatry

133

He must start by admitting with complete frankness that the ego worships not God but itself, and that it carries this idolatry into a Church, if religious, or onto the Quest, if mystical.

134

Take it as a truism that nearly every man is in love with himself. If the divine influence is to enter and touch him, much more if it is to possess him, he must be deprived of this self-love.

135

It is only idolatry on another plane, a more refined and subtle one than the physical, to worship one's ego.

136

His personal affairs are treated as cosmically important.

137

The ego seeks its own interest as its first consideration and also its last one.

138

Despite all setbacks, the ego continues to retain its misplaced confidence in itself.

139

The ego is enamoured of itself.

140

How the little ego wants to be admired, whether worthy of admiration or not! How it admires itself and, especially, how it thinks all the time about itself!

141

The egoist has eyes only for himself.

142

The self-love which the ego unvaryingly displays or cunningly disguises, in all circumstances and through its yesterdays, todays, and tomorrows alike, is simply a complete extroversion of the love which the World-Mind bears for itself, and which it reflects towards the whole universe. The ego, as a projection which is ultimately traceable to this divine source, carries with it what is nothing less and nothing other than divine love. But personalized and narrowed as it then becomes, this holy force is no longer recognizable for what it really is. However ugly or vicious, detestable or criminal, human selfishness shows itself to be at times, its essential nature remains unchanged—the love which is at God's heart, and even at the world's heart. It comes to this, that if God did not love himself, man could not do the same nor crave for love from his fellow man or give it to woman. And if God did not love man, no man and no woman would love God, seek God, and deny himself or herself for God. The corollary of all this is that since hate is the very opposite of love, and is so often the cause of murder, its birth in the human heart shuts out the human mind from the Overself's light more decisively than any other negative passion. No one can find redemption in whom it is active, nor will warring mankind be blessed with peace until it is expunged.

143

The ego's self-flattery keeps out most suggestions that its motives may be tainted, its service not so disinterested as it seems, and its humility a pretentious cloak for secret vanity.(P)

144

The earth wheels on its course through space outside and on its own axis inside. Each person who is carried by the earth has his own unseen axis, too, round which his inner nature revolves: this is his ego.

145

The ego is always its own centre of gravity.

146

The ego's self-love is so strong, its attachment to old attitudes so tenacious, its justification of wrong or foolish deeds so blind, that the likelihood of vanquishing its rule is a thin one. All this shows how absurd is man's complacent self-righteousness and smug virtue.

147

It is the ego's self-love which makes us try to defend ourselves in every situation where we are plainly at fault. It is done to justify our actions where consequences have shown that they are grievously wrong.

148

A man's pride in his own capacity to find truth, gain enlightenment, and achieve purity shuts out the humility needed to let the ego go and let the Overself in.

Egoism, egocentricity

149

Egoism, the limiting of consciousness to individual life as separate from the one infinite life, is the last barrier to the attainment of unity with the infinite life.(P)

150

The egoist has as much chance of finding real peace of mind as the historian has of finding truth in politics.

151

So long as the ego lives in him, so long will all his motives, acts, impulses, and aims be infected with egoism.

152

Egotism may take different forms and the one wherein it most successfully cloaks itself is that religio-mystical form whose theme is all "me" or "I," or the expectation of personal gain. But whether this is to be preferred to a hard, soulless materialism is questionable and arguable.

153

Those whose egoism is impenetrable by inspired wisdom or religious injunction must have it punctured by adversity.

154

When his own egoism becomes offensive to himself, and even insufferable, he may regard it as a sign of progress.

155

A man has many burdens to bear at different times during his life, but the heaviest of them all is the burden of his own ego.

156

All our movements occur within the "I." All our decisions and judgements, inner experiences and intellectual perceptions are the product of egoistic activity.

157

The disease of egoitis is neither easily nor quickly cured.

158

All his thoughts and imaginations are based on egoism, are immersed in the belief that the ego exists and is real.

159

This extension of personal egoism, this pseudo-conversion of the singular into the plural, this selfishness dressed as altruism, may easily deceive the aspirant.

160

They can keep their thoughts only upon themselves, can never relax and let go of the ego.

161

If his egoism is too strong, the highest part of the Overself's light will be quite unable to get through into his consciousness, no matter how fervent his aspiration for it may be.(P)

162

If I love the ego, then I fear other men or the opinion of other men. I will so act as to please them rather than the higher will.

163

It is not wrong that we love and serve ourselves—for who else is closer?—but only that we do so by excluding the higher purpose of life.

164

The man who asserts his ego in everyday life is often the man who is more successful than his modest fellows. But it still remains open to question whether his kind of success is worth having.

165

Everybody is devoted to his own "I" quite naturally and inevitably. But the meaning of the term "egoist" must be narrowed down to one who habitually tries to use others for his own advantage or tries always to get his own way irrespective of the needs of others.

166

He may escape from situations and from surroundings, but there is one thing from which he cannot escape, and that is himself.

167

However insignificant it be in the eyes of others, the ego carries itself with an air of grotesque self-importance. However trivial its problems, they are vast to its own thinking.

168

If egoism is a sin, we must remember that underneath it lies the basic truth that man is important to himself, and, in lesser degree, to others.

169

When egoism strongly rules the emotional life, it plainly writes itself on the physical face. You cannot have mean thoughts continually alongside of a fine countenance.

170

There is some sense in a man's holding the view that since he is not responsible for the creation of the world, he is equally not responsible for its betterment. If he takes care not to harm anyone, he cannot justly be accused of selfishness, only of self-centeredness.

171

Both emotional reactions and reasoned convictions may be wrong so long as a man is not purified of this egoism.

172

From the moment that the lower ego manifested itself, it embarked on a career of ever-expanding separativeness from the other egos and ever-increasing externalization from its sacred source.

173

The ego looks in every direction for support so that inevitably it contradicts itself from time to time.

174

His ego alternates between hating itself and adoring itself.

175

The ego is there to serve him, but the mistaken unenlightened man thinks it is to be served by him.

176

The same mixture of egoism and idealism will show in his character through most of the Quest. Only in the more advanced stages will the egoism thin down and down until its final elimination.

4

DETACHING FROM THE EGO

Its importance

Our deliverance from the miseries of life hangs solely on our deliverance from the bondage to the ego.

2

One important reason why the great spiritual teachers have always enjoined upon their disciples the need of surrendering the ego, of giving up the self, is that when the mind is continually preoccupied with its own personal affairs, it sets up a narrow limitation upon its own possibilities. It cannot reach to the impersonal truth, which is so different and so distant from the topics that it thinks about day after day, year after year. Only by breaking through its self-imposed pettiness can the human mind enter into the perception of the Infinite, of the divine soul that is its innermost being.

3

A correct estimate of the ego's strength will explain why some aspirants make such slow progress.

4

To all things there is an equivalent price. For awareness of the Overself, pay with the thing that blocks your way—sacrifice the ego.

5

The least important part of Mind gets our almost undivided attention. The illusion-attacked conscious ego—an illusion itself—forces us to see and hear the sense world, or its own vain thought-forms and dream-images, almost all the time. The real part of the Mind is ignored and left out as if it were illusory!

6

No ordinary man really knows himself. He knows only his *idea* of himself. The two are not the same. If he wants to know his true self, he must first liberate himself from this false one, this imagined one, this idea.

7

He identifies himself with all the movements of thought, emotion, or passion—and thus misses his real being.

8

The ego which gets a man into his troubles is unlikely to get him out of them—unless it reforms, learns, or lets some wisdom in.

9

In the absence of this rooting-out of ego, all the solutions of our problem are themselves turned into problems sooner or later.

10

If a man wants continual access to the Overself, he must remember that it is not free; there is a high price to be paid—the price of continual submergence of the ego.

11

It is known to everybody that a planet follows a circular trajectory, but it is hardly known at all that the spiritual path follows a similar one where this truth and teaching about the ego are not known, absorbed, and applied. For every spiritual aspirant shelters the ego in his heart, where it takes every possible disguise to keep him on this circular course that ends up where it started—in self. This is why out of thousands who seek, only a few attain, as the *Bhagavad Gita* laments.

12

Without some kind of inner purgation, they will merely transfer to the religious or mystic level the same egoism which they previously expressed on the materialistic one.

13

You may eradicate as many prejudices and eliminate as many illusions as you wish or can, but if their source—the ego—still remains, new ones will spring up to take their place.

14

The ego is Satan, the devil, the principle of evil, so long as it is not recognized and mastered.

15

So long as he thrusts his ego forward in every situation, so long does he hinder his best opportunities.

16

Rebirths, memories, occult powers—all these things exist and continue because they perpetuate the ego—the very thing we should try to escape from!

17

Consciousness as ego has cut us off from the Source. But it need not do so forever. Through the quest, we can come closer and closer to the reintegration of a subdued ego with its Source, which will thenceforth act through us.

18

So long as the ego's life is disconnected in its own consciousness from the Overself's, so long will it be unable to avail itself of the benefits and advantages which flow from connection in its subconsciousness.

19 ✓

So long as man is attached to the belief that his ego is real and lasting, or thinks and acts as if it were, so long will he be attached to material possessions and worldly desires. For the one is the root of the other.

20 ✓

Those who turn away, traitor to their higher selves, to follow the ancient lures, must travel the whole road of experience to its bitter end.

21

If he wants the best that life can offer him, he must in return offer the most that he has. He must offer himself. There can be no hidden reservations or crafty subterfuges in this offering if it is to be accepted.

22

The ego must be discarded before the Overself can be discovered.

23 ✓

The little ego may suffer under the truth, so tough, so hard. Yet it must in the end recognize that the truth is not harsh but fits neatly into the divine order.

24 ✓

Only when the ego has withered away can he know what real inner peace is.

25

It is not possible for men to live together amicably while the ego rules them. All they can do until this source of all disharmony is itself ruled is to reduce their friction to a minimum by reducing its chief provocations.

26

Only by detaching himself from the situation, the person, or the event which he is inspecting can he come to any true understanding of the one or the other.

27

The Higher Self is forever demanding this conscious relationship; the ego is forever refusing to fulfil the demand.

28

So long as the little self feels itself wise enough to make all its decisions and solve all its problems, so long will there be a barrier between it and the Higher Power.

29

The centre from which he lives is the all-important thing in a man.

30

When humans forget their source and deny their innermost being, they become creatures whose lives are empty of any higher meaningfulness— more than animals, yes, but hardly human enough to justify the dignity of the species.

31

A man can hold only one thought at a time. Even when he seems to hold two different ones (by doing two different actions simultaneously), close analysis will show that the ideas are successive but so rapidly as to appear together. Applying this, it follows that it is his holding of the thought of his personal separate ego *alone* which prevents him achieving identification with the Overself. Is this not said, in another way, by Jesus?

32

These injuries to the ego are the price we must pay for the blessings of the Overself.

33

Your handicap is the strong ego, the "I" which stands in the path and must be surrendered by emotional sacrifice in the blood of the heart. But once out of the way, you will feel a tremendous relief and gain peace.(P)

34

Until he learns that his enemy is the ego itself, with all the mental and emotional attitudes that go with it, his efforts to liberate himself spiritually merely travel in a circle.(P)

35

We must get a standard of knowledge which transcends mere individual opinion. That we can do, however, only if we look impersonally and not personally, if we drop the ego from our measuring and calculating.

36

While the mind remains so fixed in its own personal affairs, be they little or large, it has no chance to open up its higher levels. When attention and emotion are kept so confined, the chance they offer of this higher use is missed. The peace, truth, and goodness which could be had are un-touched.

37

He who lives totally within his ego, lives in a closed world even though it is within himself. He can get no direct knowledge of the divine Overself, no confirmatory experience of those truths which the revelations of great prophets have passed on to him. This is one reason why he can doubt or even oppose them.

38

The ordinary man is the unenlightened man. He lives in a kind of darkness, although he seldom understands this fact. His state is determined by the position which his "I" holds in his consciousness. Does it dominate everything else, or is it dominated itself by the Source from which it springs and borrows its reality?

39

When the ego is acknowledged as being only an existent, not a reality in the ultimate sense, then the ego's life, being in duality, will be transcended at each moment that it is being lived. Such transcendence makes ordinary everyday routine a holy and divine thing; nevertheless the routine remains quite normal, quite ordinary, undramatic, not special or apart from the spiritual life.

40

We shall discover the truth about what we really are in the measure that we discover the error of believing that we are the ego and nothing more. This discovery will take effect and bring us on the way towards realization and liberation only to the extent that we live it, for philosophy is not philosophy unless it is practised in life.

41

Man begins his search for the highest Truth with his ego and rises to its higher and higher levels, but in the end he must leave the ego if the Truth is to be found. The manner of finding truth is such that he must leave the ego's limitations and look to its origin, its universal source.

42

We sit in the ego with all its limitations as in a prison and we do not know that we are prisoners, for we identify ourselves with it and blind ourselves by those very limitations. It is there and it has to be there, but it need not be there to imprison us or to narrow our outlook. The ego imprisons us, for instance, with its memories which keep us steeped in the past when the wisdom of the spirit is to live in the eternal now—which is all we have in reality and which alone is real for neither past nor future possess any reality.

43

The more he is adequately prepared for the impact of the experience, the truer will be the enlightenment. The more his ego has been purified and controlled, the less will it mix itself into that enlightenment.

44

If you wish to be in harmony with the order of the universe, to work with it and not force yourself against it, you must stop imposing the ego—your ego—upon it.

45

The soul's presence is to be realized, its consciousness is to be attained. But the ego's conceit overshadows the one, its turbulence obstructs the other.

46

The ego is the centre of conflicts which lead to sorrow. There is no way of liberating ourselves from the latter without prior liberation from the former.

47

Man moves from Overself to ego and hence moves into suffering.

48

The man who has no other support for his activities and ventures than the ego, and no other centre for his thoughts and feelings, is verily insecure. He passes through the events and situations of life in fears and anxieties derived from the past or drawn from the future.

49

When ego confronts ego, and neither will yield, not to the other but to truth, then both will and must suffer.

50

In the consciousness of ego a man must compete with other men and the most aggressive or the most talented may win. But in the consciousness of Overself, there is no competition against him.

51

If the Overself stubbornly stays out of your range of consciousness, it is because your ego stays too much within it.

52

How true is the Bible's metaphorical statement that man shall not look upon the face of God and live. Yes, he, the ego, must die if God is to be present.

53

Imitating the example set by a spiritual leader, emulating his actions and ways and speech, may contribute helpfully toward the improvement of the self but cannot eradicate it. However improved it may become, it still remains the old self. The man is still unliberated from its thraldom and still caged inside thought patterns provided by someone else.

54

What he believes himself to be, in egoic fact, hides what he really is, in spiritual essence.

55

So long as his ego asserts its supremacy in everything he does, so long as it arranges everything for him, so long will he be the victim of its own ignorance and blindness.

56

So long as the ego is the centre of his being, he is impelled by desires and cravings, his mind covered by the cloud which hides the Source from him.

57

There are various obstacles which get in the way of truth but the biggest is the seeker himself—his limitations, his attachment to the ego.

58

No one is keeping him out of this enlightenment except himself.

59

He who asserts his own ego in conflict with others will thereby provoke them to assert theirs!

60

Truth cannot be found on the basis of what will give pleasure to one's ego. That very feeling of gratification may be a hindrance to its discovery as well as a misleading of the mind.

61

We must take care not to become straitjacketed by our identifications, by the different aspects of our ego.

62

By keeping his ego out of the way, his outlook is no longer blocked with illusions or obstructed with passions.

63

All our relations with others will be markedly affected by the way we use our own ego and function in it.

64

Men discuss gently or debate fiercely under the influence of their personal standpoints and tendencies. They are not aware how much the ego colours their thoughts and statements.

65

A man cannot extract the pure truth about a situation or about the universe if his personal prejudice and ulterior motives prevent him from seeing beyond his own selfish interest in the situation or the universe.

66

It is this personal ego which tricks us into believing that it is ourself, our true self, ever grasping and ever desiring, ever creating fresh illusions and false beliefs; it is this ego, with its wily ways, which keeps us from discovery of reality.

67

How can people find peace while they live in inner contradiction, the deeper part of their being smothered by the surface part?

68

When every thought and every feeling is directed upon his little ego, when the great questions of life itself are never asked because never relevant, a true judgement must declare his private failure whatever his public success may be.

69

While the human entity lives apart from the consciousness of its own real Self, it cannot live in peace. But when it is able to repose completely in that Self, there will be no second thing to draw it away from that peace.

70

Lost in the ego's misery, they do not hear the joyous voice which is calling out to them from a deeper level of their own being, do not know that there is a grace to be hoped for.

71

The ego digs itself into all our emotions and must be dug out again, if we are to be free.

72

When his various thoughts and feelings begin to appear as objects to his "I," it is a welcome sign that he is no longer so bound to his ego as before.

73

Such is the separative ego's hold on most men that although they carry the divine treasure with them they regard it not.

74

When the mind is clogged by memories, hoarded from the ego's past experience, it cannot free itself from the ego, and "come home."

75

The ego is a screen which a man finds between himself and the truth.

76

The patterns of habit in thinking and behaviour become so rigid with time that the introduction of a new style of life, however desirable it may seem, initiates a long struggle.

77

We are prisoners of our ego because we are prisoners of our past.

78

The ego is caught in its own theories and concepts, held prisoner by its own ideas. These are not necessary to enlightenment.

79

Most people are prisoners of their own opinions and judgements, their own point of view. The intellectual humility required either to loosen or even to let go what they hold so tightly and often defend so arrogantly or ignorantly, is one of the first qualities they need to cultivate if they are to begin the quest of truth aright. So long as men are so strongly attached to their own personal wills and limited judgements, they cannot be expected to heed the impersonal teachings and intellect-transcending injunctions of the great prophets.

80

Thoreau: "It is as hard to see oneself as to look backwards without turning round." The self is involved in the very act of seeing and may colour, distort, or obstruct the observation.

81

Ordinarily, men do not escape from their own point of view. This is one aspect of Anatole France's meaning in his phrase: "All is opinion." For all rests on the ego itself, since the latter participates in all events, both in the making of them and in the thinking about them.

82

The constant movement of thoughts and the ego's fascination with itself hide from us the divine Overself, from which both are derived.

83

People will not look at what is actual if it contradicts their expectation, but only at what they think ought to be there.

84

If anyone complains that despite all his efforts he is unable to see the Overself, it can only be because he stubbornly persists in seeing his own "I" with every effort. It is this which blocks the other from his sight. Hence it is this that he must remove.

85

Wherever he goes he brings this ego with him, looks at the world with the same eyes, the same desires and limitations.

86

The ego accompanies him wherever he goes. Let him therefore not fall into gross self-deception and imagine he has removed it.

87

Even if the highest truth were to appear in all its glorious fullness before his mind, he would be unable to recognize it for what it is—much less understand it—if there had been no preparation or purification for it. He would not even be free to look at it if the ego held him tight in its encircling network.

88

The ego can perceive only what is within itself; hence it never gets beyond its own shadow. Even when its thoughts are operating on high truth, this fact still holds.

89

The barrier to a totally clear view of truth is the ego.

90

The ego gets in its own way and shuts out the truth. It is so immersed in itself that it sees nothing else than its own views, its own opinions. And this is true even when it apparently undergoes a mental change or emotional conversion, for in the end *it is the ego itself* which sanctions the newly accepted idea or belief.

91

The ordinary man is never out of himself but always inside his ego.

92

The ego obstructs its own view, whether it is looking at a situation in its life or at God in meditation.

93

The ego should be sustained and inspired by the higher nature, but instead of that we find it barring the way to that nature.

94

The desires which operate in him, in his conscious mind and unconscious self, sway his outlook, beliefs, opinions, but are not the only factors to do so. Family, surroundings, events, and circumstances play their part, too.

95

His way to the goal is blocked by the ego; his glimpses of truth are subverted by the ego; his aspiration for the Overself is contradicted by the desires of the ego.

96

He takes only that portion of truth which suits his ego and rejects the rest.

97

Driven by the ego toward undue emphasis on one side or another, he has no interest in finding the truth. Indeed, if the emphasis is too strong, his interest lies in avoiding the truth!

98

Opinions exist where the "I" dominates; truth is where the ego does not dominate.

99

The ego sees its own picture of the world, coloured by its own characteristics and contained within its own limitations. Because of that it seldom sees people as they really are.

100

Through its ignorance of karmic operations and effects, the ego provokes many of its own oppositions and much of its own troubles.

101

Memory creates for us the patterns, traditions, values, and habits by which we live. It is the dominant authority. But it is also the tyrant which keeps us captive and denies us freedom—a deprival which effectually prevents the finding of truth and effectually builds a barrier to reality. Anyone can remember the ego-coloured past in this way, but only the sage can forget it and dissolve all these patterns.

102

Every discussion which is made from an egoistic standpoint is corrupted from the start and cannot yield an absolutely sure conclusion. The ego puts its own interest first and twists every argument, word, even fact to suit that interest.(P)

103

I am dubious whether anyone can be perfectly sincere if his actions do not come from this deeper source. He may believe that he is, and others may believe the same of him, but since his actions must come from his ego, which is itself spawned by deception and maintained by illusion, how can they achieve a standard which depends on complete truth and utter reality?(P)

104

To describe the ego as "little" and the personality as "petty" is to look at it from outside, where it is lost among such a multitude of others; but to look at it from within the man himself is to find it vastly important, dominating his consciousness, a giant holding him down. It is there, and after all the verbal analyses which reduce it to nothing, its presence reasserts itself.

105

Under the surface of ordinary consciousness he recognizes and remembers the truth when it is presented to him by a man or a book. But the false beliefs bequeathed to him by his parents and the prejudices instilled in him by his environment cause him to resist it.

106

With one part of himself he honestly seeks truth, but with another part he tries to evade it.

107

Whether he is only the victim of his own ego or also that of other men's egos—because he accepts the suggestions they force upon him from childhood—the end result is the same.

108

The ego may in the beginning miss a truth, if it is unwelcome and unpleasant, by subconscious aversion to it. In that case it will look anywhere else than the right place, if it claims to be a seeker.

109

The emotionalists are betrayed by their personal fencing-in of feeling; the intellectuals are betrayed by their shrivelling-up into personal analysis and criticism; the fantasists are betrayed by their personal imaginations. In all three classes, the personal ego limits and shapes their results. They look for God where God is not.

110

Our view of life is usually too personal to permit us to fathom its deeper truths. For the person imposes its intellectual limitations and emotional desires upon the very operation of seeing and understanding what it sees. Its hidden attachments manipulate its operations and becloud its intelligence, thus tying it to a surface view and an oversimplified understanding.

111

He is not always aware of his motives and sometimes deceives himself about them. This is either because some of them lie in the dimmer parts of his being or because they are hidden by the illusion-making power of the ego itself.

112

His personal interests put a bias into his judgements whilst his external conditions shape many of his thoughts.

113

He lives almost wholly in the impressions made upon his senses and in the emotions which may be aroused by them.

114

He tries to avoid recognizing that he is held prisoner in ignorance and in suffering by his own ego, that its condition is unhealthy and unbalanced, and that he must find some way to liberate himself from its thraldom.

115 ✓

He stubbornly persists in following his ego, not because it is superior to that of other men but simply because it is his own. Such is the condition of the average man and such the obstruction to his knowing the truth.

116

The light cannot get past his ego, or if the latter is momentarily lulled, cannot abide with him even when it succeeds in doing so.

117

The ego gets in the way, except for rare moments when the man forgets himself or when a glimpse of truth comes.

118

So long as the personal intellectual and animal ego rules the consciousness, so long will it go from error to error.

119

The ego, with its petty conceit and private desires, shuts him in on itself and cuts him off from the universal life, with its truth and reality and power.

120

The neurotic has contracted both attention and interest into his little self.

121 ✓

Each ego has its own personal version of truth, which coincides with other ego's versions only so far as they reflect its prejudices and desires, fears and favouritisms, and especially its limitations. Hence it is sure to disagree with many.

122

A situation as it appears to be on the surface may contain factors not visibly present to those who are involved in it. For egoism or emotion may cover their eyes in this matter.

123 ✓

It is an old, known fact that the truth can be very disturbing and that is why it is more honoured than practised. Let us ask, "To whom is it disturbing?" and we shall find that the answer refers to the personal ego.

124

It takes a long time, many a lifetime, before the mind discovers that its own imaginative and speculative activities hinder its path to truth or that it is the victim of powerful suggestions received from outside, and nurtured or strengthened by such activities.

125

The experience is all in his head. He thinks it is unique to himself, so it is not too easy for him to separate what is the contribution of his phantasy or his ego and what comes from the authentic source of the Overself.

126

The kind of mind which a man has will naturally put limits upon his attempts to find and comprehend the Truth. Those limits are not only the ones which all human beings possess in common, but also they will vary from one person to another.

127

We ourselves put up certain limitations, deliberately or unwittingly, which fence our thinking and our attitudes, or which may be the cause of harm to self or others.

128

Men are locked up within their little egos. They are in prison and do not know it. Consequently they do not ask, much less seek, for freedom.

129

No mind which works behind such a screen of preconceived assumptions can arrive at truth.

Why most people won't do it

130

We have to accept the fact that most people have an immense capacity for being quite comfortable within the limits of the ego, and have no wish to get away from them to a higher level.

131

They are so satisfied with their ego that they do not even question its right to dominate their minds and dictate their policies.

132

Believing in themselves rather than in God, in their ego rather than in their Overself, they act in a way detrimental to their true welfare and obstructive of their higher interests.

133

The obstacles which prevent the spread of philosophy amongst the masses are not only the lack of culture, the lack of leisure, and the lack of interest. The most powerful of all is one which affects all social classes alike—it is the ego itself. The stubborn way in which they cherish it, the passionate strength with which they cling to it, and the tremendous belief which they give to it combine to build a fortress-wall against philosophy's serene statements of what is. People demand instead what they desire. Hence it is easier to tell them, and easier for them to receive, that God's will decides everything and that the patient submission to this will is always the best course, than to tell them that their blind attachment to the ego creates so large a part of their sufferings and that if they will not approach life impersonally there is no other course than to bear painful results of a wrong attitude. This is the way of religion. Philosophy, however, insists on telling the full truth to its students even if its detached, still voice chills their egos to the bone. Acceptance of the philosophic standpoint involves a surrender of the selfish one. This is an adjustment that only the morally heroic can make. We need not therefore expect any rush on people's part to become philosophers.(P)

134

So precious is our petty ego that we strongly begrudge yielding it up to the seeming void of nonduality.

135

Human beings in general do not care to be reminded of their end, their mortality. How much more would they dislike this concept of their non-selfhood!

136

Philosophy is for the strong. Weak souls shiver in its presence and cling more strongly to their petty egoisms.

137

Most people are so unable or else so unwilling to see their faults that even when the latter are pointed out, they refuse to give assent. They prefer to wear the mask of self-deception. Why? Because the shattering truth hurts their ego.

138

The fact is that they fear to be given the answer to the question, "Who am I?" It might require them to desert their little egos.

139

No one is eager to lose himself as a person.

140

The average human being has little or no awareness of any spiritual element in his personality.

141

They are too preoccupied with passing judgement upon other persons ever to do so upon themselves.

142 ✓

They would like to have their heaven and their ego too. They would like to unite the largeness of the one with the littleness of the other. But this is impossible.

143

Engrossed as they are in personal and family life, they fail to open themselves to the delicate radiation from their innermost being and live as if it were not there.

144

In taking transport to other lands to spend their leisure or their holiday, they try, in vain and without awareness, to take transport out of themselves, out of the compulsions of littleness to the freedoms of the larger being.

145 ✓

It is perhaps not that the multitudes of people are evil as that they get so immersed in working for a livelihood, rearing a family, finding some pleasures, that the little ego provides their sole being. How much they lose if they attend only to this and never to the supreme question: Why am I here?

146

They are so accustomed to thinking in terms of the ego that it seems impossible (to them) to think in any other way.

147 ✓

The experience of being torn from one's roots is so unpleasant that the universal refusal to accede to Jesus' request to give up the ego is easily understandable. People feel the demand is an impossible one to fulfil.

148

Most people are hiding away from themselves or living only in a little part of themselves.

149

Wrapped in the narrow confines of his little self, rarely seeking to expand beyond it, without interest or aspiration outside a half-animal existence, he perishes forgotten.

As genuine spiritual path

150 ✓

If we succeed in detaching ourselves from the claims of past memories and the anticipations of future results, we succeed in detaching ourselves from the ego. This is a practical method of reaching the goal, a veritable yoga-path.

151

To surrender the ego is to surrender the thought of it, and this is done by stilling the mind whenever, in daily life, one becomes self-conscious. This silenced, ego vanishes. It is deep, mental effacement of the thought of being "XY," this quick stilling of the idea of being a particular person, this serene rejection of the intellectual movement and emotional agitation of the ego, that constitutes the "giving up of the self" which Jesus and all great mystics have insistently enjoined. This art of effacing the ego by stilling the mind, by suddenly stopping its whirling flood of thoughts, could not be practised at will and at any time if one had not practised it previously and frequently in deliberate exercises at set times. It is not an art into which the man in the street can straightway plunge. He is not ready for it. He must first get a disciplined mental nature through daily work in meditation as well as a subjugated emotional nature through hardened will. These endeavours must be brought to perfection first before the feat of giving up the ego can itself be brought to perfection.

152

Only day-by-day practice in the art of working deliberately and understandingly with the Overself by denying the ego will bring him eventually to the higher stage where he can work *consciously* with it.

153

Until it is brought to his attention, he may not know that the idol at whose feet he is continually worshipping is the ego. If he could give to God the same amount of remembrance that he gives to his ego, he could quite soon attain, and become established in, that enlightenment to which other men devote lifetimes of arduous effort.

154

There is ultimately but a single source of all power—the cosmic source—and of all intelligence—the cosmic mind. But the ego greatly attenuates and narrows down both the power and the intelligence by obstinately clinging to its own petty individuality alone. If, through the practice of philosophical mysticism, it enlarges its outlook and attunes its mentality to the cosmic mind in which it is itself rooted, then the resultant inspiration will blossom forth in a tremendous transformation of its whole life.

155

Whatever helps to lead him out of the ego's tyranny, be it an idea or a situation, an induced mood or a particular service, is worth trying. But it will be easier, and the result more successful, to the extent that he releases himself from his past history.

156

It requires a heavy effort and involves constant difficulty to live such a life. The ideal of curbing and wearing down the personal ego can be made bearable only by holding cheerfully before the gaze a picture of the satisfying spiritual condition of the ego-free man.

157

If he could stop being in love with his ego and start being in love with his Overself, his progress would be rapid.

158

The question arises: Is it possible to approach life with a mentality free from egoism? This is a question that philosophy has taken very seriously and it says: If the wish exists and the effort is made, there will at least be a less egoistic approach than there would otherwise be. It has therefore evolved a system of training the mind and feelings which, relatively and as far as is humanly possible, does free the human being from excessively egoistic approaches to Truth.

159

There is a useful technique to help attain this purpose. It is to refuse to identify oneself, one's "I," with the personal ego. This calls for frequent, if momentary, awareness of thoughts, emotions, and the body. It can be done at any time in any place and is not to be regarded as a meditation exercise.

160

The first thing to be cleared away is the arrogance and conceit, the pitiful vanity of the earthly-wise and body-held ego.

161

The more he tries to fight the ego, the more he thinks about it and concentrates on it. This keeps him still its prisoner. Better is it to turn his back on it and think about, concentrate on the higher self.

162

A man begins to come into his own the day he rejects the ego. His rejection may not last more than a minute or two, for the false self is strong enough to reclaim its victim. But the process has started which will bring it to an end.

163

It is not only that he thrusts the ego aside during certain uplifted moods but also that he steadfastly maintains this denial of self during the moment-to-moment experience.

164

It is more prudent to be habitually suspicious of his own ego, and its motives, than not.

165

The amount of energy he pours into sustaining the ego and holding to illusions to his own detriment could just as well be poured into sustaining a quest of the Overself to his own gain.

166

They dedicate their lives to worship of the ego when they might dedicate them to worship of the Infinite Power that sustains their souls and bodies.

167

If he is willing to look for them, he will find the hidden workings of the ego in the most unsuspected corners, even in the very midst of his loftiest spiritual aspirations. The ego is unwilling to die and will even welcome this large attrition of its scope if that is its only way of escape from death. Since it is necessarily the active agent in these attempts at self-betterment, it will be in the best position to take care that they shall end as a seeming victory over itself but not an actual one. The latter can be achieved only by directly confronting it and, under Grace's inspiration, directly slaying it; this is quite different from confronting and slaying any of its widely varied expressions in weaknesses and faults. They are not at all the same. They are the branches but the ego is the root. Therefore when the aspirant gets tired of this never-ending Long Path battle with his lower nature, which can be conquered in one expression only to appear in a new one, gets weary of the self-deceptions in the much pleasanter imagined accomplishments of the Short Path, he will be ready to try the last and only resource. Here at long last he gets at the ego itself by completely surrendering it, instead of preoccupying himself with its numerous disguises—which may be ugly, as envy, or attractive, as virtue.(P)

168

It is not a change of the ego's contents that is really needed, however attractive that may well be, but a change that will enable us to step out from the ego altogether.

169

The ego has enthroned itself. It asserts its supremacy in all matters. This situation may be allowed for ordinary people in the ordinary affairs of everyday living but it cannot be allowed for truth-seeking people in the graver issues of the quest. The seeker must indeed cultivate the habit of looking on his ego as his enemy, must resist rather than flatter it.

170

All this is simply to recall man to his best self, deep within, where he is made in the image of God.

171

If it could be both that which is observed and the observer itself for a single second then surely the two mental conditions would instantly annihilate each other. The task is as hard and as foredoomed to failure as trying to look directly at one's own face. Thus the inherent impossibility of such a situation stands revealed. There is only one last hope for success in such a quest and that is to abandon all attempts to know it by the ordinary methods of knowledge. What would such an approach necessarily involve? It would involve two factors: first, a union of the personal "I" into the hidden observer, of which it is an expression, although the merger must not be so absolute as to obliterate the ego altogether; second, an abandonment of the intellectual method which breaks up consciousness into separate thoughts.

172

The actual change-over from being the ego to becoming the watcher of the ego is a sudden one.

173

Thus in his onward march the aspirant has to overcome his sensations and emotions, his thoughts and reasonings, all indeed that he has hitherto known as himself, before he can wake up to the existence of the hidden observer.

174

His work is first to discover where the "I" begins; second, and much more important, where it ends and is no more.

175

It is much easier to identify with our own ego than with the Overself. This is why incessant return to these ideas and exercises is needed.

176

My dear Ego: "It is obvious that in this world I cannot live without you. Your presence is overwhelming, fills every instinct, thought, feeling, and action. But it is also obvious that I cannot live with you. The time has come to adjust our relationship. So I have one request to make of you. Please get out of my way!"

177

We cannot help living in a human ego or feeling its wishes and desires, for most of us are infatuated with it. But it can be put in its place and kept there, first through a profound understanding, next through a lofty aspiration to transcend it, and third through a following of the Quest until its very end.

178

In analysing ourselves we are helping to crush the ego. But this is true only if analysis is unbiased and if it is balanced by the Short Path attitudes. Otherwise there is excessive and morbid preoccupation with oneself, which suits the ego very well!

179

In all situations he must strive to distinguish and follow the lead of the Soul, subduing the clamour of the ego. The former will so guide him that all things will work out for the best in his spiritual welfare, the latter may merely make bad situations worse.

180

What is in your heart? Ramakrishna's was full of the Divine Mother, as he called God. Before long he found her. Saint Francis of Assisi gave humility highest place in his own. He became the humblest man of his time. Fix an ideal in your heart. That is the first step to finding it.

181

This inward exploration must be extended until it penetrates the final mystery of the *I*'s existence.

182

In the end he must untie the knot of his ego and then smooth out his consciousness.

183 ✓

Most men are very eager to appease their egos, but the earnest aspirant must fight this tendency.

184

When the lower ego consents to resign its own life into that of the higher ego, the great evolutionary turn of our times will have fully manifested itself.

185

This divided state of personality must be led to a holy integration, this civil war within himself must be brought to an end in a righteous peace. How much mental exhaustion, discordant nervousness, and emotional upset may be attributed to it!

186

The work begins by removing whatever obstructs the mind from viewing the truth, those qualities and conditions which made it impossible to see reality as it is.

187

The real struggle is not the apparent one. The real enemy is a hidden one.

188

For short periods every day he is to practise something which the ordinary experiences do not allow him to practise—going inside, being impersonal and knowing the "I."

189

Those who feel frustrated because of the absence of mystical experience in their lives, needlessly depress themselves. For their progress to higher values, their rise above egoism to principle, their choice of true well-being over mere pleasure, show their response to the Overself and mark their real advancement better than any transient emotional experience.

190

We have to learn to recognize the individual self, the person, the ego, as a mind-made thing and therefore to withdraw from it, away from it, to put space between ourselves and it, and to detach ourselves more and more and more from it. As this process develops we come more and more into the Truth, the enlightenment.

191

The more we try to put impersonality into our thought and life, the less we are likely to identify ourselves with the ego. This makes way, makes room, gives place for that which is behind the ego to begin to manifest itself.

192

It gives a definite point to one's life as also something to redeem the periods of trivial routine and the boring encounters with semi-animal, wholly egoistic people.

193

That Consciousness which men seek so variously in ecstasy or despair is already there but covered up, suffocated by their own little self-consciousness. Day and night they stay only in the narrow, the personal, be it again in ecstasy or despair. They run to others, to gurus or gods, begging to be liberated. But in the end they have to liberate themselves.

Surrender is necessary

194

The tightness with which we hold on to the ego and thus separate ourselves from the Overself's life and the tenseness with which we shut ourselves in the old miserably limited existence are the results of habit. If we are to escape from it into the free creativity of the greater life, we will have to break its vicious circle. This may be enforced upon us by the shock of drastic events or it may be made possible for us by the grace of an illumined man or it may be achieved by us through the determined arousal of a desperate will. Whichever way it happens, it will be the beginning of the end for the ego and the beginning of the best for ourselves.

195

A master counselled patience. "Can you break iron with your hands?" he asked. "File it down little by little and one day you will be able to snap it into two pieces with a single effort. So it is with the ego."

196

"Blessed are the poor in spirit," said Jesus. What did he mean? To be "poor" in the mystical sense is to be deprived of the possession of the ego, that is, to become ego-free.

197

It was a wise teacher who said to me: "Do not demand from human beings a selflessness they are not capable of giving; demand only that they understand this is the direction toward which the divine World-Idea is pushing them. Through one way or another, they will come in the end to suffer attrition of the ego until it is finally reduced to complete subservience to Overself."

198

He will advance most on the Quest who tries most to separate himself from his ego. It will be a long, slow struggle and a hard one, for the false belief that the ego is his true self grips him with hypnotic intensity. All the strength of all his being must be brought to this struggle to remove error and to establish truth, for it is an error not merely of the intellect alone but also of the emotions and of the will.(P)

199

Jesus bade his hearers forsake their ego-selves if they would find the Overself. But *how* is a man to forsake that which he has loved so long, so intimately, and so ardently. What, in definite and precise details, is he to do?

200

When all of a man's thoughts are put together, this total constitutes his ego. By giving them up to the Stillness, he gives up his ego, denies his self, in Jesus' phrase.

201

If a man wants to come to the awareness of his Overself, he must let go the awareness of his littler self, must shut himself off from its own narrow world. But this can only be effectively done if it is done *inwardly*.

202

He is to loosen himself from the ego's tyranny and thus, without unnecessary further struggle, transcend it.

203 √

"Lose yourself if you would find yourself," said Jesus. Lose the false conception that the self is something by itself, able to stand separate and alone, capable of being regarded as an object knowable by you, the subject. Let this untruth go, and you will find the truth. Cease this identification with the personality, and you will find the Overself.

204

So long as we know only the ego, that in which it abides remains unknown. The way out is to give up the I.

205

Every attempt to disassociate himself from his ego, to observe it in thought and action, to unbind himself from its desires and lusts will be successful only as it is merciless.

206 ⌄

Any direct frontal attack upon the ego as it shows itself openly involves the use of the ego itself. It may succeed in vanquishing some faults, but it cannot succeed in vanquishing that which is behind all faults—egoism. Only surrender of the will and the mind can be effectual in doing so.

207

It is a matter of changing his self-image, of moving over from the picture of a personal ego to the non-attempt to form any image at all, remaining quite literally free from any identification at all. It is not an active work of negating ego but a passive one of simply being, empty Being! For the ego will *always* strive to preserve itself, using when it must the most secret ways, full of cunning and pretense, camouflage and deceit. It takes into itself genuinely spiritual procedures and perverts or misuses them for its own advantage.

208

He clings stubbornly to his ego and cannot relax into the beautiful anonymity of the Overself.

209

It is necessary to forestall a possible miscomprehension. Subordinating one's own ego does not mean submitting it to someone else's ego.

210

The readiness to surrender his lower nature to the higher one, to give up his own will in obedience to God's will, to put aside the ego for the sake of the Overself, puts a man far in advance of his fellows, but it also puts him into certain dangers and misconceptions of its own. The first danger is that he has given up his own will only to obey other men's wills, surrendered his own ego only to fall under the influence of other men's egos. The first misconception is to take lesser voices for God's voice. The second danger is to fall into personal idleness under the illusion that it is mystical passivity. The second misconception is to forget that although self-efforts are not enough of themselves to guarantee the oncoming of Grace, they are still necessary prerequisites to that oncoming. His intellectual, emotional, and moral disciplines are as needed to attract that Grace as are his aspirations, yearnings, and prayers for it. He cannot expect God to do for him work which should be done by himself.

211

No one else can do for a man what Nature is tutoring him to do for himself, that is, to surrender the ego to the higher self. Without such surrender no man can attain the consciousness of that higher self. It is useless to look to a master to make for him this tremendous change-over within himself. No master could do it. The proper way and the only way is to give up this pathetic clinging to his own power, to his own littleness, and to his own limitations. To turn so completely against himself demands from a man an extreme emotional effort of the rarest kind and also of the most painful kind. For to surrender the ego is to crucify it.

212

"The truth shall make you free," promised Jesus. What kind of freedom was he talking about? The answer can only be—from the ego! And this is corroborated by his own statements, uttered at other times, concerning the need to die to oneself.

213

Where the crushing of a man's ego may be beyond his capacity to absorb profitably and may even paralyse his inner growth, the kicking of his ego may be exactly what he needs and what will promote his further growth.

214

The ego can effect tremendous achievements in the domain of worldly life but it can do nothing in the domain of spiritual life. Here its best and only achievement is to stop its efforts, silence itself, and learn to be still.

215

If he is willing to give the intuitive forces mastery within himself, then he will have to exert his will against the egoistic ones.

216

Those who are unable or unwilling to destroy the ego's rule from within must suffer its destruction from without. But whereas the first way brings emotional suffering and mental perturbation, the second brings that along with troubles, disappointments, sicknesses, and blows in addition.

217

All personality must be transcended finally. Even the Master's is no exception to this rule.

218

Not only does the ego, at some point on its way, have to undergo humiliation, but it also has to undergo crucifixion.

219

Every pilgrim on this quest can finish it only by dying upon his own cross. He can rise to the union with his higher self only after the lower one is crucified.

220

Before we can cultivate the best in us, we must crucify the worst in us. The ego must be hung and nailed by degrees if the Overself is to be resurrected in our consciousness. This is why it is so important to cleanse our emotions and correct our thoughts. The desires and the negatives must be overcome to make a way for the truth, the beauty, and goodness.

221

The self-crucifixion of the ego is the terminal of a long line of self-humblings, the culmination of years spent in gradually withdrawing from its thraldom.

222

To die to the ego means that he will free himself from the thought-grooves that usually dominate his life.

223

What he must do is to renounce the ego with all its pride, its greed and passion, and learn to understand his dependence on the Overself.

224

If he ruefully realizes that his most seemingly spiritual conduct and apparently altruistic deeds have been illusory, if he sees at long last that he has lived for his little self alone even when the world admired his unselfish-ness, then the time has come to live not primarily for others, but for the other self, his highest and greater one.

225

The ego is to be renounced, brought down until it is nothing more than a mere possibility.

226

The ego, when disciplined, refined, and spiritualized, can then be given a knock-out blow.

227

The Real Being is not a thing. This does not mean it is nothing. Man is so constituted that normally he can know only things. If he is to approach God, he must let go of his ego-self, his individuated being.

228

The desire to continue life in the ego contains all possible desires. This explains why the hardest of all renunciations for which a man can be asked is that of his ego. He is willing even to suffer mortifications of the flesh or humiliations of his pride rather than that last and worst crucifixion.(P)

229

When his own ego becomes intolerable to him with increasing frequency, he may take this as a good sign that he is moving forward on this road.(P)

230

The declaration of Jesus that whosoever will save his life shall lose it, is uncompromising. It is an eternal truth as well as a universal one. It is needed by the naïve as well as by the sophisticated. Only those who, under the strain and struggle of quotidian existence in these difficult times, ardently yearn for the peace of self-forgetting can begin to understand the first faint echo of that satisfaction which losing one's life brings. It means in plainer language that those who seek salvation in some deep, hidden, and fundamental part of themselves have to make this firm resolution that the physical, the emotional, and the intellectual activities of the personal self shall count less. They will not be able to do that unless they desire salvation more than anything else in their lives. Jesus' statement means that they should seek to liberate the life within them from the very limited idea which the personal ego forms around it and within which it remains confined to the physical, emotional, and intellectual planes alone, and bring it to function also in the intuitive-spiritual plane. It means that the inexorable condition which the Overself imposes before it will reveal itself in all its beauty, its grandeur, its peace, and its power is that they should abnegate this unbalanced interest in the lower activities of this world in which they are so totally immersed. If this abnegation leads to the extreme point of withdrawal from the world then they must even be willing to obey and to take the consequences. But since it is fundamentally an inner thing, it does not necessarily lead a man to take this extreme step—so long as he keeps his inner life and being inviolable even whilst trafficking with the world.

Such an achievement may seem very far off from human possibility and indeed we find in history that not many have either cared, or been able, to realize it, for it is far too painful to the ego. But the metaphysical truths of successive rebirth on earth and of the unreality of time should give some comfort here. The first teaches a great patience while men labour daily at the task of remaking themselves. The second teaches that the Overself is even now ever present with all, that in the eternal Now there is no futurity and that theoretically the possibility of its realization does not necessarily belong to some distant rebirth.

231

The attempt to subdue the ego has a better chance to succeed than the attempt to strangle it.

232

If there is any single secret of development which the successful mystic can offer us, it is that the ego must go out of us and we must go out of it!

233

The earnest enquirer who asks agonizingly how he can continue to carry his burden of responsibility for himself and of obligation to others if he scorns self, needs to make further and deeper studies into the teaching on this point.

234

Deliver up the ego to That which is beyond it.

235

Even when no longer afraid of others, a man should yet be afraid of himself—so one of the thinkers of old Rome advised. Until the ego is thoroughly conquered, vigilance will always be necessary.

236

The wisdom of Psalm 46—"Be still and know that I am God"—may be tested by experiment. For in the ego's silence there will be whispered the revelation we await.

237

The man who has enough respect for himself to realize that he could (and should) become a better man will find that the line of self-improvement stretches all the way into infinite distance. At what point is he to stop? For in the end, however much he polish and perfect the ego, it must give itself up to the Overself.

238

Give up the outer illusions and gain the inner reality. Give up considering the body as the self and gain the awareness of Overself.

239

Once the work of purification has advanced sufficiently far, the work of divesting himself of his egoism must begin. It is to be carried on as much by reflection as during action, by meditation as through watchfulness.

240

Anything and everything may be made to serve the ego and help it to become fatter. Yet they too, regarded from within oneself in the right way, may help it to become slimmer. It is the proper business of the truth-applied to show this way.

241

Every time he resists the impulse to angry action, or the urge to bitter scolding, he resists the ego. The cumulative result of many such disciplines is to thin down the ego and draw nearer the hour of its final destruction.

242

In that moment when we submit our selfish tendencies to the discipline of the Ideal, we thin down the ego and open the inner being to Truth's light.

243

I do not say that he engage himself in a vain attempt to extirpate the ego but rather its tyranny.

244

He will need strength to stand apart from the crowd, more strength to resist the world's flatteries and reject its luxuries, but the most strength of all to deny his ego and free himself from it.

245

This injunction of Jesus meant that he was to give up the old self in order to find the new one, to leave himself as a thinking animal in order to find himself as an intuiting illumined being.

246

Consider the relation that our body bears to its parents. During its childhood it was fed, clothed, sheltered, and protected by those parents, so long as it remained with them and looked to them for these benefits. If it ran away and deserted them, it was likely to lose some or all of them; above everything, it would lose the visible tokens of love that accompanied them. The finite mind, being that which dwells within the body, bears the same relation to its own parent-source, the infinite Mind God. If it strays away in heart and deed from that source, it finds itself dependent on its own unhelped small and limited resources. Its life is thenceforth beset by perils, punctuated with troubles, and clouded by errors. But if it awakens, repents, and returns; if it begins by faith, prayer, action, and meditation to surrender its personal will to the higher will; if it daily seeks guidance and strength from the Soul, help begins to come into its life.

247

What is the meaning of the parable of the prodigal son except that he is Man gone away from himself and feeding on the husks of earthly life when the bread of the Overself is being offered him?

248

The more he is unwilling to give up the ego's judgement and desires, the longer will his sufferings continue.

249

He learns to trample on the ego, to put its pride aside and resist its passions.

250

You will be saved, not by a man's suffering on a wooden cross two thousand years ago, but by your own suffering as your ego voluntarily crucifies itself today.

251

The pushing aggressive will of the personal ego is to be replaced by the passive surrendered will of the overruled ego.

252

The deeper he retires into his inmost being, the farther he retreats from the personal selfhood.

253

Discipline the ego, be hard on it, press it down to the point of crushing it. There is profit in such activity.

254

He must create the courage and realism to look the true facts about himself in the face, and for once to reject the conceited pretensions of his ego.

255

We have to pass through the life of the ego but we do not have to be enslaved by and fettered to it.

256

We all seek to fulfil ourselves, each in his own way. Let us not seek blindly, but in an awareness as complete as we can muster let us strive to see what we do from a more than personal standpoint.

257

Sufi Mystic Akhlar-I-Jalali said "One little step beyond myself was all" he found necessary to attain illumination.

258

The ego must cease its arrogance and abandon its independence. It must let itself be led.

259

The symptoms of a disease can be relieved, or even lost, without the cause of that disease being removed. It is the same with ego. So long as it dominates consciousness, so long will any physical, emotional, or intellectual change fail to be deep enough. A radical transformation is needed: the ego's dominance must go.

260

Emptying the mind of all its contents is, by itself, an admirable operation and worth trying for the sake of the benefits. But it is not, from the philosophic standpoint, a sufficient operation. It forgets the performer of the operation—the ego. He, too, ought to be emptied out along with his own thoughts.

261

A time must come, whether in this birth or a later one, when the ego must give up the struggle, which is both with itself and the Higher Power at the same time.

262

Each experience in this tumultuous world is a chance to get farther from our habitual egoism.

Its difficulty

263

For all that is talked and written about it, very few ever succeed in making the full mystical surrender of their ego.

264

This notion of the ego, acquired by ignorance and maintained by habit, persists so fixedly throughout life that ordinarily people are quite incapable of changing it, despite the suffering it constantly brings them.

265

Only the deepest kind of reflection, or the most exciting kind of mystical experience, or the compelling force of a prophet's revelation can bring a man to the great discovery that his personal ego is not the true centre of his being.(P)

266

Withdrawal from senses is hard, withdrawal from thoughts is harder still, but withdrawal from the ego is the hardest of all yogic tasks.

267

To attain relief from the ego is possible to all aspirants at times and for limited times, but to shed it altogether is possible only to the rare few who stand upon the verge of sagedom.

268

Few men are aware of their own egoism, fewer still understand it, and fewest of all are those who undertake to overcome it.

269

There is as much difference between the Sunday sanctimony of a normally religious man and the abnegating battle of an aspiring philosopher as between a stage-property landscape and a real one.

270

It requires a superhuman strength to practise the self-imposed discipline of living apart from the ego's desires.

271

Should he attempt to repudiate what is the strongest part of himself—the ego—he is likely to find how strongly attached are his desires. He has transferred the object of his attentions from the worldly sphere to the spiritual sphere, but the ego is still active. When his meditation comes to the threshold of Truth, he stops, terrified by the feeling that he is losing his very self. His little personal world is the subject that really interests him.

272

To advise a man always to remove the ego when considering a situation where a moral judgement is needed is fatuous and futile. It is like telling a man to lift himself up by his own trouser braces.

273

Some seek detachment from one thing, others from another thing, but he who seeks detachment from his ego has the highest aim—and the most difficult.

274

It is not easy for the untrained man to distinguish, among the varied contents of his consciousness, which ones originate from the Overself and which from the ego.

275

He believes he is surrendering to his higher self when all the time he is only surrendering to his own ego.(P)

276

My pen is paralysed into inactivity whenever I remember how hard it is to overcome the ego, how futile to ask men to engage in such a seemingly hopeless enterprise.

277 ✓

Only he who seeks constantly to efface his personal ego can know how hard, how long-drawn a labour it necessarily is. For it demands not only an absolute honesty of self-examination but also a complete modesty of attitude.

278 ✓

When a man's ego is inflamed with vanity, nothing can be done for him. He must then get the tutoring of the results of his vanity—which cannot in the end be other than painful.

279

Consider that all the day's activities minister to the cares or interests of the ego and emanate from it! Then realize how hard it will be to secure detachment from it.

280

The error lies in believing that the experience will deliver him once and for all time from his lower nature or implant him permanently in his higher nature.

281

If man's restless mind is hard to curb, his ego is harder still to enchain.

282

How often does the aspirant despise his ego, yet how seldom is he able to forsake it!

283

The ego is so full of subterfuges and wiles, so quick to defend its errors and sins, that the struggle against it cannot help being other than a long, drawn-out, extreme one.

284

The ego offers bitter resistance all along the way, disputes every yard of his advance, and is not overcome without incessant struggle against its treacheries and deceptions.

285

The mixture of thoughts and feelings along with the body which a man considers as himself, which is the identity that he accepts, is hard to banish willingly "and imaginatively" into a condition of oblivion and unconsciousness. It would be harder still to take out of the picture all attachment to his own person and to put into it the attributes of consciousness.

286

Men, during war, have been known to show tremendous courage in attacking other men, yet show extreme reluctance to attack a different sort of enemy—themselves, or rather that part which is baser and shameful.

287

The ego must be too often battered by life before its self-confidence can be destroyed.

Ego corrupts spiritual aspiration

288

The ego is cunning, subtle, insidious. Even when the aspirant has long left a grosser kind of life behind him, it inserts itself into his prayers and meditations alike, and enters most of his inner work.

289

The ego easily masquerades as an earnest spiritual seeker.

290

As long as the ego still dominates over, or hides behind, his spiritual activities, they are, from the viewpoint of getting a successful glimpse, in vain. Of course, from other special viewpoints, such as improving the moral character or acquiring intellectual information, they are not useless and do have valuable importance.

291

However careful he may try to be, the avoidance of personal bias in the ego's favour may only succeed in transferring it from the gross to a subtle plane. And the more the mind possesses critical capacity where others are concerned, the more it is blind to its own egoism.

292

To keep you attached to itself, albeit more subtly, the ego will make use of these very spiritual practices by which you hoped to escape it.

293

If the ego cannot keep him any longer through his animal instincts, it will masquerade as his higher self, flatter him for his lofty aspirations, insert itself into his intuitions, and seek to deceive him as he bends in prayer or sits in meditation.

294

There are today very few who have transcended their "I," and attained THAT which is behind it. Nearly all the contemporary glib talk of spiritual things or the modern advertised teachers and prophets of spiritual experience bears internal evidence of the ego's hidden presence, whatever the external signs may be.

295

The ego can take shelter under many lies, illusions, or pretexts, and this of a spiritual as well as worldly kind.

296

Endless is the procession of illusions by which man keeps his ego alive. They grow subtler in nature and finer in quality, they even rise from the materialistic plane to the spiritual, but their essential deceptiveness remains.

297

The structure of egocentric interests, attachments, tendencies, and emotions fills the consciousness of the unenlightened man and the spiritually aspiring man alike. In the second case it has either merely been enlarged to include religious beliefs and dogmas, religio-mystic experiences and feelings, or it has diminished to serve ascetic achievements and fanatic notions.

298

Messages from his higher Self, messages of guidance and of warning, of instruction and of inspiration, may come frequently to the seeker; and yet he may not receive them aright. If his emotions do not interfere with them, his intellect may do so; if his desires do not interfere, his reasoning may do so. But behind all these interferences stands the ego, sometimes open and obvious but at other times hidden, secretive, and difficult to detect. It lies in wait for every intuitive message and deliberately seizes it during the very moment of manifestation, striving to falsify and to mislead the seeker.

299 ✓

In the very act of praising God or lauding Spirit, the ego praises or lauds itself—such is the cunning duplicity with which it leads a man into thinking that he is being very spiritual or becoming very pious.

300

The ego cunningly adjusts itself to each stage of his inner growth and is thus able to remain in all his relationships and activities.

301 ✓

They seek different ways of escape, and imagine that the new way will be the final one. But this is a vain self-deception so long as the ego depends on its own activity to eliminate its own dominance.

302

Through the operation of unexpected events or unsought experiences, we are partially exposed to ourselves for what we always have been but did not always know. But such is the power and the cunning of the ego that it never exposes itself—the real malefactor—and keeps us in ignorance of the real root of our troubles. It will keep us preoccupied with thoughts of a highly spiritual kind, it will let us smugly feel we are making progress, but it will not let us see and slay the true enemy—itself!

303

Just as the evil situations in life are made to yield some good in the end and subserve the evolutionary process, so the good ones are made to yield evil results by the ego's ascendancy and craftiness. It will turn his very spiritual aspirations against him, and pervert them. If he gains a little interior peace, for instance, a lot of smugness, pride, or even arrogance may be mixed with it.

304

How easily can the ego clothe itself in false altruism or hide behind high-sounding speech! How quickly can it exploit others to its own advantage! How smoothly can it lead a genuine aspiration into a side-path or, worse, a trap!

305

Self-love hides behind most of what he does, and pursues him even into the so-called spiritual realm, where it takes on more impenetrable disguises.

306

When pushed into defending itself and justifying its ways, the ego will rationalize them and talk of their "evolutionary necessity" or of the aspirant's "higher mission and historic task." All this talk is a deceptive mental construction, not a genuine intuitive guidance. The aspirant who falls victim to his own mentally invented excuses, speculations, imaginations, or alibis falls victim to the machinations of the ego. Thus, instead of accusing it as the real source of his trouble he foolishly supports it and vainly tries to cover up its errors.

307

The ego is sitting at his side waiting to deceive him subtly into making wrong decisions and false interpretations, if they will hinder his growth into truth and thus preserve its own life.

308

He would be more prudent to suspect the presence of the ego even in his most spiritual aspirations, reflections, and experiences.

309

It is to be expected that the ego will protect itself, even if that has to go so far as engagement in a quest which apparently ends in its own utter abasement.

310

How glibly the personal ego takes over ideas and practices for the development of impersonality!

311

The ego is here, ever at work and present even when it is supposed to be absent.

312

He will not escape easily from the ego. If he transfers his interests to the spiritual plane, its imagination will transfer itself there too and flatter him with psychic experiences or visions.

313 ✓

The ego will resort to any and every stratagem to keep alive. It will consent even to any and every spiritual discipline or course, however high-sounding, except the only one that will deal it a death-blow.

314

When the ego fails to detain him in formal weaknesses, it will disguise itself anew and direct their strength into subtle and even spiritual channels. If it cannot hold him by his more obvious weaknesses, it will do so by his subtler ones; if not through his shortcomings then through his alleged virtues. It does not find much difficulty with all its craftiness and cunning in perverting his most fervent spiritual aspiration into disguised self-worship and his spiritual experiences into undisguised vanity. Or it will use his sense of remorse, shame, and even humility to point out the futility of his attempts at moral reform and the impossibility of his spiritual aspirations. If he yields to the duplicity and perversity of such moods, he may well abandon the quest in practice and leave it in the air as a matter of theory. But the truth is that this is really a false shame and a false humility.

315

The ego will creep even into his spiritual work or aspiration, so that he will take from the teaching only what suits his own personal ends and ignore the rest, or only what suits his own personal comfort and be averse to the rest.(P)

316

Although the ego claims to be engaged in a war against itself, we may be certain that it has no intention of allowing a real victory to be achieved but only a pseudo-victory. The simple conscious mind is no match for such cunning. This is one reason why out of so many spiritual seekers, so few really attain union with the Overself, why self-deceived masters soon get a following whereas the true ones are left in peace, untroubled by such eagerness.(P)

317

The ego constantly invents ways and means to defeat the quest's objective. And it does this more indefatigably and more cunningly than ever when it pretends to co-operate with the quest and share its experiences.(P)

318

To avoid the truth they accept its imitations.

319

That crafty old fox, the ego, is quite capable of engaging in spiritual practices of every kind and of showing spiritual aspirations of every degree of warmth.(P)

320

Instead of reducing the ego, it has merely exchanged its areas of interest, itself remaining as strong as before. The unworldly has been taken into its jurisdiction for the sake of its own growth and power.

321

The ego not only obligingly provides him with a spiritual path to keep him busy for several years and thus keeps him from tracking it down to its lair; it even provides him with a spiritual illumination to authenticate that path. Need it be said that this counterfeit illumination is another form of the ego's own aggrandizement?(P)

322

The ego-shadow produces its part of the inner experience or intuitive statement cunningly and unobtrusively intermingled with the real higher part.

323

If the ego can outwit his aspirations by leading him to false teachers or by deceiving him with glib sophisms or by carrying him into extravagant emotions, it will use circumstances or interpret situations so that it can do so.

324

It is in line with the limited degree of mass human development that the popular religions, both Oriental and Occidental, cater to the ego. This is visible at a number of points, such as the teachings on prayer and the post-mortem state. Those religions have had to accommodate themselves to the unevolved. And consequently in their moral aims, they have sought to thin down man's ego since he was not ready to give up trying to perpetuate it.

325

The ego takes pride in its own effort and deludes the man into thinking that therefore it is capable of leading him into the desired goal. On such a view its power is everything, the power of grace is nothing.

326

However fine the virtues which it cultivates may be, they are still ego-chosen and ego-grown, still self-centered—which may help to interpret Jesus' pronouncement about all our righteousness being as filthy rags to God.

328

The student is warned to be on guard against his own ego, which may feed his vanity and conceit with the false idea that he is much more advanced than he really is.

327

When men mistake their own desires or their own surmises for the will of God, the ego has simply transferred the sphere of its activity from the animal to the pseudo-spiritual.

329

Even when the aspirant has won his victory over the animalistic nature within himself, he often suffers a defeat from the human nature for his very victory may fill him with spiritual conceit.

330

Men suit their own self-interest. They may cover this up with tall talk or simple hypocrisy. They may try to trick others or even themselves with an outward show of idealism.

331

He has done well but not well enough. For if this part of his self is striving hard to further his quest, there is another part—his vanity—which is obstructing it.

332

A good spiritual technique may become vitiated by converting it into another way of clinging to the ego, a subtle disguised way which deceives the conscious mind.

333

The image which the ordinary person often fashions for himself of a well-developed spirituality, is usually superior to the actuality.

334

Despite its zeal to spiritualize its ways, ennoble its actions, and raise the level of its aspirations, the ego never forgets itself.

335

The ego sits in the saddle all the time that he is travelling the Long Path.

336

He is more often and more easily aware of the openly destructive traits of his character than of the subtly egotistic ones.

337

A man can carry his selfishness into his rules of self-discipline, his ambition into his aspirations, and his vanity into his meditations. The results will only stimulate his ego, and not minify it.

338

The ego creeps into spirituality and makes it self-seeking in its contacts with others or narrow in its understanding of others.

339

The "I" shields itself from all threats to complete belief in its own reality, permanence, and separateness. Consequently, it sees metaphysical-yogic work as a danger to be removed by appropriation and absorption. Such work is then misused to serve and strengthen the ego while seeming to unmask it.

340

It is inevitable for the ego to try to free itself from the restrictions put upon it, and so bring about a relapse. Its natural greed for self-indulgence comes into conflict with these restrictions. Therefore the novice who feels he has made a great advance should not exult too prematurely, or he may find that his advance is less stable than it appears.

341

Whosoever seeks his own glory in these practices may find it, but he will keep out the grace.

342

What he has done is to transfer the ego, with all its self-seeking greed, its arrogant complacency, its colossal ignorance of its own source, from his worldly activities to his spiritual activities. The ego will do everything possible to preserve its existence and devise every possible means to secure its future. This is why the man himself rarely wakes up to what is happening, and why the fates may crush him to the ground to destroy his sleep. If this event takes place while he is still comparatively young, when his powers are strong, and not at the close of life, when they are feebler and less effectual, he is indeed fortunate, although he will certainly not think so at the time.

343

"This divine illusion of Mine is hard to pierce," says the *Bhagavad Gita*. Those who imagine it is easy, and quickly done, merely move from one point to a different one within their own little ego. They mistake the false for the true, the illusion of light for Light itself.

344

So long as the ego's defenses remain intact, the man will live within its illusion as will all his spiritual experiences. They may be striking, dramatic, thrilling, rapturous, and extraordinary, but they will still be based on identification with his little personal consciousness.

345

It is the sin of spiritual pride, of pride in the fact that he is a quester. But he does not see that he is nearly always at the centre of this search: it is *his* relationship with God that matters. Always clinging to ego!

Humility is needed

346

It requires a mood of real humility for a man to acknowledge that he is in the wrong. Such a mood will benefit him in two ways. It will correct an erroneous course and it will thin down a fat ego.

347

A time will come when he will have to get away from himself. He will learn to outrage his own pride, to swallow his own vanity.

348

He knows that it is his duty to look beyond his little ego, to devise withdrawals and enter retreats from the continuous immersion in his own personality. If, in such short periods, he can achieve impersonality and attain anonymity, the result will be beneficial out of all proportion to the time given. And even though it will make him humbler in society, it will lift him to a higher place in heaven.

349

When a man can forgive God all the anguish of his past calamities and when he can forgive other men and women for the wrongs they have done him, he will come to inward peace. For this is what his ego cannot do.

350

The ego demands, fiercely and clamantly or suavely and cunningly, its own unhindered expression. But the ideal formed by intuition from within and by suggestion from without, counsels the ego's restraint.

351

Lao Tzu praised unobtrusiveness in social behaviour and minimum speech among others. Both these suggestions were intended to help put the ego in its place and to humble it.

Longing for freedom from ego

352

The longing which possesses the seeker is there because of what the Overself is and what the ego is not. There are contradictory reactions between them. The ego is attracted through an evolutionary compulsion outside itself and yet it is also repulsed through its own instinct of self-preservation. Hence the longing is not always there: again and again conflict appears and battle must be revived, victory regained.

353

The weariness of life which shows itself in the desire not to be born again at all, in the yearning for Nirvanic peace, may come from having endured too deep suffering. But it may also come from having saturated oneself with experiences of all kinds during a series of reincarnations far longer than the average one. It is then really a desire to extinguish the tired ego.

354

Will a day ever come, he may wonder, when the ego will reach the end of its own tether and lie utterly still?

355

It is both the irony and tragedy of life that we use up its strictly limited quota of years in pursuits which we come later to see as worthless and in desires which we find bring pain with their fulfilment. The dying man, who sees the cinema-film of his past flash in review before his mental eyes, discovers this irony and feels this tragedy.

356

When he finds that he has been following his own will even at those times when he believed he was following the higher self's will, he begins to realize the extent of the ego's power, the length of the period required for its subdual, and what he will have to suffer before this is achieved.

357

One day he will feel utterly tired of the ego, will see how cunningly and insidiously it has penetrated all his activities, how even in supposedly spiritual or altruistic activities he was merely working for the ego. In this disgust with his earthly self, he will pray for liberation from it. He will see how it tricked him in the past, how all his years have been monopolized by its desires, how he sustained, fed, and cherished it even when he thought he was spiritualizing himself or serving others. Then he will pray fervently to be freed from it, he will seek eagerly to *dis*-identify himself and yearn ardently to be swallowed up in the nothingness of God.(P)

358

When the wish for non-existence becomes as continuous as the thirst for repeated earthly existence formerly was, when with George Darley, the early nineteenth-century English poet, he can say "There to lay me down at peace/ In my own first nothingness," he has become an old soul.

359

He will make the depressing discovery that even when he believed he was climbing from peak to peak in overcoming the ego, he was really walking in a circle on flat ground—such is its power to delude him. When he thought he was becoming free of its chains, he was merely clanking them in another part of this circular area! It will make for melancholy reflection to find that he is still a prisoner after all these years of endeavour. Nevertheless the awakening to this fact is itself a triumph over illusion and should be used to counteract his sadness. For from then on he will be in a better position to know what are the false steps and what are the right ones in seeking to escape and he will also be more ready to look outside himself for help in doing what he must recognize is so hard to do by himself.

360

All his longings to escape from the prison of the ego and to reach the *I AM* in himself reflect themselves in his experiments with drink, drugs, sex, adventure, or ambition.

361

The impulse which impels men to seek truth or find God comes from something higher than their ego.

362

His quest has reached its end when the ego, by the Overself's grace, has come at long last to desire fully and attain successfully its own extinction rather than, as before, its own aggrandizement.

363

The desire for death which rises when suffering seems unendurable is at bottom a desire for release from individual entity.

Knowledge is needed

364

If we can first understand and then realize that we have it within us to provide channels for the higher power, we may override difficulties that the little and limited ego could not cope with.

365

It is no doubt an excellent effort to attempt the ego's curbing, restraining, disciplining, or purifying. But this is only a preliminary and cannot of itself bring enlightenment. Moreover, it is a preliminary that never seems to come to an end. As one fault is removed, a new one created by new circumstances or developments arises. So what is really required is the ego's dissolution. But this cannot be brought about without first acquiring some understanding of what the ego really is.

366

It is not to be expected that anyone can dissociate himself from the false identification with the ego before he has fully become convinced of the ego's unreality.

367

The student who wishes to progress beyond mere parrot-like book memorization will fill his mind with this great truth of the ego's unreality, permeate it by constant reflections about it at every opportune moment, and regularly bring it into his formal meditation periods. He will approach it from every possible angle and study every possible side of it.

368

"Give up thyself" is the constant injunction of all the great prophets. Before we can understand why this was their refrain, we must first understand the nature of the self about which they were talking. There is in every man a false self—the ego—and the true one—the Overself.

369

The ego stands in the way: its own presence annuls awareness of the presence of the Overself. But this need not be so. Correct and deeper understanding of what the self is, proper adjustment between the individual and the universal in consciousness, will bring enlightenment.

370

The mystic must first get a knowledge of the laws of the human psyche before he can understand what is happening to him.

371

When he can begin to see his errors, he is beginning to be self-aware.

372

To know what his real "I" is not is a first and most important step toward knowing what it really is. Indeed, it has a liberating effect.

373

The ego's rigidity must first be overcome: it shuts up consciousness within itself. If he can become *aware* of his imprisonment, this will be the beginning of finding freedom from the tendencies and impulses which largely compose it.

374

He must mentally rectify the errors of those instinctive egoistic reactions which the philosophic discipline will make him aware of—an awareness that may come quite soon after they happen or much later.

375

He has taken a tremendous step forward who comes to see his ego as ugly and unworthy, his spiritual path as self-aggrandizement.

376

Only when the ego ceases to have any existence for us can we transcend it. Only when we cease to believe in its reality can we lose the attachment for it.

377

He needs to look at himself without letting the ego get in the way.

378

He must begin by learning that the ego is very much the lesser part of himself, that it must be kept down in its place as an obedient servant, its desires scrutinized and disciplined or even negated, its illusions exposed and removed.

379

We begin by understanding the ego—a work which requires patience because much of the ego is hidden, masked or disguised. We end by getting free from it.

380

It is easy to recognize some of the attachments from which he must loose himself—the greeds, the lusts, and the gluttonies—but it is not so easy to recognize the subtler ones. These start with attachment to his own ideas, his own beliefs; they end with attachment to his own ego.

381

Insufficient insight is the cause of the power which ego-illusion retains over us. When we perceive that reality is beyond speculation, our intellectual searchings lose their utility and value and die down; the mind becomes undisturbed and calm.

382

The self-image which he holds may continue to keep him tied or help to set him free.

383

Most people exist self-sufficiently in their ego and demand nothing further from life. But if intuition can finally break through, or reason slowly work down to its deepest level, they find out how childish is such an attitude, how lacking in true maturity.

384

Both Shankara and Ramana Maharshi blame identification with the body as ignorance, which the first says results in "no hope of liberation" and the second says is "the root cause of all trouble." What they say is unquestionably so. *But what else can happen in the beginning except this identification?* It is the first kind of identity anyone knows. His error is that he stays at this point and makes no attempt to inquire further. If he did—

in a prolonged, sustained, and continued effort—he would eventually find the truth: knowledge would replace ignorance.

385

Charity, service, helpfulness, character-building—all such activities are good, but they take and leave the ego as a given fact. They are willing to curb, discipline, correct, reform, polish, or purify the ego, but its permanent and real existence is accepted not only as true but as a part of things as they are in nature.

Tracing ego to its source

386

So long as we persist in taking the ego at its own valuation as the real Self, so long are we incapable of discovering the truth about the mind or of penetrating to its mysterious depths. It is a pretender, but so long as no enquiry is instituted it goes on enjoying the status of the real Self. Once an enquiry into its true nature is begun in the proper manner and continued as long as necessary, this identification with ego may subside and surrender to the higher.

387

To trace the ego to its lair is to observe its open and covered manifestations, to analyse, comprehend, and note their everchanging ephemerality. Finally it too turns out to be but a thought structure—empty, and capable of dissolution like all thoughts.

388

Such are the demands of the personal self that they will assuredly never end if we do not check them at their source. And this source is our inborn belief in the reality of the personal ego.

389

Systems of discipline may weaken the ego, may tether it to some code or ideal, may bring it under some sort of control; but they do not bring about any root change in the man who is still himself controlled by the same old master, the same old ego. These systems may even suppress the self for a time, but that is not the same, nor can it give the same lasting result, as clearly facing the self and penetrating it by the understanding of insight.

390

Be still and know! This is to be done by practising the art of meditation deep into its second stage and then—for it cannot properly be done before—tracing the ego to its hidden lair. Here it must be faced. Being still involves the achievement of mental silence, without which the ego remains cunningly active and keeps him within its sphere of influence. Knowing involves penetrating to the ego's secret source where, in its lulled and weakened condition, it can be confronted and killed.

391

The ego is always in hiding and often in disguise. It is a cunning creature, never showing its own face, so that even the man who wants to destroy its rule is easily tricked into attacking everything else but the ego! Therefore, the first (as well as the final) essential piece of knowledge needed to track it down to its secret lair is how to recognize and identify it.

392

When the great battle is over, the Overself will give him back his ego without giving him back its dominance.

393

Everything we do or say, feel or think is related back to the ego. We live tethered to its post and move in a circle. The spiritual quest is really an attempt to break out of this circle. From another point of view it is a long process of uncovering what is deeply hidden by our ego, with its desires, emotions, passions, reasonings, and activities. Taking still another point of view, it is a process of dissociating ourselves from them. But it is unlikely that the ego could be induced to end its own rule willingly. Its deceptive ways and tricky habits may lead an aspirant into believing that he is reaching a high stage when he is merely travelling in a circle. The way to break out of this circle is either to seek out the ego's source or, where that is too difficult, to become closely associated and completely obedient to a true Master. The ego, being finite, cannot produce an infinite result by its own efforts. It spins out its thoughts and sends out its desires day after day. They may be likened to cobwebs which are renewed or increased and which never disappear for long from the darkened corners of a room, however often they may be brushed away. So long as the spider is allowed to live there, so long will they reappear again. Tracking down the ego to its lair is just like hunting out the spider and removing it altogether from the room. There is no more effective or faster way to attain the goal than to ferret out its very source, offer the ego to that Source, and finally by the path of affirmations and recollections unite oneself with it.(P)

394

The ego knows that if profoundly concentrated attention is directed toward ascertaining its true nature the result will be suicidal, for its own illusory nature would be revealed. This is why it opposes such a meditation and why it allows all other kinds.

395

The truth affronts his egoism, for if accepted, it leaves him crushed and enfeebled.

396

Each person's life is coloured by his individual attitude. This is shaped by the ego and limits both his experience and his understanding of life. At every stage of the quest, the seeker must try to track the ego to its lair, but only at the final stage can he force it into the open, to be seen at last for what it really is. It had deceived him all along into believing it was the true self.

"Dissolution" of ego

397

Being what it is, a compound of higher and lower attributes which are perpetually in conflict, the ego has no assured future other than that of total collapse. The Bible sentence, "A Kingdom divided against itself cannot stand," is very applicable to it: this is why the aspirant must take heart that one day his goal will be reached, even if there were no law of evolution to confirm it—as there is.

398

In this strange experience when his life passes before his mind's eye like a pageant but he does not feel that the figure he is watching is really himself, he learns the truth—or rather has the possibility of learning it— that even the personal ego is also a changing transitory appearance.

399

The realization of human insignificance as against the cosmic background impresses deeply. However, there is another aspect to this realization. It is an excellent preparation for the thought of the Void wherein the individual human entity is not merely insignificant but is actually nonexistent, merged or rather returned to that which gave it birth.

400 ✓

In the tremendous amplitude of this cosmic revelation, his ego narrows down to a littleness befitting its true character. Its problems diminish or disappear accordingly.

401

Hindus stress an everlasting state of bliss beyond the rebirths. Time is as illusory as its opposite number, prolonged time or eternity. Whether the ego goes out drowning in fear of bodily death or drowning in Nirvana's bliss, it goes out in the end.

402

Everyone is already practising devotion to his own ego: he loves and surrenders to it. If, by enquiry and reflection, by art or meditation, he arrives at the discovery that the essential being of "I" is none other than "He," and penetrates it deeply and constantly until he becomes established in the new identity, his ego dissolves by itself. Thenceforward he fulfils his highest duty as a man.

403 ✓

That there is an absolute end to all his existence may frighten one man but console another.

404

Who is willing to let himself vanish, even during the brief hour of meditation, into the primal origin of all things?

405 ✓

Disattachment from the world is not necessarily withdrawing from it. Getting rid of the ego does not mean destroying its existence (for metaphysically it is non-existent, a whirlpool of water) but destroying its dominant power.

406

We ascribe permanence and bestow reality on the ego, a mistake which leads to all the mistaken thoughts, attitudes, courses, and acts that follow as its effects. But the fact is that no ego can be preserved in perpetuity and that all egos are made up of ephemerally joined together activities. One of the first consequences flowing from this fact is that any happiness which depends on the ego's keeping its united state must break down with its further changes or disunion. Moreover, since the cosmic law dooms all egos to eventual merger in their higher source, a merger which must be preceded by their dissolution if it is to take place at all, their egoistic happiness is likewise doomed.

407

It would be utterly ridiculous not to grant some kind of existence to the ego within his world of appearances. This, our own eyes, our own sensations, tell us to be the case. But it is equally ridiculous for the ego to arrogate to itself a higher and more durable kind of existence than it actually possesses or a self-sufficiency that belongs only to its infinite source. None of the elements which form it is a permanent nucleus and none by itself is entitled to its name. Dissolve these elements and the ego likewise dissolves, thus revealing its temporary character. Still all thoughts, give the quietus to all passions, calm all emotions, and individual characteristics of an ego vanish.

408

All those thoughts and memories which now compose the pattern of his life have to be put aside if he is to deny himself.

409

The chains of earthly desire will be worn down to paper thinness.

410

So long as these varied thoughts hold together, so long is the sense of a separate personality created in the mind. That this is so is shown by mystical experience, wherein the thoughts disappear and the ego with them, yet the true being behind them continues to live.

411

There is no enduring ego.

412

This little creature, infatuated with itself to the point of centering its consciousness in nothing else, will have to suffer evaporation of its body and annihilation of its ego in the end.

Grace is needed

413

The subjugation of his ego is a Grace to be bestowed on him, not an act which can be done by him.

414

In that last battle when he comes face to face with the ego, when it has to put off all its protective disguises and expose its vulnerability, he must call upon the help of Grace. He cannot possibly win it by his own powers.

415

Each person is stuck in his own ego until the idea of liberation dawns on him and he sets to work on himself and eventually grace manifests and puts him on the Short Path.

416

The frontal attack on the ego's weaknesses and faults can lead to certain beneficial results, such as reducing their size and diminishing their power, or to their total surface repression but cannot lead to their total elimination. All methods which dissolve the I's faults and weaknesses still leave the I itself undissolved. All techniques which change the ego's qualities and attributes still leave the ego-root unchanged.

417

There would be no hope of ever getting out of this ego-centered position if we did not know these three things. First, the ego is only an accumulation of memories and a series of cravings, that is, thought; it is a fictitious entity. Second, the thinking activity can come to an end in stillness. Third, Grace, the radiation of the Power beyond man, is ever-shining and ever-present. If we let the mind become deeply still and deeply observant of the ego's self-preserving instinct, we open the door to Grace, which then lovingly swallows us.

418

The senses which tempt him to go astray from his chosen path of conduct may be subjugated in time by right thoughts. The thoughts which distract him from his chosen path of meditation may be subjugated by persistent effort. But the ego which bars his entry into the kingdom of heaven refuses, and only pretends, to subjugate itself.

419

He finds that no man can totally deny his ego, can step outside himself by trying to do so; some help, some intervention, some grace from outside is needed.

420

How could he see in clear light his unshakeable egocentricity, how confess it to himself when the ego would itself have to help bring about the confession?

421

That which keeps us busy with one kind of activity after another—mental as well as physical—until we fall asleep tired, is nothing other than the ego. In that way it diverts one's attention from the need of engaging in the supremely important activity—the struggle with and destruction of the ego itself.

422

This whittling away of the ego may occupy the entire lifetime and not seem very successful even then, yet it is of the highest value as a preparatory process for the full renunciation of the ego when—by Grace—it suddenly rises up in the heart.

423

The ego's interest in its own transcendence is necessarily spurious. This is why grace is a necessity.

424

It is as hard for the ego to judge itself fairly, to look at its actions with a correct perspective as for a man to lift himself by his own braces. It simply cannot do it; its capacity to find excuses for itself is unlimited—even the excuse of righteousness, even the excuse of the quest of truth. All that the aspirant can hope to do is to thin down the volume of the ego's operations and to weaken the strength of the ego itself; but to get rid of the ego entirely is something beyond his own capacity. Consequently, an outside power must be called in. There is only one such power available to him, although it may manifest itself in two different ways, and that is the power of Grace. Those ways are: either direct help by his own higher Self or personal help from a higher man, that is, an illumined teacher. He may call for the first at any time, but he may not rightly call for the second before he has done enough work on himself and made enough advance to justify it.(P)

425

The ego may have to be broken to bits, if necessary, to let the Grace enter in, to open a way through passivity replacing arrogance.

426

Virtue and compassion thin down the ego but do not confer enlightenment.

427

The destruction of our egoism must come from the outside if we will not voluntarily bring it about from the inside. But in the former case it will come relentlessly and crushingly.

428

Where is the man who does not assume the reality of his ego? He is deluded, of course, but what else can he do if he is to attend to the business of everyday living? The answer is that he can do nothing else—unless Grace comes and attends to the business for him!

429

His own self-centeredness keeps out the light. If he himself cannot open up a free way to let it in, then grace alone can crush his ego and thus reveal his sin and bring about surrender.

430

When the ego is brought to its knees in the dust, humiliated in its own eyes, however esteemed or feared, envied or respected in other men's eyes, the way is opened for Grace's influx. Be assured that this complete humbling of the inner man will happen again and again until he is purified of all pride.(P)

431

Out of this ego-crushing, pride-humbling experience he may rise, chastened, heedful, and obeisant to the higher will.

Who is seeking?

432

Who is the seeker on this Quest? It is the ego. And who undergoes all the experiences and develops all the ideas upon it? It is also the ego. Let us not therefore be too hasty in denigrating the ego; it has its place and serves in its place.

433

When the inner history of the human entity is known and its lessons absorbed, the problem offers itself: "How can I escape from myself?" The answer will necessarily show that the ego can succeed only to a certain degree in such a venture, but it not only cannot go beyond this but will not even try to do so. How can it consent to its own death?

434

The question arises *who* is to practise this annulment? The ego can feint and play at doing so, but in the very act is thereby preserving itself.

435

What or who is seeking enlightenment? It cannot be the higher Self, for that is itself of the nature of Light. There then only remains the ego! This ego, the object of so many denunciations and denigrations, is the being that, transformed, will win truth and find Reality even though it must surrender itself utterly in the end as the price to be paid.(P)

436

We are told to control, restrain, or even banish the ego. But who or what in us is to do the work? And is the ego to banish itself?

437

The attrition of the ego will come out of this incessant struggle against it, but the atrophy of the ego will not. For who is the struggler? It is the ego himself. He will not willingly commit suicide, although he will deceptively allow a steady grinding-down of his more obvious aspects.

438

Can he detach himself from himself? Can he stand aside from his own passions, and outside his own emotions?

439

The Buddhist text, *Visuddhi Magga*, declares there is Nirvana but no one who realizes it, that there is a way but not he who goes thereby.

440

Although we may grant the fact that it is the ego which is seeking truth, we must insist on the completing truth that the ego is never the finder of truth.

441 ✓

It is not the person who brings God down to a level with himself, or lifts himself up to a level with God. The ego goes when God comes.

Results of dethroning ego

442

The deep realization of the unreality of ego leads at once to sudden enlightenment. But only if this realization is maintained can the enlightenment become more than a glimpse.

443

Although the price of attainment, which is the gradual giving up of the lower self, is agonizing because the lower one is the only self we know ordinarily, there is for every such surrender a compensation equal in value at least to what is given up, and actually of more surpassing worth. This compensation is not only a theoretical one, it is a real experience; and at the last, when the whole of the lesser self is surrendered, the only description of it which mere words can give is blissful peace. Since agony of mind cannot coexist with peace, the agony falls away and only the peace remains. The warning must be given, however, that the Higher Self never yields its compensations until the requisite surrender is made. If this is done little by little, which is usually the only way it can be done, then the lovely compensation will follow also little by little.

444

"How can we carry on with our daily lives without the 'I' consciousness?" is a natural and common question. The first answer, and certainly the best one, is supplied by the personal experience of those who have done it in the past and are doing it today. Their testimony to its factuality is worth more than the theoretical objections to its possibility. Think of the great or celebrated names which proffer such testimony, of Jesus and Buddha in Asia, of Eckhart and Boehme in Europe, and of Emerson in America! And there are other names which I know, of men who lived in our own century but who lived obscurely, unknown to all but a tiny handful of seekers—men whom my own line of destiny fortunately crossed and happily tangled with in the period of my wide research. The second answer to the question of possibility is contained in the ordinary experience of awaking from the night's sleep. It is perfectly possible then to carry on with daily living without the consciousness of the self which prevailed in dreams. That self was different from the waking one since he holds thoughts and does things that the latter would never do. It certainly existed, but the morning showed it to be an illusory ego. In exactly the same way, illumination acts as an awakening and shows the everyday consciousness of self to be illusory, too. And just as we no longer need the dream ego to carry on the waking activities, so the illumined man no longer needs the waking ego to carry on his activities.

445

To the extent that he gets rid of the ego's dominance, he gets rid of self-consciousness, with its vanity or shyness, its nervousness or anxiety.

446

When the ego has dwindled away into nothingness, the Overself takes over.

447

Not until the ego is completely deflated and falls into the Void will he know, feel, and fully realize the blissfulness of salvation.

448

As a highly personal "I" competing against other "I"s, there can be only endless friction and intermittent anxiety. As impersonal I-ness, dwelling in the eternal Now, there are none to compete against and nothing even to compete for.

449

The selfish interests, which prompt man's action or guide his reflections, are destroyed root and branch in this vast transformation which attends entry into the Overself's life.

450

A correspondent wrote concerning an experience during meditation: "It was wonderful not to be limited to the personal self—joyful, peaceful, secure, satisfied. It was a revelation that this feeling of "I"-ness which makes one think one is the personal self comes from Reality itself but narrowly restricted down. It is this restriction that must be thrown off, not the I-ness feeling, and then the kingdom of heaven is found."

451

The ego in him which thinks the "I" must be rooted out. It will be followed by the Overself, which neither thinks discursively nor identifies itself with the outer person whom the world considers him to be.

452

The degree of ego-attachment which you will find at the centre of a man's consciousness is a fairly reliable index to the degree of his spiritual evolution.

453

In comparison with the ocean-depth of egolessness, altruism is shallow and charity is superficial.

454

The egoistic way of viewing life is a narrowing one. It keeps him from what is best, holds him down to what is base, and prevents him from working with the miraculous forces of the Overself. The farther he moves himself away from it and the nearer he moves into the impersonal and cosmic way, the sooner will he receive the benediction of more wisdom, better health, smoother relationships, and grander character.

455

Where the advancement has gone so far that the whole person has been unified, the ego has no chance of influencing the mind; but where it has not it will try to do so, will put forward its point of view, but will be rejected.

456

When he can look at his life-experience as something that seems to happen to somebody else, he will have a sure sign of detachment.

457

When he can release himself from the ego's tyranny and relate himself to the Overself's guidance, an entirely new life will open up for him.

458

Everything seems lost to a man when he surrenders his own personal will deep in his heart to the higher self, when he abandons his personal aims, wishes, and purposes at its bidding. Yet the truth is that only then is everything gained.

459

The same nature which, filled with ego, is such an ugly sight, becomes, when purified of it and reflecting the Overself's presence, a beautiful one.

460

He who can get outside his own ego, and leave it behind, can get to Truth.

461

To nullify the ego is the only way to perceive and identify his real being.

462

The ego collapses at this point; the weight of his burden has proved too heavy. Not only does pride go but also certitude.

463

The unawakened ego submits passively to the lower influences which come to it out of the shadows of its own long past and to the sense-stirring suggestions which come to it out of the surroundings in which it moves. But when it has found and surrendered to the Overself in the heart, this blind, mechanical responsiveness comes to an end and an aroused, enlightened, fully aware, inner rulership replaces it.

464

When the personal ego is put in its place, not allowed to dominate, when it becomes the ruled and not the ruler—and further, when meditation aligns it with the Overself and knowledge keeps it there—when finally application brings it into the day's activity, then inner directives guide the man, inner harmony gives him peace of mind. Unpleasant happenings will not be allowed to disturb this mental evenness, nor untoward ones allowed to upset his feelings.

465

Remove the concept of the ego from a man and you remove the solid ground from beneath his feet. A yawning abyss seems to open up under him. It gives the greatest fright of his life, accompanied by feelings of utter isolation and dreadful insecurity. He will then clamour urgently for the return of his beloved ego and return to safety once more—unless his determination to attain truth is so strong and so exigent that he can endure the ordeal, survive the test, and hold on until the Overself's light irradiates the abyss.(P)

466 ✓

The illusion of the ego stands behind all other illusions. If it is removed, they too will be removed.(P)

467

When a man wakes up to the discovery that his desire to teach others may only be another form of personal ambition, he may, like Saint Thomas Aquinas, stop entirely. But with the birth of true humility he may do the one or the other.

468

Only when a man is dispossessed of his ego's rule and repossessed by the Overself's can he really attain that goodness about which he may have dreamed often but reflected seldom.

469 ✓

The test of spirituality is not to be found in how long a man can sit still in meditation, but in how well he has denied his ego.

470

It is said that in *nirvikalpa samadhi* time is brought to a standstill. Obviously this can only happen when the ego is temporarily paralysed. Ramana Maharshi used to say that the ego is nothing but a bundle of thoughts and does not exist by itself as a separate entity. Nirvikalpa, being the thought-free state and involving the suspension of the movement of thought, is therefore the suspension of the movement of time in the ego's consciousness.

471

In the hour when the ego falls away from us, there is a feeling of a heavy burden being dropped, a sense of release from a condition now seen to be undesirable. This is naturally followed by a quiet satisfying joy.

472

When ego is absent, a precondition for Overself to be present exists.

473

With this release from ego there comes a sense of exhilaration.

474

If he could get the ego to withdraw from his motives and calculations and purposes and impulsions, how could his acts be other than righteous ones?

475

To the degree that we loose ourselves from the ego's grip, to that degree we loose ourselves from its mental anxieties and emotional agitations. As its power wanes, our care-free peace waxes.

476

When, and thus also, because of distracted attention, we are wholly absorbed in watching a cinema picture to the extent that we forget ourself and our personal affairs, the ego temporarily disappears and ceases to exist for us. This too means, if it means anything at all, that the ego exists only by virtue of its existence in our consciousness. If we exercise ourself in withdrawing attention from the ego, not to bestow it upon a cinema picture but to bestow it upon our own inner being, we may succeed in getting behind the ego and discovering the Witness-self.

477

You will lose nothing but your littleness. You will not disintegrate into utter unconsciousness.

478

If he will have the courage to let the ego-illusion die out, a new and real life will come to birth within his being.

479

What really happened to Descartes when he lost himself in deep meditation whilst walking the quays of Amsterdam and had to be led home to his lodging? He forgot his personal identity.

480

The man whose ego is under control will not give his mind to the effect which he has on those with whom he comes into contact, will not be troubled by his nerves.

481

The automatic, constant, and undisciplined thought-movement comes at last to an end. It is the central part of the ego which has surrendered.

482

He brings his personality into his thoughts and acts, as everyone does; but even in the next and higher stage, where he becomes a spectator of that personality, it still happens, although in a subtler and diminished way. There is a further stage where ego becomes entirely subservient and consciousness is centered on a still deeper level.

483

Take away the thoughts and feelings, including the body-thought and the specific I-feeling, and you take away the whole basis of man's personal existence. It is indeed the only mode of his life that he can conceive. After all, the personality is only a series of continuous thoughts, strongly held and centered around a particular body. He who can win the power to free himself from all thoughts, wins the power to free himself from the personal "I"-thoughts. Only such a man has really obeyed Jesus' injunction to lose his life. For what other life has man ordinarily than the personal one? But Jesus also promised a certain reward for successful obedience. He said that such a person would "save" his life. What does this mean? When the thoughts lapse and the finited personality goes, will the man be bereft of all consciousness? No—he will still possess pure consciousness, the deeper life that supports the finited self and sustains its very thoughts.

Part 2:

FROM BIRTH
TO REBIRTH

A time comes when he has to exist by himself, when aids, supports, and guides are withdrawn. This happens in meditation, dying, or between births.

Whether you ascribe the secrets of happenings in your life to karma, to fate, to other people, to blind processes of Nature, or to any other cause, leave some space for the X-factor, the unknown and unknowable which does not belong to anything which you can measure or comprehend.

1

DEATH, DYING, AND IMMORTALITY

Continuity, transition, and transformation

Life-in-Itself is infinite and unchanging, but there *is* an end to the kind of experience undergone by the living entity in its finite human phase.

2

Just as sound goes back into silence but may emerge again at some later time, so this little self goes back into the greater being from which it too may emerge again at another time.

3

We worry ourselves through the days of an existence which is itself but a day. A profound sadness falls on the heart when it realizes the transient nature of all worldly things and all human being.

4

If decay and disintegration were not present at some stage, if our life spans were extended to say double their present length, then the old would outnumber all other sections of society. Stasis would overwhelm culture because the bodily slowdown would reflect itself mentally. The World-Mind had a better idea.

5

Human life steadily and unfailingly burns away like the candle in a man's hands.

6

Individuated life is forever doomed to die whereas the ALL which receives the dying can itself never die.

7

Even stars must die one day, more violently and dramatically than most human beings, for even they come under the law that whatever had a beginning must also have an ending.

8

We hear of other people dying and make suitable comment, but we do not *feel* that the time is coming when this fate will be ours too.

9

It is not so much because death deprives man of his possessions and relations that he dreads it, as the possibility that it deprives him of his consciousness—that is, his self, his ego.

10

Those who deplore, lament, or wail at the inevitability of death are viewing it in a very narrow, short-sighted way. The more mature ought to be thankful that we humans are not condemned to remain forever confined to a single body: this would indeed become a source of anxiety, if not of hopelessness.

11

Whether this bundle of personal desires and memories which is the ego, but which some of the pious call their soul, will be annihilated at death or perpetuated, is not an anxiety for the philosopher.

12

The more they enjoy the world the more they suffer when they leave it—unless they have learnt to put detachment behind the enjoyment.

13

No force can be destroyed; it can only be rechannelled. Life is a force; death is its rechannelling.

14

The innermost being of man, his mysterious Overself, links him with God. It does not change with time nor die with the years. It is eternal.

15

Electrical fields have been detected by the use of newly developed micro-volt-meters around all living things, but there was no field around a dead man. Many years ago in the *The Quest of the Overself* the existence of an electromagnetic connection between the photograph of a man and the man himself was revealed, and its disappearance on his death was also recorded. Thus science begins to offer a basis for a part of our original statement.

16

We are tenants in this rented house of the body. We have no certainty of possession. There is no lease on parchment paper with a government stamp to guarantee even a single year's holding.

17

It would be a curious state of affairs if the sole purpose of life were to be death, a cessation of all interest in all the activities included under the heading "human existence." Has the divine intelligence nothing better to offer us?

18

The voyage of a man's life always ends in the port of death. Let him not forget this when tempted by fortune into undue elation or tossed by misfortune into undue misery.

19

This dismal fact is the mark on all things, and creatures: that they pass away, have a transient existence, and in this absolute sense lack reality. They appear for awhile, seem substantial and eventful, but are in truth prolonged mirages. If this were all the story it would be melancholy enough. But it is not. *That* whence they came, to which they go back, does *not* pass away. That is the Real, that is the Consciousness which gave the universe, of which *we* are a part, its existence. Out of that stems this little flower in each life which is the best, highest self. If we search for it and discover it, we recover our origin, return to our source, and *as such* do not pass away. Yes, the forms are lost in the end but the being within them is not.

20

Ordinarily, the date and even the place where one is to die is preordained.

21

Dying into annihilation is one thing but dying into another form of consciousness is quite different. It is the latter which happens at the passing away of the life-force from the body.

22

If the thought of death horrifies so many people, the thought of the void—of the utter annihilation of ego, of the abandonment of everything and of the cessation of suffering, frustration, and anxiety which belong to life in the world—is a welcome idea for those who think more deeply. But since life is only partly suffering, since there are also joys and satisfactions in it and positive values which ought not to suffer destruction, a better balanced view is provided by philosophy and that is that consciousness, real consciousness, cannot die, but only returns to its ultimate source.

23

We ought to be glad that we do not live forever. It is a frightening thought. If there were no death we would go on and on and on, captives in the body, having tried all experiences which promised much but in the end yielded nothing. No, it is good that in the end we are released from the physical tomb, as Plato called it, and will be able to enjoy a period of dignified rest until we plunge back again into the next re-embodiment.

24

You raise one of the points on which I happen to disagree with your respected master, and that is his experiment in the direction of attaining physical immortality. From a scientific standpoint, I would not dare to say that anything is impossible or to set any limits to human achievement; but from a philosophic standpoint I follow the Buddha whose words on this point are as follows: 1) "That which, whether conscious or unconscious, is not subject to decay and death, that you will not find." 2) "No Samana, Brahman nor Mara, nor any being in the Universe can bring about the following five things, namely, 'That which is subject to old age, should not grow old; that which is subject to sickness should not be sick; that which is subject to death, should not die; that which is subject to decay should not decay; that which is liable to pass away should not pass away.'"

25

What man undergoes in his physical life seems so real, so lasting, and so intimate—yet it is only a brief episode in the immensely larger span of his cosmic cycle.

26

Since death is the certain future of all men, being an unalterable feature of the World-Idea, and since life would be intolerable if they were not given such pauses to recuperate from its demands, and lastly since there is nothing they can do to avoid it, they might as well discard the negative but common way of looking at it.

27

Time is not only the great healer and not only the great teacher but also the true friend for it brings the Messenger of Death, who brings peace.

28

The sadness of a withered flower, its head wilted, its stem shrivelled, its leaves dry corpses, is a sober reminder of beauty's fragility and our own fatal destination.

29

Why talk only of rebirth? Do we not experience death just as often?

30

The end of life, as of journeys, is contained in its beginning.

31

The philosopher knows the higher worth of life and appreciates it. But at the same time he knows the fleeting value of life and deprecates it.

32

The inner work of philosophy results in liberation from the fear of death—whether the death which comes naturally through old age or that which comes violently through war.

33

The pillage of time can be avoided by no one. It takes his years, and in the end his life.

34

The confrontation with death is not a pleasant prospect for anyone who is not in a condition of extreme suffering of some kind, emotional or physical. The thought of being parted from everything and everyone seems hideous. And yet, in the event itself, there may happen a beautiful, smooth passing-out.

35

So long as man listens to his little ego alone, and lets the voice of the Overself remain unheard and unknown, so long will all his cunning and his caution avail him little in the end when the body has to be left and the mind must return to its own proper sphere.

36

If life is the last personal hope, death is the last social blessing. Without it the animal and human worlds would become horrors. If with its presence we complain of overpopulation, where could we all live together in its absence? The World-Idea does not include such a fault, fortunately.

37

A time comes when the prudent person, feeling intuitively or knowing medically that he has entered the last months or years of his life, ought to prepare himself for death. Clearly an increasing withdrawal from worldly life is called for. Its activities, desires, attachments, and pleasures must give way more and more to repentance, worship, prayer, asceticism, and spiritual recollectedness. It is time to come home.(P)

38

Nobody has to teach us to hold on to life and to be repelled by the thought of our death. Why?

39

When a man arrives at the biblical three score and ten years allotted to him, as I have, he is likely to hear, with some frequency, of deaths among those he has known as friends or as questers. Where I have witnessed the passing-out, I have been much impressed by the radiant smile, the strainless peace, upon the face of the dying person.

40

The ordinary human attitude towards death pushes its very thought as far from oneself as possible, prefers not to consider it; the unpleasantness and distress, possibly the pain, which too often accompany the crossing-over are too unwelcome, if not unbearable.

41

Even a little perception of, or faith in, the World-Idea redeems the littleness of so many human lives, and at their end, in dying moments, becomes tremendously important.

42

Nothing can so easily give the thoughtful man detachment from things as the news that he has only a very limited time left to live.

43

If we have all had many many previous lives on earth, we have also had many many previous deaths on earth. The actual experience of dying must leave some residual lesson or meaning or message behind in the subconscious.

44

We who find ourselves in old age with brittle bones and shrunken flesh, with wrinkled face and greyed hair, may find this a depressing experience. But like every other situation in life there is another way to look at it— perhaps in compensation for what we suffer. And that is to sum up the lessons of a lifetime and prepare ourselves for the next incarnation so that we shall better perform the necessary work on ourselves when that comes.

45

It is not pleasant to think of the decay which overtakes the faculties of so many persons who live into their seventies or eighties, yet it is a necessary thought for those who are only half that age or less to entertain. It may act as a reminder or even as a spur to quicken their pace upon the Quest.

46

It was a man very shrewd, very intelligent, very well educated, a lawyer by profession who, while he was convalescing from a heart attack, said to me, "I have been very ambitious, but I failed in my ambitions; only now however do I see that all that, the ambition and the work and the efforts which followed it and depended on it, was futile activity, mere agitation, a filling up of time." He died a year or two later, not a happy man. He had not been without spiritual feelings and intuitions, but his weaknesses, his sensuality, and his ambition overcame him until it was too late—until the shadow of death became his tutor.

47

Life is a preparation for death, just as death is a preparation for re-entry into life.

48

All instinct and all force of will resists the image of one's own ultimate passing away, one's own inevitable death. And yet this attitude depends, in part, upon one's age. Some reconciliation comes with old age.

49

There is a part of himself which cannot die, cannot pass into annihilation. But it is very deep down. The sage encounters it before bodily death and learns to establish his consciousness therein. The others encounter it during some phase in the after-death state.

50

Much confusion has been caused, and much atheism generated, by the very limited knowledge and very large ignorance of many expounders of popular religion and spiritualistic cults. They teach that the human being, after a first short appearance on this planet for an insignificant period (for what is seventy years or so against the millions of years which geology proclaims as its history?) will pass into a post-mortem state wherein it will dwell forever, that is, for all eternity. That the little ego with all its attributes and qualities, will keep the personal identity and the personal existence of that brief appearance on earth unchanged, congealed into permanency, outliving the earth itself, reunited with family and friends, finding itself among primitive people of the Iron Age and among the cave-dwellers, is a ridiculous notion. It is so utterly unscientific an idea, so appallingly opposed to real religion, as to be ludicrous.

51

When the decreed time comes the body is discarded but the mind remains. It passes through varied experiences and finally sleeps them off. After a while it awakes deeply refreshed. Then the old propensities slowly revive and it returns to this world, putting on a new body in new surroundings.

52

The eternity which we are supposed to enter after death, one where a particular form and ego are supposed to be preserved forever, is absurd. But there is a true eternity where form and ego, time and space, are transcended.

53

Since the Overself is outside time it is also outside events. Nothing happens in it or to it.

54

Spirit is not entrapped in matter, the soul is not immured in the bodily person, divinity is not asleep in the flesh. It is the ego, the I-thought, we who are entrapped, asleep, immured.

55

The notion of an immortality that keeps a single personality quite static, perpetuating its failings and foolishness, is small and mean, poor and limited. It belittles God's purpose and shames man's idealism.

56

This little bit of existence which is mine will not last. The consciousness will be removed from this world, the body will be destroyed, the relationships will be slowly or abruptly severed.

57

With death, consciousness takes on a new condition but does not pass into mere emptiness, is not crumbled away with the fleshly brain into dust. No! It survives because it is the real being of a man.

58

The same destiny which brought us to birth will bring us to death. And just as a drama of different phases of consciousness unfolded itself after birth, so a drama of changes in consciousness will unfold itself after death. It is not annihilation that we ought to fear, for that will not happen, but rather the evil in our own self, and the pain that follows in the train of that evil as a shadow follows a man in the sunlight.

59

The shadow being which emerges from the body at death, which resembles the body and lives for a while an independent existence in the world of spirits, is doomed to decay and die in its own turn.

60

Whoever has been freed from the demands of his earthly self, and from the desires of his ignorant self, does not need to return here after passing into the disembodied state.

61

Life between incarnations consists of a dream-like state followed by a period resembling deep sleep. There is, however, no remembrance of one's former birth upon emerging from this state.

62

The difference between life as we ordinarily know it and as it appears between incarnations is that here we have an apparent mixture of two worlds, the mental and the phenomenal, whereas there only the former exists.

63

We pass through the dream and deep sleep states after death just as we do before it.

64

With the understanding of life in the body comes the knowledge of what life is without the body, that is, death. Both are existences in Mind, which is their reality.

65 ✓

The multitude are brought up to be pleased with the prospect of living (after death) in eternity (as egos). But a remnant who have pondered long and deeply on what this really means shudder at the same prospect.

66

Concealed behind the passing dream of life there is a world of lasting reality. All men awaken at the moment of death but only a few men are able to resist falling at once into the astral dream. These are the few who sought to die to their lower selves whilst they were still alive. These are the mystics who enter reality.

67

Those whose thoughts are limited to earthly things, do not change with the change called death. They stay earth-bound, pathetically ineffectual and bored, unless they are able to possess or obsess someone still living in this world.

68

Whole scenes out of the years from childhood to the present unwind themselves during the post-death experience before the spirit's mental gaze.

69

Every unfulfilled desire acts as an attractive force to draw us back to earth again after every death.

70

Death is either unconscious stupor, blank sleep, partially conscious dream sleep, or fully conscious awareness.

71

If you kill a man, the Law of Consequences compels you to carry that man's corpse with you wherever you go. At first you do it in memory pictures that create fear of punishment, but after death you will *see* the victim and *hear* his cries all over again.

72

I am sorry to say that the theosophy of latter days has over-emphasized the value of individuality in contrast to the theosophy of Blavatsky, who knew the truth. Let me tell you that the so-called astral plane is equivalent to the dreamworld and nothing more. Hence the after-death state is just like a very vivid dream, after all. Therefore in the true esoteric school we do not pay much attention to such matters but concern ourselves with life here and now, on this earth, with which we have to deal whether we like it or not.

73

Our troubles are but transitory, whereas our spiritual hopes survive the incarnations and bridge the gaps between births.

74

If it be asked why this purificatory experience after death does not alter the character that reappears in the next birth, the answer is that it is a half-introverted, dreamy state which only vaguely and superficially touches the consciousness. Only here in the awakened, fully extroverted state of earth-world does experience etch itself in sharp, vivid lines on the ego.

75

This dream-like progress after death is not valueless. It acts as a re-minder during each pre-birth of the true purpose of life.

76

Pet animals do not end their existence at the body's end. Their invisible spirit form hovers around the vicinity of the master or mistress left behind. They are fully conscious and as far as they know still in the physical world. But with the passage of time, this consciousness gradually fades and they enter a sleep state which ends only with their reincarnation. Their expecta-tion of being fed or petted is also fulfilled for them by their own mental power working creatively.

77

So hard are the lessons which earth-life forces us to learn, so hard its sufferings, that it is only fair to say that the bliss to which we shall emerge after leaving it, or even now in mystic states, is not less in any way.

78

The third heaven is the loftiest and happiest state to which the spirit of those who have passed out of this body can rise. All that is finest and noblest in an individual being alone flowers here. It is blissfully peaceful but alas! must in its turn also pass and yield to a region where individuality no longer exists, where all previous existences, all personal memories must go. "From God we came, to God we go."

79

How short a time does an animal need for the rest period between its births by contrast with that needed between human births! In its case just months, in the human case, more years than it lived on earth.

80

The sense of time between incarnations varies. Five minutes to one is a hundred years to another.

81

The discarnate man naturally turns towards his memories of earth-life, dreams of those he does not want to let go, and thus unconsciously recreates his former conditions and environments. He lives in his private thought-world and among his personal thought-forms. Is it surprising then that spiritist communications are so discrepant, so conflicting, in their accounts of the other world?

82

We leave the body with the first death and the ego with the second death. But this is not the end. In the Overself we find our final being.

The event of death

83

When the end of life comes, and a man goes out of it like a candle in the wind, what then happens depends upon his character, his prevailing consciousness, his preparedness, and his last thoughts.

84

I have witnessed some advanced souls going through the process of passing to another sphere of consciousness, the process we call death, who spread mental sunshine around so that the bereaved ones gathered at the bedside felt it as a consoling counterbalance to their natural human grief. The truth made some kind of impression upon them that this universal event in Nature can actually be a change to brighter, happier, and freer existence.

85

The anonymous young airman who wrote to his mother just before he was killed in battle: "I have no fear of death; only a queer elation," possessed something more than mere courage. For the time at least he had passed over from self-identification with the body to self-identification with the mind.

86

The aspirant whose efforts to attain inner freedom and union with the Overself while living seem to have been thwarted by fate or circumstances, may yet find them rewarded with success while dying. Then, at the very moment when consciousness is passing from the body, it will pass into the Overself.

87

What sort of a death experience is he likely to have? What if he dies, as Ramana Maharshi died, as Ramakrishna died, as heroes of the Spirit— some anonymous and obscure, others famous—known to this author died, of that dreadful and contemporary malady, cancer? I can only tell what I have seen and heard when present during the last days as privileged co-sharer of the unbelievable atmosphere. To each there came a vision, a light seen, first far off, later all around; first a pinpoint, later a ray, then a wide shaft, lastly filling the whole room. And with the Light came peace; it came as an accompaniment to the cancer's pain, a compensation that as it grew made the peace grow and gave detachment, until to the amazement of doctors, nurses, family, the triumphant words were uttered before the final act, Spirit's victory over matter proclaimed. This is not to say that it makes no difference whether one dies quietly in sleep through nothing worse than age, or whether one dies through cancer, that peace and pain are equally acceptable to the emotions of an illumined man. I do not write here of the extreme fanatical ascetic. To him it may be a matter of indifference.(P)

88

If there is any loss of consciousness during the change called death, it is only a brief one, as brief or briefer than a night's sleep. Many of the departed do not even know at the time what has really happened to them and still believe themselves to be physically alive. For they find themselves apparently able to see others and hear voices and touch things just as before. Yet all these experiences are entirely immaterial, and take place within a conscious mind that has no fleshly brain.(P)

89

The dying man should cross his arms over his chest with interlaced fingers. He should withdraw the mind from everything earthly and raise it lovingly in the highest aspiration.(P)

90

This is the way a man may best die—while resting on a chair or couch or sleeping in a bed, a peaceful expression on his face as if seeing or hearing something of unusual beauty, a pleased expression around the mouth.(P)

91

It is a teaching in both India and China that by concentrating his thoughts during his dying moments on the name of his spiritual leader with full faith, undivided ardour, and sincere deep attention, a man saves himself some or all of the post-mortem purificatory torments that he would otherwise have to undergo. It is also written that if he prefers to concentrate on the kind of environment in which his next birth is to appear, he contributes toward its possible realization.(P)

92

Death is the great revealer. In that vivid but dreamlike experience which follows it, each man is shown what he has *really* done with his earth-life, what he *should* have done with it, and what he failed to do with it.

93

At death consciousness passes through an interesting phase, for it really is a passing out from the body and from the world. Memories go, the past blots itself out, faces blur and identifications of their owners disintegrate. Tired, drowsy, overwhelmed by a feeling of withdrawing: mental activities, ratiocinations, imaginings, all crumble away and then there is nothing.

94

Just when life is ebbing fast away, when death is vividly in attendance, the long-sought but little found state of enlightenment may arise and accompany the event.

95

The process of dying may become a fulfilment of long years of aspiration for the quester or a veritable initiation into the soul for the ordinary man.

96

There is a particular moment while a person is dying when the Overself takes over the entire process, just as it does when he is falling asleep. But if he clings involuntarily and through inveterate habit to his smaller nature, then he is only partly taken over; the remainder is imprisoned in his littleness.

97

The Manichaeans of medieval times assisted the act of dying by a complete fast from food and drink.

98

The act of dying has no suffocating feeling connected with it other than during the momentary swoon. On the contrary, it is genuinely a liberating process.

99

Deep into the centre of his being does a man's mind withdraw as he passes out of this life, if his karma or his aspiration, his stage of development are not obstructive.

100

There was in the dying man's room such an air of supernatural forces at work, such an awareness of the presence of another world of being, that almost no one failed to notice it. Even the attending physician, hardened agnostic in religion, a mild sceptic of survival, confessed to these strange feelings.

101

I have written of the benign peace which death may bring, but not to all. Some enter it with panic, others with fear, yet others with resentment.

102

I have seen upon the face of certain dying or just-deceased persons, an expression of joyous inner calm that reassures the sensitive onlooker not only about their inner condition at the time but also about death's aftermath.

103

Dying can be a dull experience or a thrilling one. That depends on the person, on his pre-history and his inner history.

104

When he was dying, Heisenberg said to von Weizsäcker, "It is very easy: I did not know this before." At another moment he said, "I see now that physics is of no importance, that the world is illusion." He passed away in peace.

105

The poignant realization that he is separating himself from so much that he prized or loved, regarded as essential or was hoping ardently to attain, afflicts many a dying person. I am reminded of Kahlil Gibran, celebrated author of the powerful poem, *The Prophet*, and also a talented painter. He was dying of consumption and said mournfully to another poet, who told me later, "There is so much beauty in the world and life, to see or to create, which I shall now never know."

106

The tremendous event of dying and leaving the body does not interrupt his quest.

107

When the time for exit from this world-scene duly comes, he will approach it with trust—feeling that the power which supported him in previous crises will not desert him now.

108

In these closing hours of life with its lengthening shadows, one seeks to collect oneself and be ready for the final passing. How well it is to gather those reserves and foster those perceptions which now support one with, may I humbly say, a wise divine passivity. The end will come but it will be a transformation of form and a passage to a freer higher state.

109

If he accepts the decree of destiny quietly and obediently, if he is willing to pass, without rebellion and without fighting, out of this world when the ordained hour arrives, he achieves that peace of mind which the prophet Muhammed called "Islam"—a resignation to, and harmony with, God. It is as far as detachment from the ego can go without losing the ego itself.

110

When describing the vision of the past of a dying man, insert at the appropriate place, "For a brief while the ego becomes its own spectator. For a brief time it sees itself unblinded by desire and ungoverned by vanity. Then only does it see and expect the justice behind its sorrows."

111

In the case of violent or accidental death, there will be a period of unconscious deep sleep for an ordinarily good person, but of being consciously earthbound for an evil one.

112

The process of dying is one to study. It is full of significance. So many things and interests to which the dying person has been attached are now to be left behind, so many persons to whom he has been tied with bonds of affection or repelled by feelings of dislike are about to disappear.

113

It is paradoxical that the moment of his death should automatically bring to life again all of a man's past. He has to repeat it all over again, this time from a different point of view, for the selfish, coloured, and distorting operation of the ego is absent. Now he sees it from an impersonal and uncoloured point of view. In other words, he sees the real facts for what they truly are, which means that he sees himself for what he really is. His brief experience over, he then begins to live like a man in a dream. His own will is not responsible for what happens to him as a dreamer and it is just the same with what happens to him as a spirit. He does not personally and consciously choose, decide, and predetermine the course of his spirit life any more than his dream life. It flows on by its own spontaneous accord here as there. This is more vividly brought home to him, if he is an evil man, when the after-death experience turns into a nightmare.

114

It would be wrong to say that the pictorial review of life experience when dying is merely a mental transference from one's own shoes to those of the persons with whom one has been in contact during the life just passed, as the pictures unveil before him. What really happens is a transference from the false ego to the true Self, from the personal to the impersonal. It is a realization of the true meaning of each episode of the life from a higher point of view.

115

All possessions are left behind when a man makes his exit from this world. Every physical belonging, however prized, and even every human association, however beloved, are taken abruptly from him by death. This is the universal and eternal law which was, is, and ever shall be. There is no way to cheat or defeat it. Nevertheless there are some persons who, in a single particular only, escape this total severance. Those are the ones who sought and found, during their earthly life, the inspiration of a dead master or the association with a living one. His mental picture will vividly arise in their last moments on earth, to guide them safely into the first phase of post-mortem existence, to explain and reassure them about the unfamiliar new conditions.

116

I would like to die as peaceably as Lu Hsian-Shan, the Chinese mentalist philosopher. One evening he knew his hour had come, so he bathed, put on clean clothes, sat down and remained in silent meditation until he passed away seventeen hours later.

117

As the soul prepares or begins to pass out of the body, one of two things may happen. Depending upon the direction and strength of its attachments or desires, it is pulled away from them into unconsciousness, a kind of sleep. Or it recognizes places and persons connected with it, and if knowledge or experience are present, co-operates with the passing and moves out to a higher plane for a blissful sleep. After a while both must awaken to live again.

118

(a) A lady aristocrat related this story of her uncle who was dying as the result of an accident. He found himself out of the body. It was a delicious experience, but he was told that it was not the time for his exit and although he had lost the desire for earthly life, he found himself back in the body again. He recovered and lived. (b) Another woman of high social standing related that while in deep meditation she passed into a visionary condition in which she found herself out of the body. The condition was satisfying in the highest degree. But she was told that she still had something to do on earth and unwillingly had to return. She felt that with a little effort on her part she could prevent return, but destiny was stronger. (c) An Austrian female homeopath developed the practice of meditation and eventually had an experience of leaving the body and feeling intensely happy as the result. She wanted to stay like that but then remembered her responsibility towards her daughter and came back into the body again. (d) A Jewish lady who had been miraculously saved from death in the gas chambers with her mother while at Auschwitz camp began to practise meditation after being rejected when applying for admission to a convent as a nun. She successfully reached great peace and bliss, but became too sensitive to associate with the world. She had a vision of leaving the body during meditation. She felt as if she were in heaven. She prayed not to have to go back to the world, but she was intuitively told that it was her duty to do so. She accepted it as God's will and is now trying to adjust herself to conditions here.

119

What was the name of that artist who as he lay dying asked for the window to be opened wide so that he could see the snowy summits of the mountains outside? He wanted his last thoughts, his last consciousness, to be of them. Why?

120

We may deplore our foolish behaviour in life, our stupid errors or our fleshly weaknesses, but in those moments of dying we have the chance to die in wisdom and in peace. Yes, it is a chance given to us, but we have to take it by keeping our sight fixed on the highest that we know.

121

Death can open out higher possibilities to the man who leaves this existence in faith, who trusts the Overself and commits himself to its leading without clinging to the body which is being left.

122

It is better to pass out of the physical body in possession of consciousness rather than in a state of drugged anesthesia. This applies more particularly to spiritual aspirants. But where there is great pain, local anesthesia may be unobjectionable.

123 ✓

Only in those last few days or hours or minutes do most men find out the truth that as one kind of life leaves both them and their flesh, another opens up to them.

124

The awful aloneness which confronts man this side of death does not exist for the philosopher, nor for the truly devout person.

125

When he lies almost dying he may receive verification of the belief that a dying votary will see his god or guru or saviour come to take or guide his soul to the higher world.

126

Drowning persons who were saved and survived have told of the feeling of time slipping backward and their whole lifetime being replayed. This is an experience which is not theirs alone; it happens to all who pass through the portal of death.

127

Confusion, fear, clinging to the body or other physical possessions, panic, severe depression—they make the passage through the death experience harder than it would otherwise have been.

128

Death is before me today
Like the recovery of a sick man,
Like going forth into a garden after sickness.

Death is before me today
Like the odour of myrrh,
Like sitting under the sail on a windy day.

Death is before me today
Like the odour of lotus flowers,
Like sitting on the shore of drunkenness.

Death is before me today
Like the course of the freshet,
Like the return of a man from the war-galley to his house.

Death is before me today
Like the clearing of the sky,
Like a man fowling towards that which he knows not.

Death is before me today
As a man longs to see his house
When he has spent many years in captivity.

> "Death a Glad Release"
> (Translated from the Egyptian of an unknown poet of
> four thousand years ago—by James Henry Breasted)

129

Rabelais' last words, "The farce is finished," say much in little space.

The aftermath of death

130

The best way to minister to a dying person depends on various factors: each situation is different and individual. In general it may be suggested that the first thing is not to panic but to remain calm. The next is to look inwardly for one's own highest reference-point. The third is then to turn the person over to the Higher Power. Finally, and physically, one may utter a prayer aloud, or chant a mantram on his behalf—some statement indicating that the happening is more a homecoming than a homeleaving.

131

Sympathy and understanding go to those who have endured the passing beyond of someone precious to them. Healing will, however, come in time. Those who are thus suffering should resign themselves to the will of Destiny and believe that the loved one is living still, and will return.

132

A Buddhist method of driving away obstructing spirits is to snap the fingers around the head for a while and utter the mantram "PHAT" ("crack"). This method is also used as part of the deathrite at the moment of the soul's departure from the body.

133

The student has learned that the death of the body is extrinsic to the consciousness, which lives on unchanged in itself. But when death claims the body of someone he loves, his faith will be put to test. At such a time, he must remember that the loved one has actually evolved to a more highly developed phase of life.

134

The passing away of a loved one is a heavy blow—one for which most people are improperly prepared, because they are not yet willing to face the inescapable fact that all life is stamped with transiency and loss and sorrow. Only by seeking refuge in the immortality of the Overself and in discovering the truth and wisdom of the Divine Purpose, can we also learn how to endure the suffering on the ever-changing face of life. "Letting go" is the hardest of all lessons to learn; yet it is the most necessary for spiritual advancement.

135

Although it is painful to lose our loved ones, this is often the only way by which we learn of our deep need to form some inner detachment, as well as the unalterable fact that worldly life is inseparable from suffering. Such bitter lessons are instructive; they make us aware that we must turn to the spiritual Quest if we are to find contentment and enduring happiness.

136

Loss, as in the case of death of a wife or husband, has been known to be a principle cause of the necessary receptive state of mind with which one has approached philosophy. This is significant to the student on the Quest.

137

The passing of a loved one is usually a major experience, and one's reaction to it shows the degree of development attained. He must remember that sometimes it is best for a loved one to pass away if in doing so he or she is rid of a serious and painful bodily disease. He must also be happy in the thought that the loved one has now gone on to a sphere of existence where happiness, bliss, comfort, and rest can be found as can only be imagined but not found here. He may be assured that the loved one is really in a better world where only the beautiful side of life can penetrate and where ugly and base things can never find lodgement. He may help best at such a moment by an occasional loving remembrance during the peak point of meditation. For the sensitive aspirant, such an experience as seeing death face to face as it were, is always a great one. It should mark the beginning of a new period, of a more vivid evaluation of the transient character of earthly life, and result in a powerful aspiration to wrest something of an enduring character from the comparatively few years spent on this space-time level.

138

To someone who believes that life continues beyond the body's death, a funeral seems a useless affair. But it compels the mourners to remember and think of, for a few hours, what they ordinarily forget—that they too must go, that all personal matters come to an abrupt end, and that the person himself must part from every one of his possessions. Such a ritual, otherwise boring and tedious, is a salutary reminder.

139

One hopes that those bereaved by the death of fine young men in the war may have begun to feel some of time's healing touch. It is a source of great grief to lose someone young and brilliant at such a time. One cannot answer the question so often asked as to why such a man died when he was living so useful a life. This is a mystery of the kind we must leave to the Will of God, with faith. However, this faith is not the same as blind faith, for there is certainly Divine Wisdom underlying the event. These young men still live and will live. They have passed into a brighter and happier world and there is no need to grieve for them.

140

We must bear with resignation and acceptance the coming of this inevitable visitor, Death, to those we love. It is useless to rebel or complain against a law of life which has been such since time began.

141

He who has had the good fortune to have a loving companion in marriage should not rail at Destiny when this helpmate is taken away. The same karma which brought the two together has also severed the relationship. But this is only temporary. There is really no loss, as mind speaks to mind in silent moments. Love and companionship of high quality will act as an attractive force to bring them together again somewhere, sometime. Many feel this in the inner understanding.

142

When death is properly understood, and the immateriality of being is deeply felt, there will be no more mourning funerals. If the deceased has had a long and full incarnation, his passing will be accepted philosophically.

The bereaved person faces the problem of adjusting himself to a new cycle of the outer life. During the transitional period, he may feel lonely and uncertain of the future. At such a time, the inner meaning of both this period and the coming cycle should be sought.

143

Cremation is a definite and emphatic challenge. If one really believes that the soul of man is his real self, or even if one believes that the thinking power of man is his real self, then there can be no objection to it, but, on the contrary, complete approval of it. The method of burying dead bodies is fit only for one who believes that this thinking power is a product of the body's brain, that is, for a materialist.(P)

144

I recommend the process of cremation to dispose of the body of a deceased person. An interval of three days should take place between the death and the actual cremation, because that is the transition period which makes complete the passing out of the spirit.

145

The honour that is shown to a corpse by attempting to prolong its form is misplaced. It is a glaring contradiction to accept the credo of survival and then give to dead flesh what should be given to living soul. A rational funeral would be a completely private one. A rational funeral service would be one held to memorialize the memory of the deceased, and held not in the presence but in the absence of the corpse. A rational disposal would be cremation, not burial. The psychic and spiritual health of a community demands the abolition of graveyards.

146

In ancient Egypt the common people could not afford, were not allowed, and had no reason to turn their dead into mummies; but they did practise a curious kind of burial. The corpse was put into a shallow round hole with the chin resting upon the drawn-up knees—sometimes in the sitting and sometimes in the reclining position. This was intended to imitate the exact position of the embryo in the woman's womb and to symbolize an impending rebirth into the next world.

147

Why some are taken away by death at a young age and with a lovely soul is one of those mysteries which we must leave unexplained with the laws of destiny and recompense. Despite the natural feeling of being grievously wounded, the bereaved person should resign himself in trust to the will of God and in faith that the departed will be taken care of wherever he is by the Father of us all.

148

The passing away of a loved one and what the personal loss means to the bereaved is, of course, beyond the reach of any external comment which can be made. Words seem cold and useless at such times; all one can do is to accept, and humbly resign himself to, the Higher Will.

149

When some great souls passed away they took with them the spiritual and vital essence which others felt and from which they gained some inspiration.

150

This attachment to one tomb of a relative is consciously or unconsciously meant to keep the deceased person's memory alive. But this intention can be realized in other more hygienic and rational ways.

151

He or she who has lost a loved one should concentrate on *realizing* that distance in no way alters real love, that the mental presence of the beloved must be made as nearly real as the physical presence as he can make it, and that he must rise to the ability of finding satisfaction from these meetings in the mental world. Finally, there is always the old talisman of remembering the Universal and to keep on remembering it; this in time has a curious power, not only of helping to endure the maladjustments of fate but gradually of correcting them.

152

What spiritualism is mostly trafficking with, where it is not subconscious dramatization of the mind's own content, is less often spirits of dead men as spirits of half-animal, half-human beings who pretend to be what they are not and mislead sitters, and who are antagonistic to the human kingdom because the latter has all too frequently dealt antagonistically with the animal kingdom.

153

The only way to receive trustworthy contact with the spirit of a departed loved one is by prayer and silence, practised at the same time every night. There may only be a sense of the other's presence, or there may be a clear message imparted, possibly, in a dream. Patience is needed. Moreover, this cannot be repeated more than a few times.

154

The death of the body does not mean the death of the mind. Where there is deep love there can be interludes of mental communion between the so-called dead and the living and there may be meetings from time to time when each is conscious of the other. These meetings take place in a reverie-like state. But some practice in meditative stilling of the mind is necessary, as any emotional excitement would prevent this communion. Nature, however, does not permit a continuous relation, only an intermittent one. For spirits have their own higher destinies to work out.

155

In great bereavement, it is best not to seek communication with the departed through mediums. One can never be sure that it is genuine. Moreover, it is neither the right way nor the safe way.

156

I myself find it is hard to believe that disembodied human entities are permitted by Nature, after so a long a period has elapsed, to take an interest in the affairs of our world, much less interfere with them or inspire embodied individuals. Even reincarnation would be more logical than that.

157

If familiarity between the living and the dead were as common as spiritualists claim, life would be very difficult for both the living and the dead!

158

Have the disembodied nothing else to do than to run about hither and thither with dubious messages and stale revelations?

159

Table-tipping, planchette-writing, and trance mediumship may bring us into touch with friends long gone from our world; but, on the other hand, they may also submit our existence to invading spirits of an evil order who thrust themselves, unidentified, upon our brains and pretend to be what they are not.

160

I hold with Spiritism that the ego, the personality, does survive the death of the flesh body, but I do not hold with Spiritism that this survival is a most desirable and marvellous thing. Immortality is infinitely superior for it is the true deathlessness, but it can only be had at the price of letting go the ego. Nor would I encourage anyone to use the methods of Spiritism in its attempts at communicating with the "dead," for they are dubious and dangerous.

161

Those who feel pity for a person who kills himself feel rightly. But when this feeling is not balanced by reason, it may degenerate into sentimentality. For the suicide needs, like all other human beings subject to the process of evolution, to develop the quality of strength and to unfold the feeling of hope. His failure to do so leads to this sad consequence. That some suicides occur from other causes does not displace the truth of the general statement that most of them occur from weakness and fear.

162

The desire to kill himself may really be a desire to terminate the ego's life, but the man is unaware of this. In such cases, which are in a minority, the quest will be consciously adopted later.

163

It was not considered by several ancient peoples nor by the Essenes of Judea and the Jain monks of India that suicide was a criminal act if it were performed for valid reasons. These were: a hopelessly crippled condition; an advanced age accompanied by physical helplessness; a grave, chronic, or incurable disease.

164

It is understandable, when life becomes unbearable, that a man may commit suicide. But that he should use violence when doing so, is not.

165

A man commits suicide because of one of a variety of causes: he may become completely panic-stricken; he may become utterly hopeless; he may let go of all sense of proportion; or, if to any degree mediumistic, he may be influenced suggestively by an evil spirit.

166

Is any man given more suffering by destiny than he can endure? Theoretically he is not, but actually we do see cases of those who have killed themselves or gone insane from such a cause. The manner of his death, then, must be a part of his ill destiny.

167

It was not only the Jains in India who used this form of voluntary departure from the physical body, but also the Essenes in Palestine. When they felt themselves too old, they practised a slow starvation by leaving the community and going into solitude by a river bank or mountain retreat with only a handful of raisins for support. They would eat a few each day until the supply ran out and, often, their life-current with it.

168

Several Indian mystics, such as Tukaram and Ram Tirtha, have drowned themselves by walking into river or sea, and not always for the common reason that they were too old or too infirm. But willingly starving to death was regarded as a higher way of bringing one's life to an end. However, all this has nothing to do with the barbarous murderous custom of suttee, which is forced suicide.

169

The would-be suicide seeks personal oblivion, a memory-less and mind-less non-existence.

170

It is not useful to discuss here the ethics of suicide, and the morality of mercy-killing. Those who have borne the crushing misery of chronic disease, or suffered the worst mutilations of war are at least entitled to their point of view. But what shall we say of the priest who urged Hindu widows to immolate themselves by fire and thus attain divinity and spiritual reward or, more recently, of Vietnamese monks who did the same for what was mostly a political cause?

171

Suicide by starvation was regarded as particularly meritorious by Hindus and Jains. It was not a sin, but the contrary. It was usually preceded by fasting and prayer. It was usually caused by old age, disease, incapacity, or the purposelessness of living. If caused by a great sin it was a penance.

172

When suffering reaches its zenith or frustration is drawn out too long, when the heart is resigned to hopelessness or the mind to apathy, people often say that they do not wish to live any more and that they await the coming of death. They think only of the body's death, however. This will not solve their problem, for the same situation—under another guise—will repeat itself in a later birth. The only real solution is to seek out the inner reality of their longing for death. They want it because they believe it will separate them from their problems and disappointments. *But these are the ego's burdens.* Therefore the radical separation from them is achievable only by separating permanently from the ego itself. Peace will then come—and come forever.

173

The temptation to antedate the journey out of the flesh is sometimes irresistible.

174

Is life worth living? Even if there is little reason for satisfaction with one's existence, there is equally little reason for bringing it to an unnatural end. Surely the brevity of life should settle the matter anyway.

175

What the artist may learn from ecstasy, the family householder may learn from tragedy, which brings him face to face with the nature of our existence for the first time. Birth and death are entwined in our lives. In both conditions we cross through the Source of our being.

176

There are the visible living people and the invisible living ones. None are ever lost to existence or destroyed in consciousness, but only their bodies.

177

An immortality which does not purify, exalt, and transform his life, which does not give him the new, spiritual birth, will prove as unsatisfactory to the disembodied man in the end as it is already to the embodied thinker.

178

So materialistic has the religious understanding of many men become, that they will only accept as the highest—if not the only—proof of life after death, the appeal to their gross senses and not to their fine intuition or rational intelligence. That is to say, the bodily form of a dead person has to materialize in front of their own or someone else's eyes to convince them that he has not perished after all.

179

This lesson, that a man is not his body, will be learnt in modern times through his reasoning intelligence as it was learnt in former times through his believing feelings.

180

Why did the Egyptians place their Heaven in the unseen regions into which the dying sun vanishes after sunset?

181

The answers to questions concerning immortality were given in the seventh and eighth chapters of *The Wisdom of the Overself.* However, certain points are given here again:

(a) Every person maintains his or her individuality during and after the perishing of the body-thought.

(b) The inequalities and injustices, which trouble many, are all balanced sooner or later by the law of recompense (karma). Each person receives in return precisely what he or she gives out; thus there *is* justice in the world, despite appearances to the contrary.

(c) When others ridicule the idea of immortality, the aspirant should not be upset nor allow his own faith to be weakened; he must remember that these people are merely expressing their own opinions, not passing on knowledge. The fact that many persons are not too happy about the idea of physical annihilation—and fail to take into consideration the fact that the "I" endures—has, of course, coloured their personal tastes. Their opinions are, however, incompatible with truth.

(d) The superstition that a childless person cannot reincarnate is nonsense.

(e) There are two kinds of immortality (so long as the lower self dominates consciousness): first, the "endless" evolution of the ego, gradually developing through all its many manifestations; and, secondly, the true immortality of the everlasting, unchanging Real Self—or Overself—which forever underlies and sustains the former.

(f) My reference to not clinging to the ego simply means that the aspirant must learn the art of releasing what is transitory in himself and in his existence—that which can survive only temporarily. The Real Individuality—the sense and feeling of simply Being—can never perish, and is the true immortality. No one is asked to sacrifice all interest and appreciation in "things": one may continue to appreciate them—provided their transiency is understood and one does not deceive himself into overvaluing them. The prophets merely say that the eternal life cannot be found in such things.

182

We must find heaven this side of the grave; we must understand that heaven and hell are deep inside the heart and not places to which we go; and we must know that the true heart of man is deathless.

183

The personal man will survive death but he will not be immortal. The "I" which outlives the fleshly body will itself one day be outlived by the deeper "I" which man has yet to find.

184

If death is the price of dwelling in this space-time world, then a spaceless and timeless world where there is no "here" and no "there," no "then" and no "now," no change from one stage to another, would also be an immortal one; and if death is the price of being associated with a separate individuality, then an existence which mysteriously embraces the whole world-system in unity must be imperishable.

185

The man who has studied these teachings does not believe that death can bring *him* to an end even though it must bring his body to an end. It is both a logical and biological truth for him that his inner personality will survive, his mind will continue its existence.

186

It seems that Life can very well carry on without any of us, but it does not seem that we could do the same with regard to Life itself. It depends on whether anything or nothing awaits us in the after-play.

187

The life that is in us goes at death into the life that is in the universe. It is as secure there as it was in us. It is not lost. Thereafter it reappears in another form, another body.

2

REBIRTH AND REINCARNATION

The wheel of life does not stop for long—soon it will turn again and pass from the point of death to the point of life.

2

The thought of the body, of being identified with it, guarantees that a dying person will come back here again.

3

Nature has taken a long time to prepare him for this moment—longer than he knows—and used many different forms to do so.

4

Man eagerly seeks a fleshly tenement through reincarnation or is drawn into it by his desires—describe it as you wish.

5

Tied to the great wheel of birth and rebirth as they are by desires and longings, there is in them still no wish for release.

6

The old people who walk with melancholy face, feeling condemned to die relatively soon, will do better to recognize the inexorable fatality which makes death always follow birth, but which then makes rebirth follow death.

7

The mental wavelength on which we tune in helps to determine the kind of life we have, the kind of environment we get.

8

Both the things we desire and those we dread bring us into incarnation again.

9

Better than being born to wealthy parents is being born to wise ones, for then the child will not only be taught spiritual values but will see them demonstrated before his eyes.

10

To be born and brought up in an atmosphere of high thinking and wide searching—this is the chance which reincarnation gives.

11

A child is born into a family not by mere chance but as the resultant of forces set agoing in the previous births both by the newly born and by its parents.

12

Parents may do what they wish to encourage the good and discourage the evil in the characters of their offspring, but in bringing them into the world they took a chance. For the children brought their own characters with them from previous incarnations.

13

When a child is born or a man dies, the new world of his experience cannot be said to be either a ready-made one or an entirely personal one. The truth lies in a combination of both. The mystery of existence lies in the wonderful way in which such a combination is brought about.

14

None of us is thrown into this world against his will. All of us are here because we want to be here.

15

We reincarnate in part through the pressure of accumulated karma and in part through the pressure of habitual tendencies.

16

Some are eager to descend into a body again, but others are reluctant and are half-dragged down.

17

All men come back to bodily life again if they leave a residue of karma. All karma that is not brought to an end by bringing the mind's bondage to the ego-thought to an end, makes reincarnation inescapable.

The influence of past tendencies

18

The tendencies brought over from past births, the experiences and contacts made then as well as in the present one, explain his acting as he does, and his being what he is.

19

He excuses his weaknesses by complaining against nature, which has provided him with instincts and passions leading to them. But that which he calls nature is really the inheritance of his own tendencies from former lives.

20

At any given moment, a man thinks and acts according to, and as a result of, his whole mental and physical experience of life and his whole character and nature. These cannot be limited to the single short life on earth he now knows, for that will not explain many of his tendencies and traits. They must include all his previous lives.

21

All things contribute to the making of man—the history of his past and the climate of his land, the people among whom he is born, and his own particular tendencies. The most important is his karma.

22

The modern world is a crucible, into which is thrown all the ideas so far recovered from the past, together with those born in the present.

23

He finds himself within the frame of the tendencies he has brought over from earlier births, modified or corrected or supplemented by the conditions of his present birth.

24

Whether or not the advance of age and the accumulation of experience has caused new ideas to supersede his older ones, the unconscious mind keeps its own register of every occasion and situation.

25

The past puts itself into every thought, every act, every perception even.

26

The materialists stretch the tenet of heredity to an irrational degree. No man merely reproduces the characteristics of his parents or of his distant forefathers. The differences exist and are plain in most cases. On the contrary, there is always some variation which separates him from his ancestry, always something original to himself. And this is explicable only on a basis of reincarnation.

27

Theoretical acceptance of the doctrine of reincarnation leads us to cancel out part of the claim of the materialists that the influence of environment makes the whole of man. For as a spiritual being, the man's essential self is already there even from birth, and is really unfolding himself into a material environment. The latter provides him with conditions which enable him to express himself, or by failing to provide those conditions hinder that expression. But the environment cannot wholly change a man or cannot wholly eliminate his true character. What he really is will sooner or later come out and show itself, with or without the help of environment. It is true, however, that a part of him might be unable to express itself altogether owing to a completely adverse environment or set of conditions. Nevertheless, the unexpressed part would still remain latently existent within his character and even if it never expressed itself at all throughout the whole of his lifetime it would reappear and express itself in a later reincarnation.

28

We are as much the victims of our own tendencies as of our environment. They shape happenings, deeds, reactions, decisions, aspirations, and grovelings.

29

The belief is common in Europe and America that we start life as babes with a blank character or with one inherited partially or totally from parents and ancestors.

30

The complexes and tendencies pre-existing the present birth and hidden deep in his subconscious mind, must sooner or later come through to the surface mind.

31

In the final accounting it is less what a man receives from education than what he receives from former lives that matters most. His education may help to bring it out and round it out but his innate stock will largely be the measure of his assets.

32

Ancestry may bring a man's body: it does not bring his genius.

33

The traits and tendencies which a man receives from the preceding births constitute in their totality the personal self which he knows as "I."

34

What a man brings over from former births are the fixed ideas in his consciousness, the habitual direction of his feelings and the innate impulses of his will.

35

The habits of thought, feeling, and conduct which settle upon a man really constitute the man. For it is those which are brought over from the experiences of earlier births, which sprout up in his youth and ripen in his maturity, and thus express themselves through his particular personality.

36

What a man is, needs, or has done puts him just where he is.

37

That character is shaped by circumstance and environment only spiritual dreamers may deny, but that it is wholly shaped by them only materialist dreamers may affirm. A keen, subtle, and sensitive intelligence can trace by logic, imagination, or intuition the fact of its own previous existence and hence accept the necessity of its development through reincarnation.

38

The ego inherits the tendencies, the affinities, and the antagonisms which have shaped themselves in a long series of births behind the present one.

39

The innate tendencies of his mental life give rise to the natural compulsions of his active life. He cannot behave differently from the way he does—that is, if he is not on the quest and therefore not struggling to rise beyond himself. His own past—and it stretches back farther than he knows—created the thoughts, the acts, and the conditions of the present.

40

There is a definite relation between a man's character, capacity, and talent in combination and his fortunes, opportunities, and frustrations.

41

The future of any individual is partly foreseeable to the extent that his character, past history, and his capacities give a clue.

42

We are hit in the face by our own sins.

43

These thoughts have become, by constant repetition, long-standing and deep-rooted. That is to say, they have become inherent tendencies and governing complexes of the man's character. He himself seldom realizes how much and how often he is at their mercy.

44

There is a sagacity which comes from ripened experience and another which comes from deepened experience.

45

The more I reflect about my global travels, observations, and studies, the more I hold firmly to this truth: "Character is fate."

46

The imperfections in our character measure accordingly the unpleasantnesses in our experience.

47

Men are not separated from each other by the yards between their bodies alone, but even more by the inequality of their characters and the discord between their attitudes. Men do not become neighbours merely because their bodies live near to each other, but because there is affinity between their characters and harmony between their attitudes. Two loving friends are near each other even though their bodies are in separate continents; two hating enemies are far from each other even though their bodies are in the same room.

48

A complete knowledge of what men are ought to lead to a complete foreknowledge of how they will act. But actually there is always a margin of unpredictability.

49

It is true that the whole of what man experiences is not wholly of his own direct making and that only a part of it is so. But that is the largest part. It is true that his nation's life affects and is responsible for some of the colour which his own takes on. But why was he born in that particular nation during that particular period? The answer must again be that he is getting the recompense of his own past making. For his nation may lie defeated and wounded, or it may stride triumphant and prosperous.

50

We automatically try to repeat the old patterns of behaviour created in former lives whether they are beneficial or injurious to us. This happens because we can hardly help doing so.

51

The recurrence of these old situations will go on lifetime after lifetime until the lesson is learnt.

52

We are victims of our own past: it creates a groove of impetus and momentum along which we move. This leaves no room for the new, the creative, to enter in.

53

We may have forgotten the early and original source of a present belief, an inveterate attitude, or an intense feeling, but yet it may have a powerful hold upon us and exert a powerful influence on our acts.

54

An aspirant may resolve to drop the past from memory after he has absorbed its lessons, to let it go because it still belongs to the illusion of time. Nevertheless its consequences are still there. They are present in him in what he is now.

55

Tendencies, habits, and desires inherited from past lives may be worth following. But they may also be harmful, or negative and not easily dislodged.

56

It is neither feasible nor desirable to eliminate all traces of the past from his mind.

57

What we were in the past is not important. What we are now is important. What we intend to make of ourselves in the future is vitally important.(P)

58

A man can respond to events or to prophets, to demands or to experiences, only on the level of his own capacity and mentality. We have no right to ask that he shall be better or wiser.

59

Character and culture are to be graded by the inner attributes which former lives have developed but which may not yet, in the present life, be fully unfolded.

60

The pathetic thoughts of what might have been torment him. But are they futile? If they show how actions could have been improved and decisions bettered, they sow seeds for the next birth.

61

This clinging to habits stands in the way of our health and even of our salvation.

62

We come into birth as distinct persons—even babies begin to show their individual differences with characters formed already in previous existences. This is one reason why some amount of tolerance, some acceptance of one another as we are, is necessary if we are to live peaceably together.

63

Wisdom happens. It may be found among the rich or respectable, or it may take a playful turn and dismay snobs by being born among the poor or pariahs. Only fools try to tie class, race, or nationalist labels onto the soul.

64

The essence of countless experiences and states through which he has passed is here and now with him as the degree of character, intelligence, and power which he possesses.

65

He who has taken many births has a great wealth of total experience behind him. This manifests itself naturally in wiser decisions and better self-control.

66

Memory is a spiritual faculty inasmuch as it gives us the chance and means to extract teaching wisdom and guidance from the past. It enables us to visualize past experience and make it either a guide or a warning in dealing with present problems.

67

That a truth which is so clear to their own minds could be so obscure to other minds, is easily explicable by the grading processes of reincarnation. Each man's present state and views are the outcome of his past experiences in past lives.

68

Some spend a whole lifetime trying to get enlightenment, others get it in a few years. The difference is accounted for by the difference in readiness, in growth, and in balance.

69

In reactions and desires, in needs and mental patterns, in tastes and interests we may search the planet's millions but find no two individuals absolutely alike. Difference and variety are imprinted upon the human race.

70

Wild animals are merciless but human animals are a mixed lot. Some are kindly, others cruel. The difference between the wild and human varieties is simply a difference in evolution. The distance between them is filled with births, experience, the resultant lessons absorbed leading to traits developed.

71

The same situation which leads to one man's development leads to another man's degradation. This is so because their capacities to draw right lessons from experience are unequal.

72

Just as each man has a separate identity, so all men have distinctive traits and marks, form and appearances. Nature does not indulge in the monotony of uniformity.

73

Whenever there is a choice to be made between the truth of the philosophic view and the falsity of the materialistic view, the man's spiritual age will reveal itself.

74

Where experience of life is limited to a small area, knowledge may be just as small. The result really depends on what a man does with his mind, if we assume that he has had a lot of experience in previous incarnations, even though he may have had little in this present incarnation.

75

The notion that wisdom comes with age is ridiculed by the young people of today. They see senile fools or middle-aged failures or leaders whose people fall into newer and more numerous difficulties and conclude that they themselves not only know better but can do better. Yet the notion is not to be dismissed so lightly. There is a deep ground for its truth, too deep perhaps for common sight, and hence only for those of insight. The age which is grown into after many births, rather than many years, *is* mellow with wisdom quite naturally.

76

We ought not to ask men to express qualities of character and mind which neither experience nor birth enable them to express.

77

Men actually defend themselves against the Truth, so attached are they to their ancient thought-forms and beliefs.

78

The advanced mystic reaches a point in his life where he finds it necessary to overcome the pull of those past periods, when he was able to live in a more congenial atmosphere than present-day civilization provides. Because of the world crisis which dominates every aspect of life, he knows it is necessary to look forward and not backward. And he knows, too, that this is why he feels immensely attracted to a particular place—Egypt and India are common examples.

79

We are all biased and blinded by the past. We need to force ourselves to face the present by the light of the future, as a man forces himself to bear the burden of prolonged hard work wherefrom he hopes to reap his high reward.

80

This incarnation will be worthwhile if only it is used to rectify some of the mistakes of earlier incarnations.

81

The man who finds his mind suddenly illuminated, but does not know why it came about, may find his answer in the doctrine of "tendencies"— prenatal and karmic—reappearing from former lives and held hitherto in the deeper mental levels.

82

It is easy to despise as stupid those of obvious inferior intelligence, but it would be well to remember that we were once at the same level. The notion of rebirth teaches tolerance.

83

Of what use is it to quote the need for following tradition and obeying authority or for joining in protest and rebellion? Men move into action of the one or the other kind as their tendencies dictate, in accordance with the pressures from their previous births. This is what Buddha saw when he penetrated and analysed human nature and why he insisted on the emancipation of oneself from oneself.

84

Why do some take to the True Doctrine at first glance whereas others—and they are the majority—spurn it? The answer is to be found in the internal age or prenatal experience or reincarnated tendencies.

85

When intuitive recognitions of truth, swift flashes of understanding, come on hearing or reading these inspired statements, this is a sign of having been engaged in its quest during former reincarnations.

86

We are in bondage to our own past. Who can deliver us, save ourselves?

Reincarnation and Mentalism

87

That men are at varying stages of mental capacity, different degrees of spiritual response, and unequal in character, manners, self-control, or reactions, is a matter of everyday observation. The theory of reincarnation in mentalism offers a logical explanation of these differences, and a deeper one than materialism's.

88

The truth about the universe cannot be had unless at the same time we get outside the limited views and emotional prejudices of the personal life. Nor can we get at the truth about ourselves so long as we think in terms of a single earthly lifetime. To do so leads to mental short-sightedness and gives an incorrect visual image of human life. All this shows why we need both the quest's discipline and philosophy's knowledge.

89

There is no direct and incontrovertible proof of reincarnation, but there is logical evidence for it. Why should there be certain abilities almost without previous training? Why should I be possessed at an early age of the mental abilities of a writer, or someone else of a musician? Heredity alone cannot account for it. But it is perfectly accounted for if we consider them to a subconscious memory. I am unwittingly remembering and using again my own capabilities from a former birth. This is possible only because I am *mind*. Mind alone can continue itself. Capacities in any field cannot appear out of nothing. The individual who shows them forth is repeating them out of his own deeper memory. There is the evidence of Nature. When I wake up in the morning, I pick up all that I had the day before. I remember my own individuality and use the same literary talents as before. Otherwise, I could never write again, or someone else could never sing. The basis of this reminiscence is not a physical occurrence, but a mental one.(P)

90

It is necessary to know *how* men think in order to understand *why* they think as they do. The structure of the mind in human beings explains why they arrive at particular conclusions or accept certain beliefs in each particular case. But without the idea of rebirth this explanation remains incomplete.

91

The views which anyone holds intellectually are relative to his experience and status, his innate character and reincarnatory history.

92

Is it true that soon or late after death we emigrate to another physical body? Can such a doctrine be part of a reasonable man's views? The answer is yes. Nor need reason alone guide us in this matter, for the varied evidences have been collected and stated by a very few authors. Psychical sensitivity to invisible records of the past offers, for what it is worth, some confirmations.

93

The capacity to commune with the Overself exists in all men; it is a universal one. But it does not exist to an equal degree. For those who can accept the doctrine of rebirth, the explanation of this inequality lies there.

94

Whether we have lived on this earth before and shall live on it again is a matter susceptible only of metaphysical and not of physical proof.

95

The very nature of reincarnation prevents anyone from completely proving it. But there is no other theory that is so reasonable to help us understand our evolution, history, capacity, genius, character, and inequality; no other so useful to help us solve the great problem of why we are here on earth at all. This doctrine, that the ego repeatedly visits our plane in fresh physical forms, is demanded by reason, supplied by intuition, and verified by revelation.

96

Any man is free to use his memories and experiences either destructively or constructively: it is up to him which use he makes of them. That environment, circumstances, heredity, and other well-known factors may influence what he does with them is true enough; but what he *is*, what character and tendencies he expresses, were transmitted from former births, were present before he acquired the attributes mentioned.

97

All his experiences during the ages upon ages of his existence as a finite centre of life and consciousness have left their record in the mysterious and measureless seed-atom of his body.

98

Freud's postulate of the Unconscious mind as a structure of forgotten unrecoverable memories is a precursor of the rebirth theory. It prepares the way for scientific acceptance of the latter and should inevitably lead to it. In turn, it throws light on the doctrine of karma. For the ego which revives out of apparent nothingness is the conscious mind which reappears out of the unconscious. When the production of these idea-energies (that is, tendencies, *samskaras*) is brought to rest, then they can never again objectify into a physical environment, a fresh rebirth, and thus man becomes karma-free and enters Nirvana. As long as he believes that he is the body he must reincarnate in the body.(P)

99

The reincarnations which precede the present one contribute to its characteristics and help to shape its happenings. But this does not mean they give all its characteristics and happenings. Some develop out of the outer facts and inner reactions of this present birth.

100

The strange feeling of having lived before and therefore of having been someone else may flash briefly through consciousness.

101

His conduct while alive will contribute to the kind of body and environment he gets next time, his thought and feelings too. We earn from life and pass up higher or go down lower like pupils in graded school.

102

One who knows something of his past lives has something to throw light in some way on his present one.

103

Where is any man's biography which is more than fragmentary, opinionated, and biased? For without the background picture of earlier lives in other bodies the materials are thinner than the compiler believes them to be.

104

The common complaint against the idea of a human re-embodiment is that we have no remembered knowledge of what happened and, therefore, of the causes of present troubles for which we are personally responsible. It is forgotten that such knowledge could only be had at the cost of re-suffering all the horrors and miseries of the past as well as its joys.

105

The benevolent shield of Nature protects us from the unhappy past; otherwise we would suffer futilely, as Taylor Caldwell, famed American novelist, suffered when she had recurrent nightmares of living in a dungeon during the Middle Ages.

106

If thousands of prenatal memories were to come crowding in together, the mind's life would be horrible, crazy. Worse, one's own personal identity would be lost, merged in all the others.

107

It is not at all necessary to learn how we lived in past lives in order to know how best to live in this one. Such knowledge might be useful but it also might be quite dangerous. It could lead to attempts to evade what is coming to us as a consequence of what we have done before. Such evasion could rob us of a chance to learn the lessons of that experience, while the attempts to gain this knowledge could itself lead to psychism. A sufficient practical guide can be found in Philosophy's moral wisdom, together with one's own conscience.

108

Speculations on former births can develop into hallucinations. It is wise to keep off these useless imaginations and attend to the here and now.

109

Whether a man's life be governed by a morality based upon religion or an ethics inculcated by breeding, or upon neither, there is a subconscious conscience always present which is a hidden underground factor in his outlook and decisions. It comes from former births.

110

One may experience a sense of loss if he has not recovered the degree of awareness achieved in previous incarnations.

111

What we know from past births does not have to be learned again from experiences of the same kind in the present birth, unless we do not know it or feel it strongly enough.

112

If he must seek to remember previous existences now lost to consciousness, let him seek only those wherein he rose to his spiritual best, wherein he came closer to God than in the others.

113

The unenjoyable lesson may be assimilated but the past has been recorded. Memory cannot change it, cannot remove its unpleasantness. So the blankness of the newly reincarnate blots out such morbid souvenirs.

114

This feeling that we have seen this place before, passed through that situation, comes from a former personality. The soul is the same, but the outer man is not.

115

Reincarnation. We tell our children strange tales that bring a yearning wonder into their eyes, for out of the far past their simple and unstained souls remember lands peopled with fairies and gods.

116

Is it so foolish a thought to say to oneself, "I sometimes identify with the Indians so closely, so sympathetically, that this belief that I was once one of them is quite acceptable"? When I first heard of it the idea of reincarnation seemed in harmony with Nature and needed no further argument in its favour.

117

There are some who feel a special affinity with the Orient, or rather with a particular Oriental country. This feeling has significance about their past pre-natal history, and should be valued for what it is. But to let the present lifetime be wholly overshadowed by the dead past is unwise.

118

If the physical memories of earlier lives are lost, the mental capacities and emotional trends persist.

119

A man may sit alone in his solitary room and stir but little from it, yet the wisdom of strange lands and stranger ages will float into his mind. Such a one has received a high inheritance down through the turnings of Time, a goodly power that is the testament to his strenuous efforts in search of knowledge in former lives. Some men are such natural mystics that they are born, as it were, with the thaumaturge's wand in their hands.

120

It is common enough to hear of people who want a place in the reincarnatory sun, compensating for their present obscurity by the discovery that they were formerly Cleopatra or Julius Caesar or the like in their previous reincarnation. We laugh at such weakness and vanity but we might ask such persons why should the presence of remembrance stop with the last birth. What about the birth before that? What about the dozens of births before that ultimate one? What about the births during the prehistoric period? Why pick on only the first and not on the hundredth birth from the present one?

121

The same forces which bring us into the experience of a new reincarnation also deprive us of the memory of previous reincarnations.

122

We may feel the pull or the repulsion generated by events or by persons met with in other lifetimes. The meaning of such meetings should be sought, although it may take some time and experience before it is found. If a place or a person seems strangely, even eerily, familiar, so that one enters into a relationship whether as friend or as enemy very quickly, this can often be taken as a strong confirmation of a pre-natal relationship.

123

What we learned in previous lives comes back again in the present one, but it may not come early, it may come later. Much depends on the environment as to when these old qualities can reappear. It also depends upon the events and the history of the individual.

124

Each new birth is neither a total replay of past ones nor totally different from them. The relation to each other is not only there, but also to the World-Idea, hence to the far goal.

125

The human being does not reach full physical development until the skeletal structure, particularly the wisdom teeth, reaches it. This happens between the ages of twenty-five and thirty. With the new body fully ready, recapitulation of the old one's experience soon ceases.

126

The conditions which surround a man are no accident. They are there because he is what he is and his past is what it was. If anyone ignores the Law of Recompense and limits his past to the present known lifetime, ignoring previous appearances on this planet, those conditions will many times be inexplicable.

127

His experiences in this life were largely decided for him in a previous life on earth.

128

Just as in the playing of billiards the impact of a ball hitting a second one gives the latter an impetus and a direction, so the *karma* of one birth is brought over to the next birth. This is not the same as a particular entity, a thing called ego, being carried over.

129

The feeling of familiarity with someone met for the first time, of vague indistinct recognition which we sometimes get, may have varying significances. But one of them is an echo of remembrance of previous contact in a past birth.

130

Imagine how much inconvenience would be caused if scenes and occurrences from previous lives kept on intruding into the affairs of the present one.

131

Some find it fascinating to speculate about whom they are the reincarnation of, but they ought to keep clear in mind that this is imagination given free play. In other cases, however, there is genuine remembrance, which may appear in either waking or dream states.

132

The saints were martyrs. They accepted all their suffering as coming from God and even embraced it. The Philosophic way is to realize that it is often karma, self-earned and brought upon oneself; hence one should analyse it and try to understand why it has come so that the lesson won't have to be repeated.

The Christian, Muhammedan, and Jewish religions must accept the doctrines of reincarnation and karma if they want to establish a reasonable place for suffering in the scheme of things.

133

There are people whom, at a single glance and in a single second, one feels one has known well before. With them one may drop the conventional preliminaries, the tedious circumlocutory play of more words and further meeting as being unnecessary.

134

Whatever he learned in the past years and births was a step—not always a forward one—to be regarded as a source of further instruction, experience, understanding, and practice.

135

When the balance is struck at the end of each re-embodiment, whatever he has achieved falls to the credit of his advancement: its value will show itself in his next births. But it is up to him to earn it, just as he is free to a limited extent to diminish what he had already. The Egyptian *Book of the Dead* refers to a "Day of Judgement." This is it.

136

Since it is not from the animal but from the human state that the Essence of Being can be realized (because the animal does not possess the necessary faculties), the processes of rebirth must fill the gap between lowest animal to highest human.

137

When the energies have run out, and the advance of years must be measured sadly; when a man knows at last what he ought to have done, it is too late. This is why another chance, another birth on earth is needed.

138

Something does get distilled from these repeated existences, however slowly. That men learn little or nothing from history seems true to many moralistic critics; they have a good case, but its truth is only on the surface of things.

139

Only when the desire for perpetuation of personal existence finally leaves him is a man really near the point where even a little effort produces large results on this quest. But getting tired of the wheel of rebirth's turnings does not come easily.

140

Why should that which is perfect need to be born again and again? The tenet of reincarnation is true only from the point of view of the ego and its senses. It is not true from the ultimate point of view. It explains all the inequities and some of the sufferings of life within the world-dream, but it is meaningless when we awake to the real world.

141

But who can count the number of times a living being must incarnate in the plant world before it is ready to enter the animal kingdom? Nearly a half of the average life is spent in recapitulating the previous incarnational development so that the work of a new incarnation does not really begin until then.

142

It would seem that the experience of a whole lifetime is wasted when people exist in such spiritual torpor, merely keeping their animal bodies alive. But of course it is not really so; for however slight and outwardly unrecognizable inward growth may be, it must be there, or Nature's process of reincarnation would be meaningless and useless mechanical repetition.

143

If a new birth is a new opportunity to gain spiritual experience, it is also a new opportunity to commit errors and acquire vices.

144

Looking at the monstrous wickedness and folly in the world today, it would seem a stupid and hopeless effort to believe that human character will become any better than it was and still is. But the fact of reincarnation, with its tremendous possibilities, restores this hope.

145

We change a little in appearance with each incarnation; we have to. But sometimes we change altogether.

146

We are incarnated to be educated. Experience provides the lessons, and necessity gives the disciplines.

147

His reappearance on earth would be justified by two results alone—that it gives a man a chance to start life anew and to mend character.

148

It would be absurd to regard every fresh rebirth as a fresh advance in wisdom and virtue. The human entity is not a mechanical entity. There are lapses, regressions, failures, and stagnations in its long journey.

149

Just as the impetus of one wave causes another to come into being, so the impetus of one human reincarnation causes another to follow it in succession. And just as the second wave may be similar to but not identical with the first one, so the later ego may be similar to, but is not identical with, the earlier one.

150

All the reincarnations which are necessary to the unfoldment of his character and capacities must be lived through.

151

The prospect of an endless existence, however cyclical and intermittent it may be, keeping on and on and on is not attractive to everyone and certainly not to those who have weighed well the measures of joy and suffering in earthly life. All desires are melting down into a single desire for non-existence, but they have done so only partially.

152

Living entities come here from less-evolved planets just as we go on to higher ones. But, in both cases, this must be accomplished within certain limited periods. After that the possibility of entry ceases.

153

The notion that we humans return to earth for a renewed life thrills some persons with pleasure but others with dismay. This reaction depends on the personal history, and on the physical-mental condition.

154

It is hard to understand why Adam and Eve needed angels with flaming swords to drive them out of the Garden of Eden. Surely the boredom of such a place was enough inducement for them to leave voluntarily, even eagerly? Men pass through heaven during the period between earthly embodiments, yet they do not remain there but must return to "this vale of misery." Why? Do they come to a time when unalloyed happiness, without a flaw and without an opposition, can be sustained no longer and a change from this Eden-like state, any change, seems more preferable?

155

There would be little advantage in gathering more experience only to repeat every mistake every time. Although this seems to happen quite often, it cannot be a permanent pattern.

156

Why do we have to learn these simple basic truths through so many reincarnations and at so high a cost? This is a complaint some people make.

157

In another body, born in another land, life's persistence brings us here again. The old game intermittently recurs, bringing its joys and griefs.

158

The development of these faculties, the unfoldment of these capacities, and the expansion of this consciousness are also incipiently present even in the animal reincarnation of the entity.

Beliefs about reincarnation

159

Reincarnation accounts for the predisposing factors, the specific urges, the particular additions, and the natural qualities of each ego.

160

When he looks back upon the long series of earth lives which belongs to his past, he is struck afresh by the supreme wisdom of Nature and by the supreme necessity of this principle of recurring embodiment. If there had been only one single continuous earth life, his progress would have been brought to an end, he would have been cluttered up by his own past, and he could not have advanced in new directions. This past would have surrounded him like a circular wall. How unerring the wisdom and how infinite the mercy which, by breaking this circle of necessity, gives him the chance of a fresh start again and again, sets him free to make new beginnings! Without these breaks in his life-sequences, without the advantages of fresh surroundings, different circumstances, and new contacts, he could not have lifted himself to ever higher levels, but would only have stagnated or fallen to lower ones.(P)

161

The law which pushes us into, or out of, physical bodies is a cosmic law. There is no blind chance about it.

162

(a) Not until the fourth century when one Christian party became successful enough to be armed with worldly power did the persecution of Gnostics begin.

(b) In the attempt to eliminate unpalatable tenets, no less than seven Councils were held in those early centuries. Here such tenets were branded as heresies and arrangements made to exterminate them thoroughly. Especially at the Council of Nicea (325 A.D.) and the great Council of Constantinople (381 A.D.), rebirth was pronounced a heresy, all the books teaching it were ferreted out and destroyed, and its advocates threatened with severe punishment.

(c) Yet not only had several Christian sects believed in reincarnation but some of the early Christian Fathers, too. The Fathers who held metempsychosis to be true included Origen, who flourished about 230 A.D., Justin Martyr, 140 A.D., Clement of Alexandria, 194 A.D., Tertullian of Carthage, 202 A.D. The sects who held it included Basilidians, the second-century Marcionites of Pontus, the Valentiniens of Egypt, also second century, and the Simonians. Moreover, all Gnostic sects held it and they were once more numerous than any other group of Christians. This is important, that most of the *early* Christians believed in this doctrine.

(d) The Manichaeans also taught rebirth and, together with the Gnostics and Samaneans, formed a considerable part of the early Christian world.

(e) Where the literature was not destroyed it was so adulterated or interpolated as to make it appear either quite ridiculous or utterly er-roneous. The historians among the later Fathers even accused the Gnostics of eating children!

(f) The early Gnostics came closer to the truth, but the later cults which sprang up among them departed from it by intermixing it with nonsense and corrupting it with falsehoods.

(g) Philo, himself a Jew, explicitly states that the Essenes got their knowledge from Indian Brahmins. Everyone knows that rebirth was an essential feature of the Brahmins' faith, so it is fair to assume that it was taken up by the Essenes, too.

163

We are given one life, one day, one present time, one conscious space-time level to concentrate on so that Nature's business in us shall not be interfered with. Yet other lives, other days, other times, other levels of consciousness already exist just as much at this very moment, even though we do not apprehend them, and await our meeting and experience by a fated necessity.(P)

164

I was not surprised when Jung told me that he could not accept the idea of reincarnation but could accept the idea of karma.

165

We repeat these appearances on earth in a constant process and a long cycle of time. But contrast it with the beginninglessness and endlessness of life itself. What is this but a fraction of a fraction of a moment?

166

Can the invisible inner being migrate at death, after a suitable interval, from one body to another?

167

Reincarnation is now one of the most romantic and abused of the Orient's commonplace ideas. It is like a servant strutting in the elegant clothes of a Countess.

168

If we believe that our personal life has no more significance than a ripple on the surface of the ocean, it is either because we are blinded by material-ism or because we are blind to the ultimate secrets of human personality.

169

The belief in reincarnation is not so foolish as it seems to some people: there is reasonable foundation for it.

170

To descend into the body, to reincarnate in the flesh is itself a kind of crucifixion. Note that the head and trunk are right-angled by the right and left arms forming a cross. This is symbolic partly of the loss of higher consciousness which this descent entails and partly of the pains and miseries which appear intermittently during embodiment.

171

From my understanding of the teachings of the Buddha, the man who has annihilated the illusion of a personal self and who has brought his mind under complete control will not be reborn against his will, even though he should indulge in such non-Buddhistic practices as wearing leather shoes and eating cheese.

172

When a man has established himself in the Universal self, in the awareness of its oneness, the series of earthly reincarnations of his personal self comes to an end. For himself, they would serve no further purpose.

173

Bringing rebirth to an end has two esoteric meanings: (a) The Arhat is free from *ignorance*. (b) Even though he is reborn physically in order to help others, still, as he enjoys the awareness of Atman, which he knows to be deathless and unborn, *he* does not look at himself as being reborn.

174

It is well to realize that belief in reincarnation, or rebirth, is not the sole determining consideration of our activities, as it is among many institutionalized approaches to Truth in the Orient.

175

The Christian Church wanted to emphasize its doctrine that the newly disincarnated soul went straight to heaven or hell. This is one reason why the belief in rebirth was later stamped with the mark of heresy. Another is that it contradicted the teaching of the resurrection of the body.

176

I often wondered in the past why it is that the land of Britain which, nearly two thousand years earlier, accepted and valued the doctrine of reincarnation and therefore looked on death as an interval between two earth-lives, should have so far forgotten its former allegiance as to dwell in the dusk between the narrow limitations of single-embodiment belief and the hopeless outlook of agnosticism or atheism. It is pleasant to welcome the contemporary revival of interest, in many cases, and acceptance in others, where rebirth is discussed.

177

Somewhere in Shakespeare there is that phrase about our human "exits and entrances" which, with its reversal of the natural order of birth and death, I take to mean our reincarnation.

178

In 1938 Somerset Maugham wrote, in *The Summing Up*, a fair reference to the theory of reincarnation but ended it by saying he found it incredible. In 1944 he referred again to the same theory and found it "the only plausible explanation for the existence of evil," although beyond human verification.

179

If all those prominent persons who hold this belief in rebirth were to come forward and boldly proclaim it, and if all those Protestant ministers of religion and Catholic priests or bishops who hold it secretly were to confess, the world would be astonished.

180

We glibly use the term reincarnation when, under certain conditions, the term metamorphosis is more pertinent.

181

If a sharp intellect shuts the door on all authorities except one, it has only its own foolishness to thank when it shuts truth out with its action. So keen, witty, and logical a mind as Saint Augustine's brusquely rejected the doctrine of the human entity's successive reincarnations on earth. Yet, in the same book, *The City of God*, he unhesitatingly accepts the computation that the age of the human race is less than six thousand years. He bases his reckoning on nothing more than the petty tribal histories contained in the Old Testament. He rejects, too, the grand conception of the pagan thinkers who preceded him, that the world has passed through countless cycles and consists of an infinite number of worlds.

182

Another result of a full comprehension of mentalism is that it makes possible a change of attitude towards the doctrine of reincarnation. Those who reject this doctrine because they are not interested in any past or future person who is not completely identical with their present person, do not perceive that this lack of interest arises out of their total self-identification with the physical body. They regard it to be the real "I." But this is utter materialism. For they do not see that the mental "I" is more really their self than the fleshly one. Mentalism can help greatly to rectify their error.

183

The doctrine of transmigration of souls into animal forms was given out for, and led to the same effects as, the doctrine of after-death punishment in hell. Timaeus Locrius, the teacher of Plato, said as much and observed that "if the mind will not be led by true reasoning, we restrain it by false." The Buddhist and Christian picture of the souls of murderers being burnt in the fires of the underworld serves the same warning and disciplinary purpose as the Hindu picture of those souls incarnating into the bodies of wild beasts. Transmigration of this kind is not to be taken literally. Brahmin priests who teach it publicly do not, if they are also initiates in philosophy, believe it privately. It is the exception, not the rule, and opposed to the evolutionary course of Nature.

184

If the doctrine did nothing more in its practical effects than inspire its believers with a sense of life's continuity and impress them with a warning of personal responsibility for their fortunes, it would have done enough.

185

We may be surprised that so many intelligent people refuse to believe in reincarnation and karma, even though they cannot explain God's justice without them. The truth is that they are defective in intuition and dependent on intellect and emotion. But emotion and intellect alone are too limited as instruments for finding truth.

186

Whatever we constantly concentrate on provides one of the factors in reincarnation. If we love a race or an individual strongly enough, we shall sooner or later necessarily be drawn into their orbit when reincarnating. It is equally true, however, that if we hate a race or an individual strongly enough we shall have the same experience. Both love and hate are forms of concentrated thought. The nature of concentration, whether it be that of like or dislike, attraction or repulsion, does not alter its strength.

187

The transmigration of souls from human to animal bodies is a fiction. The individual consciousness which has one or more specifically human attributes, cannot be brought naturally into the brain and nervous system of any creature which has only animal attributes. That millions of people still believe in its possibility merely shows how widespread is superstition.

188

The popular Hindu theory of the transmigration of souls is not quite the same as the philosophic theory of the evolution of souls. According to the first, a man may once again become an animal or a tree; according to the second, this is not part of the ordinary processes of Nature. Many superstitions, however, hide some truth among their nonsense, and this is one of them. Just as every biologist knows that Nature sometimes produces freaks, and every physician knows that monstrosities are sometimes born into the human race, so there are cases where a deranged mind frantically thirsting for a physical body after the loss of its present one may succeed in driving out the inner being of an animal form and taking possession of it. If this mind is also very evil as well as deranged, it will utilize that form to terrorize a human community. But such happenings are breakaways from the ordinary processes of Nature and, therefore, uncommon. The penalty for such unnatural transmigration is insanity, which is the price which will have to be paid in the next human birth. The ego will then be tied to a body which it will be unable to use, yet unable to escape from.

189

Whatever the worldly and physical experiences of a man may be, however materialistic his mental attitude and personal feelings may become, his essence-being remains untouched and unpolluted. But his link with it is another matter. If he falls too low this link may be so thinned that he is thrown back into an animal body in his next birth, to make another attempt at normal progression into the human condition.

190

It is something rare, abnormal, and exceptional, but not impossible, for a human being to be put back in an animal body. Then it becomes an imprisonment for one lifetime, and as such a punishment.

191

Had the tenet of rebirth not been rejected from official Christian doctrine but incorporated into it, European and American history would have moved to a slower tempo and Western material achievement would have reached a lower height.

192

Several of the early Church Fathers taught the doctrine of reincarnation. Origen even calls it a "general opinion." Justin Martyr declares that the soul inhabits a human body more than once, and Clement of Alexandria asserts it was sanctioned by Paul in Romans 5:12, 14, and 19. Despite this, the Council of Nicea pronounced it a heresy in 325 A.D., the Council of Chalcedon condemned it in the same century, and finally in the reign of Justinian at the Council of Constantinople in 553 A.D., it was again repudiated and its supporters anathematized. There was no room for it along with the rest of Catholic theology and especially with the teachings on redemption and purgatory. There is no room for both the doctrine of reincarnation and the doctrine of everlasting torment in purgatory; one or the other must go. So the first was branded a heresy and its believers were excommunicated or persecuted. The second reason for opposing it was that, the doctrine of Atonement was brought in little by little until it displaced the doctrine of metempsychosis, as it was intended to do. These two also could not exist side by side, for one contradicted the truth of the other. The third reason was that in the contentions for supremacy among the various Christian sects, those which later arose in Greek and Roman peoples triumphed over those which existed earlier among Oriental ones who believed in reincarnation, as most Orientals do even today.

193

The common interpretation of the Biblical sentence, "Dust thou art, and to dust thou shalt return," was interpreted by the Jewish medieval Kabbalists and by initiated Rabbis of antiquity as referring to reincarnation.

194

Greeks who believed strongly in the idea of rebirth were not only the initiates of the Orphic Mysteries, but also among the most celebrated thinkers, especially Plato.

195

Some upper-rank members of the Catholic hierarchy who privately believed but publicly rejected the tenet of reincarnation gave me, as the principal objection among a few others, that it allowed too long a time for people either to work for salvation or receive punishment for sins.

196

There is something awesome in the thought that birth and death within the human species have been going on for millions and millions of years. Today we see the outcome of all this vast line of experience.

197

Buddha tried to get his followers to abandon the will to live, but he did not try to get them to commit suicide of the physical body—rather to kill out the cravings and desires which tied them to reincarnation and led to their return to that body.

198

If death is so much a feature of the divine arrangements in the universe, we must accept that the divine wisdom is not faulted here and that, like the phoenix, out of the death of every creature shall arise a new one, a new form, apparently a new life.

199

To carry the burdens of existence in one body after another through a long series may seem an unpleasant prospect to some minds, as it did to Gautama in India and Schopenhauer in Germany.

200

Certain religious beliefs have come quite close to the idea of rebirth but at the crucial point have gone off at a wide tangent and missed the truth altogether. One belief leads to the expectation of a physical resurrection of the dead; the other to the practice of a physical preservation of the dead, as in mummification.

201

To assert that time does not return on itself, that history does not repeat its story, is to show an ignorance of the fact of human re-embodiments.

202

It is not often worth all the troubles and pains of being born and enduring all its consequences, even allowing for the pleasant interludes. Buddha would certainly not agree with any optimist about this matter.

203

In the lengthy writings of the fathers of the early Christian Church, we can find approval of belief in the doctrine of reincarnation expressed by Saint Methodius, Origen, Synesius, and Pamphilius.

204

Each comes to the front of the stage, plays out his allotted role, and moves away. Shakespeare's picturesque statement of the human predicament comes to larger meaning when interpreted in terms of rebirth in series. All mankind become a company of actors, appearing in play after play, each story different, each part acted in a new body.

205

The periodic return to earth-life was a belief shared by poets like Goethe, Shelley, and Browning, by thinkers like Plato, Schopenhauer, and Swedenborg.

206

Has the celebrated thinker, the Very Rev. Dr. W. R. Inge, become an adherent of the Hindu doctrine of the reincarnation? This is the question asked following his confession in a London newspaper article in March, 1944, that he believes there is an "element of truth" in this theory of personality common to the Indian masses and mystics of all countries.

Declaring that the error of Western civilization in crisis lies in a wrong idea of the human personality, he says that the truth is expressed in the "most famous Indian poem" which says, "Never the spirit was born; the spirit shall never cease to be; birthless and changeless and deathless, the spirit abideth for ever; death cannot touch it at all, death though the house of it seems."

This means, he says, that immortality is not a string with only one end, which is difficult to believe. Within the time series, that which has no end can have had no beginning. "The Indians and Greeks, both convinced of survival and pre-existence, stand or fall together."

Dr. Inge considers the absence of memory no fatal objection for there may be unconscious memory. "Who taught the chicken to get out of its egg? I cannot tell, but there is no mystery about all this.

Defending himself against the criticism that a dignitary of the Anglican Church has no business to dabble in such "heathen beliefs," Dr. Inge declares that rebirth is not alien to Christian thought and asserts that it is implied in many texts."

Coming from one of the intellectual leaders of the English Church and a former Dean of Saint Paul's Cathedral, the foregoing admission is of outstanding historical importance. The doctrine must now be considered worth serious discussion by all Western educated persons and no longer left to a few queer dreamers as something bizarre and exotic. Its increasing acceptance will also be a triumph over materialism. Rebirth identifies a man more with his mind than with his body. It thus accords perfectly with mentalism.

207

Gurdjieff and his one-time disciple Ouspensky revived the doctrine of Eternal Recurrence and put it forward as a better alternative to the doctrine of Reincarnation. If we examine the historic Tibetan Buddhist symbol called "The Wheel of Life," we see pictures of human beings being moved through contrasting phases of experience as the wheel turns round. But after it comes full circle they are subjected to exactly the same conditions, the same phases as before. It is pertinent to remember that Gurdjieff learnt about Eternal Recurrence in a Buddhist monastery in Central Asia, where the same version of Buddhism prevails as in Tibet. It is also pertinent to remember the monotonous movement of life for the somewhat primitive inhabitants of that wild region for centuries until very lately. The pattern of their existence recurred again and again in the same way. What more fitting in their beliefs than that their rebirths would be similar too?

208

By different turns in the course of his mental existence he takes different bodies. Widespread in Asia from the earliest times, accepted by many of the thinkers in ancient Greece and Rome, by the Druid priests of Britain and the Dacian priests of the Balkans, the theory of reincarnation has been both known and favoured.

209

In the Buddhist symbolism the wheel of life rolls on, dragging man with each complete turn through another reincarnation. Again and again he goes through the same experiences until he gets worn out and tires of them and seeks release from being tied to the wheel, the release which is called Nirvana.

Reincarnation and the Overself

210

We have to become in actuality what we are in potentiality; all our rebirths are engaged in this process.

211

Whether we confront the mystery called death or the equal mystery called life, the revelation must come in one or the other state: there is a connection with HE WHO IS. For this are we born and our oscillation between the two happens at the Mind of the World's behest. As, so sleepily and unwittingly, we shape and light up these fragments of being that we are, quite simply the connection gets uncovered more and more.

212

Until he finds his Overself, no man can escape this coming back to the earthly life. And this remains true whether he loves the world or is disgusted by it.

213

The lotus-flower of the soul unfolds but slowly through many births, yet it is certain and sure. This is indeed better than the mere stuffing of the brain with learned lumber that has to be abandoned with each death.

214

We come back to this earth of ours and not to some other earth because it is here that we sow the seeds of thought, of feeling, and of action, and therefore it is here that we must reap their harvest. Nature is orderly and just, consistent and continuous.(P)

215

We need more lifetimes and plenty of them—even half a hundred would not be enough—to do the work upon self which has been assigned us as our highest duty. This is why reincarnation is a fact, and not a fable.

216

Patience, little men, there is no possibility of your missing salvation. What if you have to wait through a number of reincarnations! You cannot lose this wide-stretched game, played all over the planet, for you cannot lose your innermost being. The Covenant with your Creator has been made and must be fulfilled in the end, however dubious the prospect seems today.

217

Hope comes to him from this benevolent source, evil departs from him as he draws on these higher energies for defense, and ethereal purpose surrounds his entire life like an aura. He knows that his history did not begin in the country where he was born. He knows that it will not end in the body in which he dies.

218

The passage from quest to conquest would be impossible for most humans if they had only one life to live, one body for the start and the finish.

219

There can be no Second Coming of Christ—the Consciousness—for it never went away. There can be a return of Jesus—the man embodying and reflecting that Consciousness—for the person may be born and reborn as God wills.

220

The Long Path idea of reincarnation is illusory. The Short Path idea of it is that it is an undulatory wave, a ripple, a movement upward onward and downward. Since there is no ego in reality, there can be no rebirth of it. But we *do* have the *appearance* of a rebirth. Note that this applies to both the mind and body part of ego: they are like a bubble floating on a stream and then vanishing or like a knot which is untied and then vanishes too. We have to accept the presence of this pseudo-entity, the ego—this mental thing born of many many earth-lives—so long as we have to dwell in that other mental thing, the body. But we do not have to accept its dominance; we do not have to perpetuate its rule, for all is in the Mind. Where then are the reincarnatory experiences? Appearances which were like cinema shows. They happened in a time and space which were in the mind. The individual who emerged lost the individuality and merged in the timelessness of eternity. This is the unchanging indestructible Consciousness, the Overself.

221

Are all the varied joys and sufferings undergone only to come to a complete end in death? Is all the vast intelligence of this universe which gave birth to our own minute fragment to be forever separated from us? No! We shall live again, die again, and return again unless and until we have fulfilled the divine purpose which brought us here.

222

If it had been possible to attain salvation in the non-physical worlds, we would not have been born in this one. We are here because nowhere else could we, in our present state of progress, find the right environment to ripen those qualities which will lead us further toward this ultimate goal.

223

The eventual trend of evolution is through and away from personality, as we now know it. We shall find ourselves afresh in a higher individuality, the soul. To achieve this, the lower characteristics have slowly to be shed. In this sense, we do die to the earthly self and are born again in the higher self. That is the only real death awaiting us.

224

The possession of moral values, metaphysical capacities, and spiritually intuitive qualities which distinguish more evolved from less evolved men takes time to acquire—so much time that reincarnation must be a continuous process.

225

If it were true that a bad man must always remain bad, where would the hope be for mankind? But in the perfect wisdom of the Infinite Mind, human lives are so arranged that the bad man will go on garnering the untoward results of his deeds until his mind, first subconsciously but later consciously, perceives the logical and causal connection between his act and his suffering and begins the attempt to control his evil tendencies. Both this education and this effort will continue through many births for a single one would be too short in time, too poor in opportunity, for such a total reformation to be achieved.

226

Even those who are well-intentioned and spiritually minded make many mistakes in life simply because they cannot see the unfortunate results to which their wrong decisions and actions must necessarily lead. Only experience can lead to their correction and only reincarnation can give enough experience.

227

Life in the flesh is a gift if we are using it rightly but it becomes a curse if we are not. Every incarnation should be used to help one get somewhat farther in doing this job of achieving an Overself-inspired existence.

228

What is happening to his characteristics, what he is learning from experience lies, in more or less degree, below the threshold of consciousness. Only time, with its repetitions, and thought, with its conclusions, will shift the lesson or ability into visible manifestation above the threshold.

229

The difference between savage and sage may be only two letters in spelled words but it may be two thousand incarnations in historic meaning.

230

Whatever mistakes the aspirant has committed in the past and whatever results from them he is suffering in the present, he should look to the future with some hope and never let it desert him, for even if that hope cannot be realized in the present incarnation it may be in the next. Time is passing, we come and we go, and in the end time is illusory, but we remain: the best in us remains, the rest will go.

231

The changes of personal identity under the process of reincarnation alone show that the little ego's immortality is a religious illusion. Only by finding its higher individuality is there any chance of preserving any identity at all, before Nature re-absorbs what it has spawned.

232

Plant, animal, and human bodies pass through this cycle of growth, maturity, decay and death. All this means being exposed to different forces, different experiences, resulting in the development of consciousness.

233

To become Man as evolution intends him to be, he must draw out all his latent resources, fill out a wide experience. This is why so many reincarnations on earth are needed. Until then, his realization as Man will be an incomplete one.

234

In the strictest meaning of the term, no man can give up himself, for no man can give up his innermost being. But what is really meant by the term and what every man could give up is the false sense of self which makes him think that he is only the ego or only the body.

235

There, in this necessity of developing, balancing, and coordinating all the parts of one's being, is a further argument for the necessity of reincarnation. A single lifetime is too short a period in which to fulfil such a task.

236

The ripe wisdom of a sage could not possibly be the fruit of a single lifetime, but only of many lifetimes.

237

The experiences of life will in the end overcome these inner resistances. The silent instruction multiplied during the re-embodiments will defeat the psychological defense mechanisms set up against unpalatable truths or new ideas. It is the repetition and deepening of all these lessons through the accumulating rebirths that enables wisdom to penetrate consciousness completely and effectively.

3

LAWS AND PATTERNS
OF EXPERIENCE

Defining karma, fate, and destiny

In karma we find a key to many puzzles of contemporary history. It is a doctrine which warns us that we have prepared the cocoon of our present lot largely by the thoughts and deeds spun out of ourselves during bygone earth-lives and the present re-embodiment. Now the doctrine is as applicable to the history of whole peoples as to the history of single individuals. Its corollary is that our characters and minds are in travail through the ages; some are old with the rich experience of a hoary past but most are young, unwise, and ungoverned. Its lesson is that the changing tides of public fate and private fortune are not meaningless. On the contrary, they invite our philosophical consideration so that we may understand how neglected duties or positive wrong-doing are the hidden root of our troubles. Those who understand the principle of karma aright, who do not misunderstand it as being an external independent fate but see it as a force originally set in motion by our actions, understand also the significant part played by suffering in the lives of men. It is educative rather than retributive. Merited punishment is really a crude form of education. Thoughtful men learn lessons from their sorrows and resolve not to commit the same sin or the same error a second time.

2

The unexpected events which happen to us apparently without cause or connection in our conduct constitute fate. The tendencies by whose influences and the circumstances by whose compulsion we act the way we do, constitute necessity. The results of those actions constitute Karma (recompense).(P)

3

What a higher power has decreed must come to pass. But what a man has made for himself he can modify or unmake. The first is fate, the second destiny. The one comes from outside his personal ego, the other from his own faults. The evolutionary will of his soul is part of the nature of things but the consequences of his own actions remain, however slightly, within his own control.(P)

4

Karma's will could not prevail in one special part of our life and not in any other parts, nor in one special event of our life and not in the others. It could not be here but not there, in the past but not now. Nor, going even farther still, could it confine itself only to major items and not to minor ones. It must be ever present or never present at all. If it puts more destiny into the happenings we experience than lets the Westerner feel comfortable, we must remember that other facet of truth, the creative and godlike intelligence in our deeper humanity and the measure of freedom which accompanies it.(P)

5

Whereas fate (in the original and Greek sense of the word) is decreed by whatever Powers there be, karma is the result of our own doing.(P)

6

The correct meaning of the word "karma" is willed action through body, speech, and mind. It does not include the results of this action, especially those which produce or influence rebirth. Such inclusion has come into popular concepts, but shows a loose use of the term. Karma is cause set going by the will, not effect at all. The phrase "Law of Recompense" is therefore not satisfactory and a better one is needed.(P)

7

In the universal drama every man is playing the role required of him. Neither the drama nor the role depends upon his personal choice. The very circumstances which instigate his decisions or prompt his actions are written into the script in advance. Even the attempt to change his part or the refusal to continue in it is also in it.

8

No one will deny that the past is now absolutely fixed and completely unalterable.

9

All the karmic tendencies are not present in consciousness at the same time; some have yet to pass from the potential to the kinetic condition.

10

If we could really know what was going to happen to us, it would certainly be important to us. But who *really* knows? The future is in God's hands.

11

Every creature comes to earth with a certain potential of life-force which, ordinarily, must exhaust itself before it leaves.

12

The same destiny which brings two persons together, also parts them.

13

Since in the end the entire universe is destined to turn to ashes, what future is there for the human species?

14

The workings of the law of recompense are carried out by a means as beyond human comprehension as are most of the other workings of the World-Mind behind it. They are not thought out step by step but appear suddenly by a single magical stroke just as the result of a problem presented to an electronic calculator suddenly appears on its dial.

15

The law of recompense may possibly be better named the law of reflection. This is because every act is reflected back to its doer, every thought is reflected back to its source, as if by a vast cosmic mirror. Perhaps the idea of recompense carries too strong a moral implication and hence too limited a meaning to be the correct equivalent for the word "karma."

16

A doctrine which has the power to deter men from wickedness or to stimulate them to virtue, not by fear of punishment or hope of reward but by convincing them that the Good is to be followed for its own sake, is valuable both to society and the individual.

17

It is not that some mysterious superphysical angel, deva, or god intervenes personally and manipulates karma as a puppet performer pulls the wires of his suspended figures, but that karma is part of the equilibrium of the universe, bringing a come-back, recording a pressure, allowing each reaction to come about by its own momentum.

18

If life is a drama put on the stage of this planet for us (and others) to play in, then karma is the audience, the witness of it all.

19

Quite logically it is taught that some sort of a balance is struck between the two kinds of a person's karma, so that the bad may be mitigated or even outdone, but equally the good may be reduced or even offset.

20

Events happening to us are not necessarily karmic in the sense that we earned them. They can also have a non-karmic source. No physical doing on our part brought them on, but they are what we need at that point for character or capacity, development or correction. Both kinds are fated. In that sense they are God's will.

21

Human instruments *are* used to cause suffering to others and they *do* cause it out of human viciousness. Both statements are correct. They are complementary, not contradictory as we may think. Destiny naturally looks around for a vicious person when she wants to do harm, or a foolish one who can be led emotionally by the nose for a time, or an impulsive one who may do in a moment what he regrets for years. She will not waste time looking for ultra-wise and ultra-good people when she wants to do harm.

22

The *destiny* of man is whatever happens to him, be it self-earned or ordained by a higher power. The *fate* of a man is the special kind of destiny which is so ordained and hence beyond his control.

23

The victory of the spiritual nature in man is foreordained and unavoidable, but the hour of that victory no man knoweth.

24

If he could see his present path and goal more clearly, he could foresee his future ones more correctly.

25

Man's destiny always exists potentially and only waits the propitious moment when it may rightly reveal itself.

26

Destiny follows tendency. What we are makes us go in a certain direction. Philosophy sees the end from the beginning.

27

This tenet is not offered as consolation to the afflicted; indeed it would be a poor panacea for them. It is offered because we see no other that appears to possess its truth, harsh though that be.

28

Ouspensky's theory of eternal recurrence is both true and false. We repeat ourselves and our circumstances but always on a different level. It is a spiral not a circle. An event or a period in life corresponds to a previous one but is not identical with it. The future is analogous with the past but does not duplicate it. The spiral does not bring you back identically the same self or the same work: it brings you to what corresponds to it on a different level.

29

There is an inescapable balance between our principal thoughts and deeds and our principal life experiences. And this balance shows itself where it is least expected—in the moral sphere. Our wrong-doing produces sorrows, not only for others but principally for ourselves. Our good action produces a rebound of good fortune. We may not escape from the operation of this subtle law of moral responsibility. Causation is the top of a wheel whose bottom is consequence. This is just as true collectively as individually. When, for instance, a nation comes to believe that the conception of right and wrong is a false one, it marks itself down for destruction. We have seen this in our time in the case of the German nation. The moral law is not a figment of man's imagination. It is a divinely established reality.

30

It would be an error to separate karma from the universal power and to treat it as an independent power. This error accounts for the difficulty in understanding its role in bringing the cosmos into manifestations. Treat karma rather as an aspect of God and as inseparable from God, or as one of the ways in which God's presence manifests itself.

31

Karma, being made by human will, is subject to human modification. Fate, being decreed by the higher power, is not. The general fact of death is an example of fate, and in this sense the poet James Shirley's line: "There is no armour against Fate," is true. But the particular fact of death, its time and manner, may be alterable.

32

If it be true that the course of life is predetermined, this does not necessarily mean that it is arbitrarily predetermined. No—the good and bad qualities of your character, the development or lack of development of your capacities, and the decisions made in passing or by reason are the real determinants of your life. There is an inescapable equation between conduct and consequence, between thought and environment, between character and destiny. And this is karma, the law of creative equivalence.

33

It is because this tenet has been so often ill-understood that it has taken extravagant or erroneous forms and consequently ridicule has been cast upon it.

34

In philosophical tradition, the sword has been the symbol of God's Law of Recompense and Justice.

35

The law of consequences is not primarily an ethical law: more properly it may be said to have an ethical side.

36

Destiny is not working blindly and unintelligently, arbitrarily and antagonistically against us as most of us are likely to believe when enduring through a cycle of unfavourable karma. On the contrary, it is Absolute Wisdom itself in operation.

37

The processes of imagining are endless and incessant. It is inherent in mind that one idea should give rise to another because of the dynamic character of mind itself. Karma is the law that links the two.

38

The experience of hearing inner music is an interesting and significant happening. It is rare when it happens upon meeting, being more apt to occur at parting—usually with someone who is very dear, whom Destiny has decreed cannot stay with us.

39

Things act according to their nature. The World Idea records these actions in a secret way and reflects back their appropriate results. And as with things so with persons. Each of us sings a note out into the universe, and the universe answers us in the same key.

40

Whether he looks under a microscope at the lowest form of life or whether he looks deep within his own consciousness, this one law prevails unbrokenly.

41

Where misfortune seems to have visited a man through no contributory cause of his own, where he does not seem to have deserved in any way the poor cards which have been dealt out to him by destiny, he has no other alternative than to ascribe it to the deeds and thoughts of a former existence on earth, or to the necessary education of his inner nature by his higher self.

42

Every man is really on trial. Life itself is his judge with the working of karma, the ignorance or wisdom of his fellows, the voice of his conscience, and the capacities or incapacities of his personality.

43

As he looks back over all the events of his outer life, they seem like pages in a book he has been reading, already written out, with the events yet to happen being the unread pages. Or he is only a character in the book's story, seemingly acting out of his own choice but really and quite unconsciously working out the author's choice.

44

Buddha's statement of the karmic law, as made in the *Dhammapada*, is brief, lucid, firm, and confident. We are inescapably confronted with its truth as if it were a granite-hard mountain—a fact, fixed and undeniable.

45

The Greeks of antiquity believed in three Fates (The Moirai, or spinners): three old women, sometimes thought of as past, present, and future, or the holder of the distaff, the one who pulls the thread of destiny, and the one who cuts it. The early Romans believed in the birth-fairy who writes down the child's destiny when it is born.

46

Life owes you only what you have given it.

47

Karma is the king who rules this earth.

48

Life has no real purpose for its own essential self; it has just gone on and on. Man lives and lives, but the iron law of Compensation guards it, producing effects from Cause, good or bad, and adjusting the good or bad acts of man to the consequences.

49

The action which completes a thought is thrown back at him by Nature in the guise of karma. In this view he carries the responsibility for himself. He cannot turn it over to any human institution such as a church, or to any other human being such as a guru or saviour.

50

Karma is an impersonal force. It is not to be swayed by prayers as a Personal God is supposed to be.

51

When rendering an account of good or bad fortune, people usually forget to include the ethical values which were acquired from each experience. But when a man has attained some understanding of such matters, he will involuntarily bring the truth of personal responsibility into this light, not merely as an intellectual dogma but as a heartfelt conviction.

52

He has to foresee the consequences not only of an action but also of an attitude or an outlook.

53

He may deceive himself or others, but he cannot deceive the power of karma. Before it, he must stand responsible for his acts and receive their due effects. There is no other way he can go.

54

Those who will not learn from correct reflection about their experiences will have to learn from kicks delivered by the fresh karma they make.

55

Each birth makes fresh links in that chain of consequences which is karma.

56

From our study of the law of karma, we may deduce that a man must grow up, become adult, and learn to be responsible for his actions, decisions, emotions, and even thoughts. It is he who is accountable for which ideas, especially which impulses, he accepts and which he lets pass or pushes away.

57

Whoever ignores these higher laws and especially flouts the law of karma is opening a volcano under him.

58

Karma puts a certain responsibility upon every man alike—upon the philosopher no less than the primitive.

59

The man who imagines that he can go through life and manage his various affairs in independence of any alleged higher laws is following an illusion. Somewhere or at some time his awakening is inevitable.

60

A life that is not directed towards this higher goal, a mind that is entirely uninterested in becoming a participant in the Overself consciousness— these failures will silently censure a man both during his bodily tenancy and his post-mortem existence.

61

Men act out of self-interest; but through ignorance of the higher laws, especially that of karma, they may act against that interest.

62

Many groups in many lands demand justice from their governments, with varying definitions of the word. Apparently the claims are not easily satisfied for there are more today than ever before. Some individual persons go farther and demand justice from God. In a world where mischief and misfortune are so active they too seem only partly satisfied, if that. Here the notion of karma may seem fairer than governments are, but it is tied to other births in which these persons have lost interest!

63

It is largely their own doing which makes men suffer their own karma. But this is no reason why we should stand aside and leave them to their destiny.

64

Each of us carries a certain amount of responsibility for himself: none of us can justly renounce it on the plea that fate governs, directs, and arranges all things.

65

Let us not imagine that we are merely puppets bewitched hither and thither into pleasure and pain by an unseen showman.

66

If men ascribe to the overwhelming nature of fate the miserable weakness of their own inertia, they worsen their bad situation.

67

If men complain that life brings them its worst, they ought to pause and consider whether they have prepared themselves inwardly to receive anything better than the worst.

68

Too many people complain that they have been unfairly singled out by fate from others for unwarranted troubles, that they have had more misfortunes than they can bear, and that the good life they have led has availed nothing against such cosmic ill will. The fact is not that they have been specially harassed but that they have convinced themselves they have been harassed!

69

I am well aware that there are "occultists" aplenty who can furnish full and detailed descriptions of the operations of karma, who know its Alpha and Omega, who can trace its activity among men as easily as a heraldist will trace your pedigree. They have led many into their camps with their glib "knowledge," and they shall lead many more. But they are only tendering the counterfeit coin of mere opinion for the rare currency of factual knowledge.

70

We are seldom fair to fate. When events do not happen in the way we would like them to, we refuse to accept the idea that it is our own fault, so we blame our harsh fate. But when they do happen favourably, we personally take the credit for bringing them about!

71

It is quite possible to trace the world's troubles to any cause—from eating certain food to the presence of certain people—which human fancy picks upon. For there is nothing which is not in some way and however remotely connected with some other thing. All that is needed is some imaginative faculty and some logical facility.

72

Too many people are praying to be delivered from the consequences of their errors or weaknesses, too few are trying to set themselves free from the faults themselves. If the prayers of the larger group are answered, the weaknesses still remain and the same consequences are bound to recur again. If the efforts of the smaller group are successful, they will be delivered forever.

73

When we think of all the possible permutations and combinations of destiny and compare them with what actually happens, and note its relation to our inner being, condition, fault, virtue, or need, a line that is more than merely coincidental can be traced.

74

A man need not sit all night under a peepul tree to get the revelation of this truth about the law of recompense. He can get it sitting in a professional office or walking in the marketplace, if he will watch what happens with his eyes and put two and two together with his brain.

75

This blaming of others for one's misfortunes or even for one's misdeeds is, for the quester, a device whereby the ego directs attention away from its own guilt and thus maintains its hold upon the heart and the mind. For the ordinary man, it is merely the emotional expression of spiritual ignorance.

76

Everyone has to feel and think and act and speak. But everyone does not perceive the consequences, near or remote, swift or slow, of these operations.

Whoever chooses a wrong aim or an unworthy desire must endure the consequences of his choice. In every evil act, its painful recoil lies hidden.

The process is a cumulative one. Each act begets a further one in the same downward direction. Each departure from righteousness makes return more difficult.

77

To bemoan and bewail one's lot helplessly on the plea of inexorable fate is to pronounce oneself a slave. Whence came this fate? It was not arbitrarily forced on one. The very person who complains was its maker. He therefore can become its un-maker!

78

If the cause of his troubles is left unremoved, it will in time lead to new effects and simply add more misery to his existing burden. All his so-called escapes from them will be illusory, so long as this cause is still operative.

79

There is a spiritual penalty to pay for every intellectual misbehaviour and every moral misconduct, whether there be a worldly penalty or not. For the one, there is the failure to know truth; for the other, there is the failure to find happiness.

80

Man is responsible for his own acts. The belief that any Saviour can suffer for his sins or any priest remit them is incorrect.

81

He may resent and resist the law, but it requires him ultimately to go forward alone.

82

To ascribe the results of man's negligence to the operation of God's will is blasphemy. To blame the consequences of human stupidity, inertia, and indiscipline upon divine decrees is nonsense.

83

Those who say they deem it unjust to be forced to accept the painful consequences of deeds somebody else has done, who consider the lack of remembrance between the two earthly incarnations sufficient excuse for their lack of belief in the doctrine of re-embodiment, utter reasonable objections.

84

If men knew that the law of compensation was no less operative than the law of their country, they would unquestionably become more careful.

85

People should be warned that cause and effect rule in the moral realm no less than in the scientific realm. They should be trained from childhood to take this principle into their calculation. They should be made to feel responsible for setting causes into action that invite suffering or attract trouble or lead to frustration.

86

When men come to understand that the law of compensation is not less real than the law of gravitation, they will profit immensely.

87

It is not only a misfortune for which he is to be pitied, when a man endures trouble of his own making, but also a fault for which he is to be blamed.

88

Where a man will not put himself under his own discipline, life eventually compels him to accept its sterner one. Where he will not look his defects in the face, sufferings that result from them will eventually remind him of their existence.

89

Sins of omission are just as important karmically as sins of commission. What we ought to have done but did not do counts also as a karma-maker.

90

The same man who is responsible for our mistakes is likewise responsible for our misfortunes.

91

If the teaching of Karma (the law of recompense) imbues men with the belief that it is not all the same whether they behave well or ill, if it arouses their sense of moral responsibility, then none can deny its practical value.

92

He who discovers these moral truths and reveals them to his benighted fellows is not only their educator but also their benefactor. For he saves those who heed him from much avoidable suffering.

93

There is a justice in human affairs which only impersonal eyes can see, only impartial minds can trace.

94

Once a man really takes the law of consequences to heart, he will not willingly or knowingly injure another man. And this is so primarily because he will not want to injure himself.

95

Modern man needs this awakening to the fact that he is responsible for his fate and must not seek to saddle it on a whimsical God or blind chance. And so far as he has brought evil upon himself he should acquiesce in the justice of it, confess his sins, retract his deeds, and reorient his conduct.

96

When we thoroughly imbibe this great truth, when we humbly acknowledge that all human life is under the sway of the law of consequences, we begin to make a necessity of virtue.

97

When considered from the long-range karmic point of view, each of us creates his own world and atmosphere. Therefore, we have no one but ourselves to thank or blame for our comfort or wretchedness. It should be remembered, too, that present correct or incorrect use of free will is right now deciding the conditions and circumstances of lives to come.

98

It is absurd to treat the idea of karma as if it were some outlandish Oriental fancy. It is simply the law which makes each man responsible for his own actions and which puts him into the position of having to accept the results which flow from them. We may call it the law of self-responsibility. The fact that it is allied with the theory of reincarnation does not invalidate it, for we may see it at work in our own present incarnation quite often.

99

The attempt to evade karma may itself be part of the karma.

100

Foolish actions damage a man's life and may damage other men's lives, too. Wicked actions claim him as their first victim for he will suffer morally at some time in life or death, and physically if the karma justifies it.

101

Since it is demonstrably true that it is the degree to which events affect your thoughts or move your feelings that they have power over you, it must also be true that to gain control over thought and feeling is to become pleasurably independent of fortune. If you let your life be managed entirely by the hazards and chances of outside happenings instead of by your own intelligence, you imperil it.

Our outward miseries are symbols and symptoms of our inner failures. For every self-created suffering and every self-accepted evil is an avoidable one. It may not depend entirely upon yourself how far events can hurt you but it does depend largely upon yourself. If you had the strength to crush your egoism by a single blow, and the insight to penetrate the screen of a long series of causes and effects, you would discover that half your external troubles derive from faults and weaknesses of internal character. Every time you manifest the lower attributes of your internal character you invite their reflection in external events. Your anger, envy, and resentment will, if strong enough and sustained enough, be followed eventually by troubles, enmities, frictions, losses, and disappointments.

Yes, if you wish to understand the first secret of fate, you should understand that its decrees are not issued by a power outside you, but by your own deepest self.

102

Will the West ever admit the notion of karma to its mind? I feel assured that it will do so. This is because it will have to admit the idea of rebirth which, once accepted, introduces karma as its twin.

103

Do they notice the sequence of cause and effect in the lives of others, as well as in their own?

104

His own actions will in turn lead to someone else's further actions.

105

It is because of this pressure of their limitations that men are driven sooner or later to seek the inner life.

106

Men will moan about their unhappy past, and ache because they cannot undo it; but they forget to undo the unhappy future which they are now busy making.

107

The weapons which wound us today were forged by our own selves yesterday.

108

Know thou also that the woes of men are the work of their own hands:
Miserable are they, because they see not and hear not the good that is
    very nigh them; and
The way of escape from evil, few there be that understand it.

—Pythagoras: "Golden Verses"

109

So long as men love only the ephemeral and lose themselves in it, so long will they continue to suffer from that portion of their troubles which is avoidable. This was a chief element in the Buddha's message twenty-five hundred years ago and it is still as true today.

110

We reject the fatalism which would preordain every happening in such a total way that there is nothing left to personal initiative, nothing more that the individual man can do about it. We accept the existence of a line of connection between actions and their ultimate effects in one's life, even if those effects are deferred to later reincarnations.

111

Nobody succeeds in extinguishing karma merely because he intellectually denies its existence, as the votaries of some cults do. If, however, they first faced up to their karma, dealt with it and used it for self-cultivation and self-development, and then only recognized its illusoriness from the ultimate standpoint, their attitude would be a correct one. Indeed, their attempt to deny karma prematurely shows a disposition to rebel against the divine wisdom, a short-sighted and selfish seeking of momentary convenience at the cost of permanent neglect of the duty to grow spiritually.(P)

112

If we look at men in the mass, we *must* believe in the doctrine of fatalism. It applies to them. They are compelled by their environments, they struggle like animals to survive precisely because they are not too far removed from the animal kingdom which was the field of their previous reincarnational activity. They react like automatons under a dead weight of karma, move like puppets out of the blind universal instincts of nature. But this is not the end of the story. It is indeed only its beginning. For here and there a man emerges from the herd who *is* becoming an individual, creatively making himself into a fully human being. For him each day is a fresh experience, each experience is unique, each tomorrow no longer the completely inevitable and quite foreseeable inheritance of all its yesterdays. From being enslaved by animality and fatality, he is becoming free in full humanity and creativity.(P)

113

The old Japanese method of cultivating rice yields larger crops on poorer soil than the old Indian method. It was introduced and publicized by the Indian Republic's Ministry of Agriculture with such favourable results that it has become unnecessary to import the annual balance required to meet the population's growing needs. It is estimated that cheaper and more plentiful rice will within a few years reduce or remove the traditional hunger of this vast country. The people have hitherto religiously interpreted their starved existence as the will of God. The episode may teach them the philosophic truth that they are here to become co-workers with God by developing their intelligence, knowledge, and abilities. By improving themselves, they are able to improve the environment. The supine fatalism saddled on them by a mistaught religion and a miscomprehended mysticism may yield at last to the correct kind of fatalism taught by their own highest philosophy.

114

Such an enlightened and qualified fatalism need not lead to a paralysis of the will and passivity of the brain. It emphatically does not lament that man can do nothing to change his lot for the better nor, worse, leave him without even the desire to change it. No—the submission to fate which a doctrine teaches is not less enlightened and qualified than itself. Its effect upon those who not only believe in it but also understand it, is towards the striking of a balance between humble resignation and determined resistance, towards the correct appraisal of all situations so that the truly inevitable and the personally alterable are seen for what they are. It yields to God's will but does not therefore deny the existence of man's.

115

Can the puniness of man pit itself against the immensity of the universe? This is the attitude behind Fatalism.

116

The believer in such rigid fatalism finds himself trapped; there is nothing he can do about a situation except let it take its own course. Whichever way he turns he feels that he is caught. No choice that he makes is really his; it is always an imposed one. He cannot act of his own free will.

117

The belief that he can do nothing to control his future is paralysing to a man. Why try to become a better person if the matter is already totally arranged, if the same result will come about whether he acts well or evilly?

118

Philosophy refuses to acquiesce in a wrong or foolish deed merely because it has happened. Therefore it cannot acquiesce in it even if and when the happening is asserted to be God's will.

119

Philosophy teaches the truth of destiny but not the half-error of fatalism.

120

This utter dependence on destiny, this refusal to lift arm or limb to change one's circumstances, this complete acquiescence in every miserable event that time and others may bring us—this is not fatalism, but foolishness.

121

The fatalist who believes his future is irrevocably fixed, loses ambition, initiative, and other valuable spurs to human effort.

122

The malignant spirit of fatalism cannot be exorcised by a word or by a sentence, but when religion consistently entreats men to come up higher, to live out the fullness of their being, it is certain to have a wholesome influence upon those who hear.

123

The materialist doctrine of "determinism" is a mixture of truth and falsity. It rightly points to the way our outer lives are determined by our outer circumstances and events. It wrongly deprives us of the freedom to react as we choose to those circumstances and events. It is quite untrue where moral choice is concerned.

124

That the course of our actions and decisions has been unalterably fixed for us by an external power is manifestly an exaggeration. If it were really so, it would be useless for prophets to preach their religion and for philosophers to teach their system.

125

When the belief in fatalism is pushed to the Oriental extreme, the believer assumes no more responsibility for his life, his misdeeds, his health, his errors, and his fortunes. All these have been decided long beforehand by a power completely outside his control; it is not for him to question the decisions or complain against the actions of this power.

126

No man need resign himself to utter helplessness in the face of fate. Let him try to change what seems inevitable, and his very trying may be also fated!

127

In other words, what is destined to happen, paradoxically comes to pass through the exercise of our free will.

128

The choice between right and wrong can only exist where there is freedom of will to make it. Man is neither responsible nor free, declares materialistic determinism. If he is or becomes a criminal, environment is to blame, heredity is to blame, society is to blame—but not he. Spiritual determinism, karma (recompense), does not give him so wide a license to commit crime. It asserts that he was and is in part the author of his own character, consequently of his own destiny.

129

How can a man hold at one and the same time a belief in the existence of destiny and a sense of personal responsibility? Philosophy reconciles the two, solves the dilemma, and makes this position quite reasonable.

130

Three ways of looking at the world, out of many: (1) young optimism, such as that of Christian Science, New Thought, and so on, which solves problems by ignoring them or by dismissing them as imaginary; (2) individual optimism which believes that man can conquer all difficulties by supreme self-exertion of will; and (3) the fatalistic acceptance of all difficulties as unavoidable and unmodifiable.

131

A freedom which permits everything to man is quite deceptive. A fatalism which denies everything to him is quite depressive.

132

He can accept neither the arrogant Occidental attitude which believes itself to be the master of life nor the hopeless Oriental attitude which believes itself to be the victim of life. The one overvalues man's creativeness, the other undervalues it. The one believes it can banish all human ills, the other regards them as irremediable.

133

That the future already exists in time does not necessarily mean that we must become fatalists, that it cannot be changed, and that escape from its confinement is impossible.

134

That the retribution of guilt is as much a haphazard thing as the reward of goodness—this is a logical conclusion from the doctrine of materialism, as dangerous to the individual who believes it as to the society in which he lives.

135

The rigid fatalism which ignores the fact that what we do now is contributing towards the making of the future and which resigns itself to endure the effects of what it has made in the past—that rigid kind of fatalism which is mesmerized by those effects and makes no effort at all—has no place whatever in philosophy or in the philosophical understanding of the law of karma.

136

The idea that everything is already preordained and that nothing we can do will alter the destiny is accepted with a melancholy finality by millions of Orientals, but resisted by millions of Occidentals.

137

There is a large and decided factor between the original meaning of karma and that which has come to be assigned to it through the efflux of time. Once I rented a house in India and had to take the gardener into my employ with it. After a few days he asked my secretary to approach me to give him an increase in wages. As his former pay was by Western standards pitiably small, I instantly agreed to grant an increase. But as a student of human nature I took the opportunity to send for him and pretend that it could not be granted. He blandly raised his eyes to the sky and muttered: "It is your karma to sit comfortably inside the house but mine to toil fatiguingly outside it in the grounds. If the Lord had willed that you should give me an increase in wages you would surely have done so. As it is, my karma is bad and yours is good. There is nothing to be done but to accept it." He went back to his work, scraping the ground with a shaped piece of wood as his ancestors had scraped it two thousand years earlier. I saw that piece of wood as a symbol of inertia and unprogressiveness which the misunderstanding of karma had stamped upon his character. For whereas karma has come to mean that a man's life is predestined and patterned for him all the way from conception before birth to cremation after death, its original meaning was simply that a man could not escape from the consequences of his habitual thoughts and acts. It meant that success or failure in life lay largely in his own hands, that satisfaction or sorrow followed inevitably upon the heels of virtue or wrong-doing.

138

There is certainly a distinction to be drawn between determinism and fate. Those who have never been determinists, in the materialistic sense of the word, showed intuitive powers even in the earlier stages of the Quest of Truth.

139

If by determinism it is meant that something outside of oneself is the cause that determines one's actions, this can be only partly true. For the thought and energy behind them must come out of oneself.

Karma's role in human development

140

That which compels us to act in a certain way is in part the pressure of environment and in part the suggestion of our own past. Sometimes one is stronger, sometimes the other is stronger. But the root of the whole problem lies in our mind. Its proper cultivation frees us largely from both compulsions.

141

If you want to change your karma, begin by changing your attitude: first, toward outer events, people, things; second toward yourself.

142

The centuries-old debate between those who believe that all happenings are predetermined and those who believe they are the mere play of chance, can be resolved only by understanding that both predetermination and chance take their rise out of the divine Void.

143

When he fails to admit this first blunder, the way is opened for more blunders linked with it and possibly, emerging as a larger consequence of it.

144

His efforts to modify the effects of evil karma (recompense) must, where he can possibly trace any of them to causes set going in the present life, include remorse for wrongs done to others, as well as for harm done to himself. If the feeling of remorse does not come naturally at first, it may do so after several endeavours to reconsider his wrong actions from an impersonal standpoint. Constant reflection upon the major sins and errors of his past in the right way, setting the picture of his actual behaviour against the picture of how he ought to have behaved, may in time generate a deep sense of sorrow and regret, whose intensity will help to purge his character and improve his conduct. If, by such frequent and impartial retrospection, the lessons of past misbehaviour have been thoroughly learnt, there is the further likelihood that the Overself's grace may wipe out the record of evil karma waiting to be suffered, or at least modify it.

145

What he has brought upon himself may come to an end of itself if he finds out what positive quality he needs to develop in his attitude toward it to replace the negative one.

146

We learn in time to accept everything that happens to us as the will of the Supreme Father, and hence never grumble or complain about misfortunes. The karma made in past births is like a shot from a gun; we cannot recall it and must endure the consequences. But once we have surrendered ourself to the Spiritual Preceptor, he guides our hands and prevents us from shooting out further bad karma.

147

Although karma is clinched by what a man does in fact, it is built up also by what he long thinks and strongly feels.

148

If a man will not repent his ill-deeds, will not make restitution where he has wronged others, and will not try to change his thoughts and doings for the better, then his bad karma (recompense) must run its inevitable course.

149

It would be an error to confuse this serene peacefulness, this calm acceptance of life with mere stagnation or unfeeling sluggishness. The latter makes no effort to improve circumstances or to progress personally whereas the former is ready to do so at any time. The latter is stupefied by its situation, whereas the former patiently endures the necessities of its situation only so far and so long as it is unable to change them.

150

He will naturally try to smooth his destiny but he will not do so at the expense of his character. If there be no other way to keep his ideals, then he will be prepared to endure and suffer.

151

Only when a man can judge his own fortunes with impersonality and without complaint, can he develop the capacity to understand the mystery of his destiny and why it has taken one particular course rather than another.

152

Although philosophy considers all attitudes to be relative, it makes use of particular attitudes as and when necessary. Because it recognizes the factor of destiny and tries to detect the trend of events and to adjust itself to that trend, at certain periods it is optimistic, at other periods pessimistic. It knows there are times when the greatest efforts will still go badly. This is why the philosopher disciplines himself to endure with equanimity misfortunes which are such that none can avoid them, but on the other hand he seeks to overcome with resolution those which need to be fought against.

153

When a man finds that a condition is beyond his power to change, he may better endure it by holding the faith that all things and all conditions are ultimately ordered by the Universal Mind, and that they will work out for the best in the end.

154

When he becomes a philosopher, he will become strong enough to bear his fate with submission, if he finds that he cannot or should not modify it. Then neither grief nor distress, neither other people's evil-doing nor their evil-speaking will force him into emotional self-betrayal of the inner peace which has been won with so much effort.

éternels

tome 1 : evermore

155

We must learn to let go, to renounce voluntarily that which destiny is determined to take away from us. Such an acceptance is the only way to find peace and the only effective path to lasting happiness. We must cease to regard our individual possessions and relationships as set for all time.

156

The man who can live without troubles has yet to be found, but the man who can live without worry about them may be found wherever philosophy is found.

157

There is no capacity of mind which will always and easily give the foresight of consequences; but there is a capacity which will give an insight into truths which, when applied to practical affairs, guarantees the best possible consequences.

158

Before a man can submit to his destiny he needs to know what it is. Because something has happened to him in the past and is again happening in the present, must it necessarily happen in the future?

159

He will then see that the ego is not his true self, that the evil and error which it spawns are the avoidable causes of avoidable distresses.

160

The same illness whose enforced inactivity brings boredom or despair to one man, may bring literary discoveries or spiritual awakenings to another man. It may quickly dull the first one's mind but directly stimulate the second one's to reflect about life, suffering, and death.

161

It takes time, and plenty of it, before the new ideas and ideals become established in the mind, the feelings, and the actions.

162

It is a valuable exercise for him to find out just where his own responsibility for his troubles begins, to separate what is really an outward projection of his inward defects from what is being saddled upon him by an untraceable destiny or a formidable environment.

163

When we discover how small is the measure of freedom we possess, the first reaction is one of stunned hopelessness; the second, which may come months later, is of weary surrender to it all.

164

Let him place his trust in the universal laws and turn his face towards the sun.

165

In the making of our future, a mixed result comes from the mixed and contradictory character of the thoughts feelings and desires we habitually hold. Therefore our very fears may contribute their quota in bringing about what we do not desire. Here lies one advantage of positive affirmations and clear-cut decisions in our attitude toward the future.

166

The unpaid mistakes and debts from former lives are now here to haunt us. If we want release from them, we must either get release from our egos or else set up counteracting thoughts and deeds of an opposite character and in overwhelming amount.

167

The measure of this counter-influence will be the measure of the sincerity of his repentance, of the refusal to take any alibis from himself, of the effort to change his mode of thought, and of the practical steps he voluntarily takes to undo the past wrongs done to others.

168

A wiser attitude carries its outward problems into the inward realm of character, to intelligence and capacity, and deals with them there.

169

By watching our thought life, keeping out negatives, and cultivating positive ideas, full of trust in the higher laws, we actually start processes that eventually bring improvement to the outer life.

170

He is wise who sifts, screens, and absorbs the bygone years, taking only their lessons, counsels, warnings, and encouragements. In this way, he frees himself from much of it.

171

He must use his combined reason and intuition, that is, intelligence, to discern the handiwork of karma in the pattern of some of the external events of his own life.

172

Repentance for wrong-doing may not commute its karma but will at least provide the indispensable preliminary condition for such a commuting.

173

Life is largely what we make it by our way of thinking about it. How important then to remove error from the mind and to put truth in its place! How different would our fortunes be if we recognized this need and always acted upon it!

174

It is a Jain belief that bad karma can be cancelled by practising austerity, penance, and self-mortification. The harsher the asceticism the quicker will be this process of destroying the results of an evil past. There is a certain logic in this belief, for by suffering this self-imposed pain one is also suffering the bad karma, albeit in a concentrated form, and not evading it.

175

He may have to learn how to accommodate what he cannot control or avoid. This is resignation, the very name—Islam—of the religion given to the world by Muhammed. But if he has to accept certain things, this is not to say that their accommodation implies his approval of them. It means rather that he ceases to grumble or worry about them.

176

He is content to leave them, these evil-doers, to the judgement of time, knowing that the power of karma is inseparable from it.

177

Your karma is being speeded up; everything is being accelerated to a certain extent. This is necessary for a period to bring quicker progress through forcing different parts of mind and character into activity.

Think how much has been accomplished since you took up these studies. Look back to your state of mind before that.

178

Only when he sees that he himself is the prime cause of his own troubles, and that other people have been not more than the secondary cause, does he see aright.

179

Where it is possible to undo the past, he will try to do so, but where it is not he will remember the lessons but forget the episodes.

180

To state the doctrine is one thing; to apply it to practical problems is another.

181

Even deliberate inaction does not escape the making of a karmic consequence. It contains a hidden decision *not* to act and is therefore a form of action!

182

The law of recompense is not nullified nor proved untrue by the objector's proffered evidence of hard ruthless individuals who rose to influence and affluence over the crushed lives of other persons. The happiness or well-being of such individuals cannot be properly judged by their bank account alone or their social position alone. Look also into the condition of their physical health, of their mental health, of their conscience in the dream state, of their domestic and family relations. Look, too, into their next reincarnation. Then, and only then, can the law's presence or absence be rightly judged.(P)

183

We humans have to bear the decrees of Allah as best we may.

184

Forces out of his own reincarnatory past come up and push him towards certain decisions, actions, and attitudes.

185

Men being what they are, the results of their actions must be what they will be, too.

186

One of the greatest misunderstandings of karma by its believers, and perhaps one of the chief hindrances to its acceptance by others, is the idea that it produces its effects only after very long periods of time. What you do today will come back to you in a future incarnation several centuries later; what you experience today is the result of what you did hundreds or even thousands of years ago; what you reap here in this twentieth century is the fruit of what you sowed there in Rome in the second century—such are the common notions about reincarnation and karma. But we have only to open our eyes and look around us to see that everywhere men are getting now the results of what they have done in this same incarnation.

187

Karma waits for a proper time before calling in its accounts; its settlements being periodic and grouped together explains why good and bad fortune so often run in apparent cycles.

188

Our intellect acknowledges the justness of this law, but our heart craves for the mitigation of its harshness. We pray for the forgiveness of our sins, the remission of their penalties.

189

The Day of Judgement is not only on the other side of the grave. It may be here, on this side, and now, in this month.

190

A man may break these higher laws through his own personal weakness or moral failure, or through deliberate rebellion and refusal.

191

Quite unwittingly, the criminal, the evil-doer, or the sadist is trying to punish himself. Soon or late he will succeed in doing so, and in proportion to the extent that he hurts others.

192

When the cause is put too far from the effect, as in some beliefs about karma, the moral effectiveness is weakened.

193

Karma is really neutral although to the human observer its operations seem to be rewarding or punitive.

194

All through history we see men inflicting suffering upon other men. This shows their ignorance of the higher laws, for by their own sin they punish themselves.

195

Not to harm others is as much in one's own interest as theirs. For if one does harm them he sets up causes which lead in the end by a mysterious cosmic working to a consequential suffering. Cosmic justice is then self-provoked.

196

The working of karma may often seem a grim affair, dragging in the past when he would prefer to forget it—whether it include unpleasant things done or pleasant things not done—permitting no appeal and offering no pardon.

197

The good merits of conduct in former lives bring pleasant benefits in the present one.

198

Retribution comes, even if it comes so late as to be deferred to another lifetime on this earth. Some ancients thought it came down too heavily, especially when the sin was only one of pride or folly, and complained to the gods.

199

Trotsky made a point of being merciless to the enemy during Russia's Civil War: it is not surprising that his own murder was a merciless affair.

200

If in the end—and sometimes well before—karma catches up with a man, it is not all painful; the term need not fill him with foreboding. For the good he has thought and done brings a good come-back too.

201

There are times when the karma of an action comes back to a man with the speed and precision of a boomerang.

202

The working of karma traces complicated effects back to complicated causes.

203

The web of karma tightens around a man as the lives increase with the centuries or thins away as the ego gets more and more detached.

204

The brutal egotist who ruthlessly knocks others aside on his way upward will himself receive harsh treatment when the time is decreed.

205

Most men do not learn the practical wisdom of life the easier way. They do not heed the true seers, the far-seeing sages, the inspired prophets. There is a harder way, which they choose because it appeals to both their animal instincts and their selfish purposes. This is why they must be tutored by necessity—that is to say, by harsh circumstances of their own making, by karma.

206

Man rules this planet but the gods rule man. Take them into account in your mortal reckonings.

207

It will be asked: Why should the innocent suffer because of the activities of wicked men? Their innocence belongs to the present; we do not know of their past evil deeds and misdeeds!

208

The errors and disorders in his consciousness reflect themselves eventually in his general fortunes and outward conditions.

209

History shows that there are implacable forces around man which can elevate him in a day or cast him down in a night.

210

Events and environments are attracted to man partly according to what he is and does (individual karma), partly according to what he needs and seeks (evolution), and partly according to what the society, race, or nation of which he is a member is, does, needs, and seeks (collective karma).

211

The law of compensation does *not* measure its rewards and penalties according to the little scale of little human minds.

212

It is sheer nonsense habitually to interpret karma (recompense) as something which is operative only in remote reincarnations. Actually it is mostly operative within the same lifetime of a man or nation.

213

The working of karma from former lives is mostly in evidence at birth and during infancy, childhood, and adolescence. The working of karma made in the present life is mostly in evidence after the maturity of manhood has been reached.

214

We invite the future through our aspirations. We get the consequences of our thinking, feeling, and doing. Nature has no favouritism but gives us our deserts.

215

A man's sins are the outcome of the limitations of his experience, faculties, and knowledge.

216

Retribution must one day overtake the wrong-doer. His sins and mistakes will pile up until one day the karmic hour strikes and they come down on him with a crash. All failure to wake up to responsibilities constitutes an ethical error for which a man must bear the consequence eventually. Thus the failure to do a right deed in a certain situation may be a karmic sin, although very much less so than doing a wrong deed.

217

Every infraction of the great law of compensation on its moral side is cumulative, piles one eventual affliction upon another into a heap, which is one reason why we often hear the complaint that afflictions are not in just ratio with sins.

218

The working of recompense (a piece of karma) also affects those who are closely associated with the person whose own acts or thoughts originated it.

219

The course of karma is not rigidly predetermined. It may have alternative patterns. If an evil deed does not find retribution in some other way, then it will always find retribution in the form of disease. This must not be foolishly misinterpreted to mean that all disease is the result of evil karma. If we live in an unhealthy manner, the disease which is thereby generated is the karma of our present ignorance or bodily imprudence, not necessarily the expiation of moral faults committed in other lives.

220

When at length he will be called to account by karma, he will be judged not by the certificates of character which others bestow upon him, whether good or bad, but by the motives felt in his heart, the attitudes held in his mind, and the deeds done by his hands.

221

These doctrines assert that those unlucky wretches are merely paying for their misdeeds in former bodies. Why, if that is correct, should they suffer for errors which they cannot possibly remember and which might have been committed by others, for all they know? I can understand and appreciate the philosophical arguments for the doctrine of rebirth, but I cannot understand the justice of punishing men for misdeeds of which they are completely unaware. Such is a reasonable criticism.

222

For some errors we have to pay with the misfortune of a few years. But for others we have to pay with the misfortune of a lifetime. An injury done to a Sage who incarnates compassion may easily, if not repented and amended, fall into the second class.

223

Any man who artfully hurts another in the end hurts himself. For he denies the principle of love in his relationships, a principle that is part of the higher laws set for his development, and must pay the penalty of his denial.

224

The karma of a man cannot be measured by the world's yardsticks. Wisdom is worth a fortune at any time and goodness is a solid protection. Those who live for the immediate moment, the immediate enjoyment, may not perceive this; but those who wait for the ultimate result, the ultimate event, know its truth. Indeed, how could it be otherwise in a Universe where infinite intelligence and infinite benevolence have made the laws which make the destiny of mankind?

225

It is a mistake to regard the karma of a deed as something that appears later in time, or comes back to its doer soon or long afterwards. It is not a sequence to follow after what was done before. On the contrary, the karma is simultaneous with the deed itself.

226

A grievous marriage situation may itself change completely for the better or else a second marriage may prove a happier one, if there is sufficient improvement in thinking to affect the karma involved.

227

If men behave like wild beasts of prey, violent and greedy; if they show an utter lack of conscience, we may write them down as doomed to suffer themselves one day the painful consequences of their misdeeds.

228

A callous egotism is a bad-paying investment. For it means that in time of need, there will be none to help; in the hour of distress, none to console. What we give out we get back.

229

The war showed in the plainest possible way that the cost of wrong-doing is painful retribution. For we lived to see Hitler destroyed by his own hand, his Nazi hierarchy with its loathsome deviltry destroyed by all humanity's hands, and his deluded followers eating the sour fruits of their own planting.

230

The karma of a thought-habit or a deed becomes effective only when it reaches maturity. The time this takes is variable.

231

Karma expresses itself through events which may seem to be accidents. But they are so only on the surface.

232

The moral fallacy which leads a man to think that he can build his own happiness out of the misery of other men, can be shattered only by a knowledge of the truth of karma.

233

If you throw a pebble into the sea, its ripples go on and on, until they are exhausted. In the same way, there comes a time when the accumulated effects of doing or thinking lets loose a ripple of karmic come-back.

234

The consequences of several years of wrong doing and wrong thinking may crowd into a few months.

235

In the final test, they may show by their own words and actions during the next decade whether they honestly wish to enter the path of reconciliation. Their last yet first hope is to purify themselves by discipline and to make restitution—either physical or verbal—to those whom they have wronged.

236

His situation in the world is highly paradoxical, at once comic and tragic: comic because he knows that he is not so sure of himself as he appears to others, tragic because he does not know if adversity's sudden blows will miss him and strike others.

237

The prophet becomes the butt of the vulgar and violent mob, but in heaven the mob itself is gibbeted and hung. So justice works.

238

Each period of a life has its own evaluation, and opinions differ about them. Some say the early years are best, others the middle years, and so on. But the truth is that it depends on a person's karma more than on his age as to which shall prove best for him and from which he shall extract the most satisfaction.

239

Failure to act at the right time in the right way may bring its own karmic consequences.

240

Although the higher laws bring man the kind of experience—pleasurable or painful—which is so just, so right, and so fitting to his true deserts and need, he is mostly unable to see this, being blinded by his ego or his ignorance.

241

Here are facts which are vital to our conduct of life, primal to our search for happiness, yet which he leaves ignored or, worse, deliberately sneers at. Karma is one of them.

242

It is a fact in many people's lives that some of the troubles which befall them have no origin in the karma of former lives but belong solely to causes started in the present life.

243

The spiritually ignorant are to a large extent makers of their own misery.

244

Whoever fails to take advantage, by his co-operation and effort, of the right time for beginning an enterprise or the right opportunity that fortune thrusts in his path, will never again be able to do so to the same extent, if at all—for neither he nor circumstance can remain the same.

245

For the lucky few, life is pleasure spotted by suffering. For the unlucky many, it is suffering relieved by pleasure. For the rare sage, it is ever-flowing serenity.

246

Every prophet knew and taught that virtue rewards itself as sin punishes itself.

247

If his evolutionary need should require it, he will be harassed by troubles to make him less attached to the world, or by sickness to make him less attached to the body. It is then not so much a matter of receiving self-earned destiny as of satisfying that need. Both coincide usually but not always and not necessarily. Nor does this happen with the ordinary man so much as it does with the questing man, for the latter has asked or prayed for speedier development.

248

The wisdom which he has the chance to gain from his sufferings should lead not only to some self-renunciation, but also to some self-resignation to destiny's will when it reveals itself as inexorable. Once he brings himself to this submission, time will then more quickly heal up its own wounds and inner peace will more easily be obtained. So destiny shows itself also as a teacher.

249

There are times when, for a man's inner evolution, his ego has to be crushed, and he may then find himself bent under harsh events or melancholy reflections.

250

Fate is fashioned in such a way that it gives people at times what they want, so that they shall eventually, through this experience, learn to evaluate it more justly. They have then the opportunity to see the adverse side of the experience, which desire too often prevents them from seeing. Fate is also fashioned to go into reverse and block the fulfilment of the wishes of other people. Through this inhibition they may have the chance to learn that we are not here for a narrow, egoistic satisfaction alone, but also, and primarily, to fulfil the larger purposes of life as formed in the World-Idea.

251

The Law is relentless but it is flexible: it adjusts punishment to a man's evolutionary grade. The sinner who knows more and who sins with more awareness of what he is doing, has to suffer more.

252

The subconscious connection between wrongs done and sufferings incurred leads him to feel more uncertain and more uncomfortable the more he engages in such acts.

253

To look upon the encounters with suffering, misfortune, mistakes, and disappointment as the principal offering of each reincarnation is one view, and especially the Indian view. To see in them the requitals and rewards of the Goddess of Justice is another.

254

When man knows the results of his actions, he has the chance to know the value of those ideas which led to these actions. In other words, experience will bring responsibility, if he allows it to, and that will bring development.

255

Everyone has periods of pleasurable delusion when he affixes a rosy label on life but the awakening to what lies on its other side must follow sooner or later. Only after both experiences is he able to form a fair judgement upon it. The philosopher however does not want to wait for this tutoring by experience alone. By a deliberate detachment from every feeling likely to falsify the picture of life, he puts himself in a position to see it as it truly is.

256

The spiritual inertia which keeps most men uninterested in the quest is something which they will not seek to overcome by their own initiative. Life therefore must do this for them. Its chief method is to afflict them with pain, loss, disappointment, sickness, and death. But such afflictions are under karma and not arbitrary, are intermittent and not continuous, are inlaid with joys and not overwhelming. Therefore their result is slow to appear.

257

If this is the way his life has to be, if this is how the cards of his destiny have fallen, and if the inner voice bids him accept it after the outer voice has led him into unavailing attempts to alter it, then there must be some definite reason for the situation. Let him search for this reason.

258

As a man flings his cigarette suddenly upon the floor and stamps his heel savagely upon it until the red spark is extinguished, so too life flings some of us to the ground and stamps upon our ardours and passions until they are dead.

259

Life will bring him, if he is teachable, through the tutelage of bitter griefs and ardent raptures to learn the value of serenity. But if he is not, then the great oscillations of experience will tantalize him until the end.

260

Life is not trying to make people either happy or unhappy. It is trying to make them understand. Their happiness or unhappiness come as by-products of their success or failure in understanding.

261

The modern struggle for existence is nothing new. It is the same sky and the same world of pre-historic times. The scenes have been changed only in details; the actors, men and women, remain the same but they are now more experienced. Incessant struggle has ever been the lot of the human race.

262

No human existence is without its troubles at some period or without its frictions at another. The first arises out of the element of destiny which surrounds human freedom, the second out of the element of egoism which surrounds human relations.

263

Sorrow, loss, and pain may be unwelcome as evils but they are at the same time opportunities to practise the philosophic attitude and to train the will.

264

There is peace *behind* the tumult, goodness *behind* the evil, happiness *behind* the agony.

265

The painful elements in your destiny are the measure of your own defects. The evils in your conduct and character are mirrored forth by the troubles which happen to you.

266

Despite its insistence that suffering is always close to life, it tries to charge its message with the flavour of hopefulness, and to inspire men to make efforts and be daring in their inner lives. When suffering stimulates a man to re-adjust his life on sounder philosophical lines, it can hardly be called an evil.

267

I believe in love, not hate, as a motivating force for reform. At the same time, I see karma at work, punishing the selfish and the heartless, and I know that it will inexorably do its work whatever anyone says. God never makes a mistake and this universe is run on perfect laws. Unfortunately, suffering is one of its chief instruments of evolution and especially so where people will not learn from intuition, reason, and spiritual prophets.

268

How priceless would be the knowledge of the outcome of our actions at the time we did them! How invaluable the capacity to foretell beforehand the consequences of our deeds! We would then certainly avoid the tragedy of error and the misery of failure—so runs our thinking. But life is wiser and lets us profit by the commission of error and the experience of failure to find out what needs correction or cultivation in our own personalities.

269

Everyone has his burden of bad karma. What kind and how heavy it is are important, but more important is how the man carries it.

270

While fulfilling its own purpose, karma cannot help fulfilling another and higher one; it brings us what is essential to our development.

271

When his life does not develop along the line he has planned, his mind will become confused and self-doubt will creep in. It is then that the ambitious man is taken in hand by his higher self, to learn through frustration and disappointment released by the new cycle of bad karma those lessons he could not receive through success and triumph.

272

He makes many wrong decisions in the course of a lifetime, suffers their consequences, and learns the lessons of these results. If he is willing to learn them, they will be more quickly, fully, and consciously learnt; if not, they will be only partially, slowly, and subconsciously learnt.

273

All relative truths are fluctuating truths. They may become only partially true or even wholly falsified from a higher standpoint. The case of evil is a noteworthy instance of this change. A karma (recompense) which is outwardly evil may be inwardly spiritually beneficial.

274

The deer which lies mortally wounded by a hunter's shot is not capable of asking Life why it should suffer so, but the man who lies mortally wounded by a murderer's shot *is* capable of doing so.

275

When he accepts affliction as having some message in it which he must learn, he will be able to bear it with dignity rather than with embitterment.

276

When justice is done to a man for the injuries he has done to others, when his wrong actions end in suffering for himself, he may begin to learn this truth—that only the Good is really able to triumph.

277

It is true that sometimes the past, or at least some portion of it, will not bear looking at. It hurts to know that its unworthiness was created by his own actions, its foolishness by his own choices. Yet it may help somewhat to reconcile him to mistakes which are now unmendable, to recognize that they arose out of his inheritance from former lives, out of the nature this caused him to be born with, and out of the circumstances this allotted as his destiny—that, in short, he could hardly have acted or chosen differently. It would be futile to be angry with himself or resentful against fate.

278

Generation follows generation. Of what avail all this striving and struggling which always ends in death and dust? It is salutary at times to sink in this mournful thought, provided we do not sink to the point of despair.

279

People bound by their littleness, uninterested in Truth and unable to see it, dominated by puerile aims and petty desires—their way is long and slow, it is the way of instruction by karma.

280

The iron of man's character turns to tempered steel in the white-hot furnace of trouble.

281

We do not easily grow from the worse to the better or from the better to the best. We struggle out of our imperfections at the price of toil sacrifice and trouble. The evil of these things is not only apparent nor, in essence, in any ultimate conflict with divine love. Whatever helps us in the end towards the realization of our diviner nature, even if it be painful, is good and whatever hinders, even if it be pleasant, is bad. If a personal sorrow tends towards this result it is really good and if a personal happiness retards it, then it is really bad. It is because we do not believe this that we complain at the presence of suffering and sorrow in the divine plan and at the absence of mercy in the divine will. We do not know where our true good lies, and blindly following ego, desire, emotion, or passion, displace it by a fancied delusive good. Consequently, we lose faith in God's wisdom at the very time when it is being manifested and we become most bitter about God's indifference just when God's consideration is being most shown to us. Until we summon enough courage to desert our habitual egoistic and unreflective attitude, with the wrong ideas of good and evil, happiness and misery which flow out of it, we shall continue to prolong and multiply our troubles unnecessarily.

Destiny turns the wheel

282

When he knows that no good phase can last, that fortune will never let him rest durably in its undisturbed sunshine, he is ready for the next step. And that is to seek for inner peace.

283

It is as foolish to attribute all events to fate as it is to claim that all decisions and choices are free ones.

284

It is possible to take any and every situation and assert that it is in entire conformity with God's will. It is possible to find reasons to support the assertion. And the argument would be right, for if the universe with all its complications, ramifications, and connections, with all its network of relations and events, is not a manifestation of God's will in the end, then what is it? But two opposing events, or two hundred varying and contradictory ones happening at the same time as each other, can be brought into the same argument, thus making nonsense of it.

285

"Mektoubi!" exclaims the North African Arab. "It is written (fated)," implying that there is nothing to be done as action is useless. "Mektoubi."

286

There are events which a greater power than man's has preordained. Some he can modify, change, or prevent altogether but others he cannot. All of them exist already in future time. He will meet them in present time. He never leaves present time. Therefore it is not he that is moving to meet the future but the future is moving to meet him.

287

He clanks the earth in iron chain, each link stamped with the word "destiny." But because he neither sees nor hears his chains, he imagines that he walks where he wishes and as far as he wishes.

288

A man's whole destiny may hang upon one event, one decision, one circumstance. That single cause may be significant for all the years to follow.

289

There are times when events *have* to happen as they do, because such is the decree of the higher power which governs life.

290

Sometimes, here and there, a man foresees his fate, but to most it is a blank page.

291

What is the message of Greek tragic drama, what do these doomed figures who make us shiver as they commit or endure horrors have to tell us? Is it not that do what you will circumstances will catastrophically overwhelm you, that the gods will drive you to an allotted disastrous end however much you may plan the contrary? From this depressing view, we may gladly turn to Shakespeare's, arrived at in the last maturest years of his life, expressed in the final four plays, ending in the philosophic view of *The Tempest*, that out of all life's troubles good somehow will emerge.

292

The same opportunity does not recur because it cannot.

293

No man is, or can become, fully free.

294

Some events in the future are inevitable, either because they follow from the actions of men who fail to amend character or improve capacity or deepen knowledge, or because they follow from the basic pattern of the World-Idea and the laws it sets to govern physical life.

295

He cannot withdraw from this destiny, try as he may.

296

When he reaches the end of a cycle, there will necessarily come with it some inner adjustment and outer change. This may also produce a little mental confusion.

297

Cycles of destiny make their periodical returns, for individuals and for nations. The prudent man foresees the coming one in advance and lets neither adversity nor prosperity overwhelm him but bears the one well and the other calmly.

298

All too often does an important enterprise, a long journey, or a serious undertaking carry in its start the insignia of its end.

299

However carefully we choose our course and plan our actions, we discover in the sequence that what is to be, will be. We have no power over happenings.

300

Life itself will work out his future course without consulting him.

301

"The fault, dear Brutus, is not in our stars, but in ourselves that we are underlings." Shakespeare's bold words sound reassuring, but he omitted to add that Brutus and Cassius were both struck down by violence. Does this not show that the last move was with fate after all?

302

But the ordinary man, who has not yet come to scorn time or seek a higher consciousness, will not like this terrible truth.

303

If all men knew all that would happen to them, how many would be willing to go on living into the worst period? Even if deprived of hope most perhaps would not abandon the body.

304

The feeling of being trapped by fate, held down by forces beyond his control, is partly true.

305

He becomes penetrated with the thought of his personal helplessness as against this inexorable and impersonal power controlling his life. He feels that there is nothing he can do when confronted by the unfavourable situations it creates for him, no way in which he can help himself. He sees himself in a little boat tossed by the waves of this immense power, a boat whose drift toward catastrophe he may observe but not prevent.

306

Atlantis shaped itself out of the condensing fire mists. Land hardened. Animals appeared. Men and women appeared. Civilizations appeared. The continent was developed. Then the wheel turned. The continent sank and all went with it. In 1919, Germany lay at the feet of her victors. She was disarmed and dismembered. She was weak, depressed, and fearful. Nobody was afraid of her. The wheel turned. Germany armed to the teeth. Her frontiers grew. She was strong, optimistic, and aggressive. Everybody was afraid of her. Today she is again disarmed, weak, and fearful. Arabia was unknown, insignificant, unimportant, obscure, her people barbarous, semi-savage. The wheel turned. A prophet arose, instructed and inspired his people. They spread out and took an empire that spread from the Atlantic to China. The wheel turned. The Arab power dwindled again. Arabia itself became a mere province, or colony, of the Turks. Empires are formed but to dissolve again; continents rise but to sink. Peoples collect but to be redistributed once more. Cycles operate, the wheel turns, evolution becomes involution. Only the intellectually blind, the spiritually paralysed can fail to perceive this. And the seeker of truth needs to be brave to be a hero, if he would tear down the veil and behold the Goddess Isis as she really is. Our own decade has witnessed strange things but things which prove this truth up to the hilt.

307

Even if his intuitive feeling warns him of an impending event in such a manner that he knows it to be unalterably preordained and inevitable, his inability to prevent it from happening need not prevent him from making all possible preparations to protect himself and thus to suffer less from it than he might otherwise have done. Such a warning can only be useful and saves a man from falling into the panic in which fear of the unexpected may throw others.

308

When a favourable cycle of destiny is operative, a little right action produces a lot of fortunate results. But when an unfavourable cycle is dominant, a lot of right action produces little result. The man and his capacities have not changed but his destiny has. At such a time, the new sequence of events in his life is dictated not by his individual will but by a higher will.

309

You can win if at the beginning of any enterprise you determine to do so, unless the fates are equally determined that you shall not. This is the "X" factor, the unknown hand which can gather up all your winnings in one grasp and toss them all aside. You may call it Luck if you wish. The wise man will in all reckonings allow for this mysterious factor and accept its existence as a fact.

310

If we accept the fact that man is as predestined to suffer as to enjoy life, that both experiences have been allotted to him, sometimes in juxtaposition but more often in rhythm, we can better prepare ourselves for life. If we refuse to accept it, we may have to pay the price which Oscar Wilde had to pay. The same Wilde, who until he was forty years old said that he did not know what it felt like to be unhappy, who repeatedly said, "We should seek the joys of life and leave the sores alone," lived to utter this confession and commentary upon his earlier attitude: "I seem dead to all emotions except those of anguish and despair."

311

Professor Don Mackenzie Brown, of the University of California at Santa Barbara, told me the story of a professional Hindu seer who visited that city. Under the strictest scientific test conditions, the man correctly predicted a number of headlines which would appear in the local newspaper within the next week. Did this mean that the events to which they referred were already present? If so, did that lead to the corollary that they were fully preordained and ruled by Fate? Or was there some entirely different explanation?

312

Many events in a person's or a nation's life are foreseeable, but only if existing trends of thought and existing courses of action are continued.

313

There is always some part of a man's person or fortune which remains wholly beyond his control. Do what he will he cannot alter it. It is then more prudent to acknowledge the inevitability of this condition than to waste strength in useless struggle. Sometimes he may then even turn it to his advantage. But how is he to know that this inevitability, this decree of fate, exists? By the fact that no matter how much he exerts himself to alter it, he fails.

314

We meet our destined experiences, for we have been given sealed orders at the beginning of our incarnation.

315

He knows that fate moves in rhythms of gain and loss, in cycles of accumulation and deprivation. The force which brings us loving friends and hating enemies is one and the same.

316

The wheel of life is a fixed one. Its turning spokes bring now elation, then depression, now prosperity, then adversity. There are periods of years when good health and good fortune crowd together, but then there are succedent periods when death and disasters try to break one's heart.

317

If, for instance, he is not destined to enjoy marital happiness, it would be futile for him to go on seeking it. If he does, he will one day get tired of beating the wings of desire against the bars of fate. But it is not always possible to know through past experience or present reasoning what his destined lot really is. For the past may be quite misrepresentative of the future, and thought can only throw light on some of its mysteries, not on all. Consequently he is forced to seek aid from revelation. This may come to him unreliably through the channel of one of the predictive arts or, most reliably, through a deeply felt intuition granted by his own higher self.

318

Those ignorant of the dark power of Destiny struggle with their lot and try to alter Fate's decrees. As well might they try to stop the roar and rush of a Niagara, alone and unaided. Even the mighty Napoleon, who nearly conquered all Europe, could not conquer Fate. He had to bow before its terrible sentence, as his own pathetic words at Saint Helena testified later. It is better to bow to the inevitable, and endure bravely what we cannot alter, than to cast our strength away in vain struggles.

319

We imagine we are the masters of destiny, when the truth is that we are as the barges that float down the Thames with each tide. I am never tired of telling myself, when things appear to go wrong, that the Gods rule this universe, and not man, that the last word lies with them, and if they see fit to dash all our plans to the dust, perhaps it is as well.

320

There is one striking passage wherein Emerson's pen neatly turns out the truth about the problem. I give it in its entirety because it is worth passing down intact. "I lean always to that ancient superstition (if it is such, though drawn from a wise survey of human affairs) which taught men to be beware of unmixed prosperity . . . Can this hold? Will God make me a brilliant exception to the common order of his dealings, which equalizes destinies? There's an apprehension of reverse always arising from success."

321

Destiny gives him hills of difficulty to climb because of its own impersonal balancing activity. But if he is thus able to, he demonstrates the superiority of the Man over the inferiority of the Position. Destiny befriends him.

322

He could not have met any person whose contact left deeply felt or important after-effects at any particular time in his inner life without the almighty power and infinite wisdom behind life having brought the meeting about for his own eventual development.

323

So many seemingly unrelated occurrences and inconsequential events shape into a pattern when looked at later, when they have long fallen into the past.

324

The wheel of life keeps turning and turning through diverse kinds of experiences and we are haplessly bound to it. But when at last we gain comprehension of what is happening and power over it, we are set free.

325

The broken fragments of destiny's mosaic are put into their correct places by his growing insight and thus an intelligible pattern eventually appears.

326

Internally and externally, we find through experience that a certain arc of fate has been drawn for us and must consummate itself. Futile is the endeavour to try to cross that arc; wise is the submissiveness that stays within its limits. We must leave to it the major direction which our mental and physical life must take. The thoughts that shall most move us and the events that shall chiefly happen to us are already marked on the lines of the arc. There is nothing arbitrary, however, about this, for the thoughts and the events are related and both together are still further related to an interior birth in the long series that makes up human life on this planet.

327

There are tides of fortune and circumstances whose ebb and flow wash the lives of men. There are cycles of changes which must be heeded and with which our plans and activities must be harmonized, if we are to live without friction and avoid wasting strength in futile struggles. We must learn when to move forward and thus rise to the crest of the tide, and when to retreat and retire.

328

Time and thought have fixed in my mind the unpleasant but unescapable notion that the major events of a man's life are as preordained for him as are the destinations of a million different letters all posted on the same day.

329

It was not blind fatalism but clear perception which made Mary, Queen of Scots, say that her end was in her beginning.

330

Can the oracular writing of destiny be deciphered? Can its mysterious pattern be foreseen?

331

Destiny may bring them together for the purpose of the spiritual birth of the younger one of them, may confront them so that the elder may pass his living vision and enlarged understanding to the other.

332

He misses the road-signs of life, the events which could tell him where he is going, the episodes which indicate success or disaster as a destination if he does not heed their meaning.

333

That the human will is but a thin straw floating on an irresistible tide, is a hard conclusion for the human mind to accept. Yet it is not less reasonable than it is distasteful.

334

For long I fought desperately against the notion of fate, since I had written screeds on the freedom of will. But an initiation into the mysteries of casting and reading a horoscope began to batter down my defenses, while an initiation into profounder reflection caused me to suffer the final defeat.

335

Human will may plan its utmost for security, but human destiny will have something to say about the matter. There is no individual life that is so secure as to be without risk.

336

Every man's personal freedom stretches to a certain distance and then finds itself ringed around by fate. Outside this limit he is as helpless as a babe, he can do nothing there.

337

Envy not those with good fortune. The gods have allotted them a portion of good karma, but when this is exhausted they will be stripped of many things, except those inner spiritual possessions.

338

If fate's decrees are preordained but a man's prayer seems to bring result, then his prayer too was part of his fate and also preordained.

339

But after we have listed all these various sources and influences which make us what we are, it would be an exaggeration to assert that they do so inexorably, immovably, and inevitably. We are not condemned to be the plaything of all these forces. There is a mysterious X-factor in every human being which he can call upon if he will. The fact that so few do so merely means that through ignorance they condemn themselves to remain as they are.

340

What different course our life might have taken if we had not casually met a certain person—a meeting which led to momentous consequences—

affords material for tantalizing speculations. Fate sometimes hangs upon a thread, we are told; but it always hangs upon such a tangled knot of dependent circumstances that the game of speculating how different it would have been had a single one of them been changed, is futile though fascinating.

341

We are at one and the same time both the consequence of our environment and the creator of it. The philosophic mentality sees no contradiction here, knows that there is a reciprocal action between the two.

342

Those who look for some swift miraculous renaissance of peace and goodwill in the Occident look in vain, for such miracles do not happen. The world is making its own destiny, and nobody can neutralize it. Nobody can abrogate the past. A grim Justice rules all worlds, from the strange and weird places where ghosts foregather to the more matter-of-fact haunts of earthly cities. Only the psychically blind and the spiritually sightless ever hope to evade this Justice or to escape the final accounting which tracks down individuals and nations alike with mathematical accuracy.

343

That our mortal destiny is made up of welcome and unwelcome circumstances or happenings is a certainty. There is no human being whose pattern fails to be so chequered—only the black and white squares are unequal in number, and the proportion differs from one person to another. It hurts to confess this duality of pain with joy, this temporality which threatens every happiness; but this truth is unassailable, as Buddha knew and taught.

344

You cannot defraud self-made Destiny. It enters unannounced upon your best-laid plans.

345

Life whirls us around as the clay is whirled upon the potter's wheel.

346

If good cycles seem to pass all-too-quickly, the bad ones seem to linger.

347

His spiritual destiny remains hidden far out of sight in the future.

348

Our lives are like a jigsaw puzzle; we collect our little queerly shaped pieces and then one day the pattern is seen.

349

Where nothing is certain, nothing is really predictable.

350

That an irresistible power dictates the major events of our lives, who can doubt that has lifted a little of the veil?

351

"We trail our destiny with us wherever we go. Even the gods cannot alter the past," says a Greek aphorism.

352

The disintegration and disappearance of things is an inescapable part of their history if they are to come into existence at all. Nature could not be formed by God on any other basis than this. But it is followed by their reappearance.

353

In the story of life there is misfortune and suffering, frustration and calamity; but it is not completed by them alone. It usually includes other chapters which bring out some of its positive, attractive, and happier sides and even its potential glory.

354

Only the sage perceives with deadly clarity how like the dust blown hither and thither is the weary labour of their days; how frail are the timbers of the ships which men send out, laden with their self-spun hopes and fears; how dream-like are their entire lives.

355

Whatever happens to a man or a nation is self-made or God-decreed. And this is still so even when some other human agent or other nation is the outward doer.

356

Whether he enters birth in penurious squalor or in palatial grandeur, he will come to his own SPIRITUAL level again in the end. Environment is admittedly powerful to help or hinder, but the Spirit's antecedents are still more powerful and finally INDEPENDENT OF IT.(P)

357

One man's power may prevail against his circumstances, whereas another man must accept them simply because he lacks both the power and the knowledge to contend with them.

358

The ugly woman has the right to ask why others are born beautiful and she not. The deformed man has an equal right to ask why other men are born well-formed, healthy, virile and not he.

359

We are often not doing the ideal actions, but those which the circumstances necessitate, which are forced on us for the time being.

360

We are forced to discover in the end how little is the freedom which illusion deceives us into believing is our own. We are drawn to move in environments and mix with people scarcely of our own choice.

361

There was a period when the Roman Imperial grip on Europe and the Near East was so firmly established, and for so long, that few could foresee how it could ever be relaxed, let alone removed.

362

He despises the snobbishness which despises others less fortunate, yet he acknowledges that caste is a fact in Nature. Is this a contradiction?

363

Caste differences may be accepted but caste rigidity need not. There ought to be free passage upward for those who seek to qualify by self-improvement, who have widened their horizons and started to respond to the meaning of quality.

364

When the low castes rule society, do not expect a high result because inferior sources must yield inferior results. But if the low castes rule society, it is because the high castes were indifferent to their welfare or even exploited them.

365

Newspaper quote: "While a man may inherit wealth and position he does not necessarily inherit brains and wisdom." P.B.'s comment: But he does inherit upbringing, atmosphere, and standards.

366

Many individuals may be caught in the wave of a common destiny, may have to share a group karma.

367

Each of us lives at a certain time in history and occupies a certain place (or certain places) during that period. Why now and here? Look to the law of consequences for an answer, the law which connects one earthly lifetime with earlier ones.

368

The ability or cupidity, the opportunity or inheritance, which brings a man into the possession of riches, is itself the product of his karma.

369

If a man can come up out of the squalor, discomfort, and ignorance of the slums into cleanliness, culture, and refined living, we may read into it either the favourable working of karma and rebirth or the power of the person to conquer his environment. But others who fail to do so may read into it the belief that luck is against them or else their lack of capacity to overcome environment. Thus we see that some glean a message of hope from reading the biography of such a man while others glean only frustration, if not despair. In both views there may be an element of truth but how much will differ from one person to another.

370

He has unconsciously taken a decision. It lies there, implicit, within his obedience to, and faith in, the credo or the party he follows. He is still responsible, still making personal karma.

371

Who is to say whether contributory circumstances which totally change our plans are merely pure coincidence or really the writings of the hand of destiny?

372

Duty and destiny must be reckoned together in one's life account. It is often a matter of not only what one should do but also of what circumstances allow one to do.

373

Suppose you had to carry the hunchback's cross? Would you not be bitter? Would you consider God's dealing with you a just one?

374

Nobody has been betrayed, either by God or by life. We have contributed to, and in some measure earned, the tragic happenings of our time.

375

When we say that a situation is caused by circumstances, we mean that it had to happen. *That* is fate. But does this imply that nobody is responsible for it, no individual is to blame for it if it is tragic or distressing?

376

It is quite untrue to say that we are created by our environment. It is true to say that we are conditioned, assisted, or retarded by our environment, but it is only a half-truth. We bear within ourselves a consciousness which, at several points and in different attributes, is independent of and sometimes quite opposed to all environmental suggestions. For, from the first day on earth, we possess in latency certain likes and dislikes, aptitudes along one line of thought and action rather than along others, whose sum, as they disclose themselves and then develop themselves, constitutes our personality. Of course, such a process necessarily takes time. Biological heredity contributes something quite definite toward this result but former incarnations contribute much more.

377

The face, brain, and form of the body will partly be molded by his destiny, partly by his character-tendencies and mental qualities.

378

The bad environment does not *create* the bad character. It brings it out and encourages its development. The weaknesses were already there latently.

379

The man who is born with a silver spoon may have great talents but never use them. They may die with him, because he never felt the spur of necessity. Insufficient or moderate means may give a man incentive. The worse the poverty the greater the incentive. This sounds a hard gospel but for some men it is a true one.

380

You want your exterior life unfoldment to meet your own conceptions. But if your have not found your interior harmony with God, in spite of all your efforts it will never do so.

381

Circumstances or other persons may be contributory but cannot be wholly responsible for a man's failures and misfortunes. If he will look within himself he will *always* find the ultimate causes there.

382

The average man is not so heroic or so angelic as all that and soon finds out that his soul cannot rise above his circumstances and that his nerves are unquestioningly affected by his environment.

383

To regard man as the product of his thinking only, to ignore the existence and influence of his surroundings, would be to place him in an utter vacuum.

384

Man's body and mind inherit his past, and the body can move freely only within the limits imposed by this past karma, just as a goldfish can move freely only within the limits of its globe of water.

385

He may be predestined to live in certain surroundings but the way in which he allows them to affect him is not predestined.

386

Karma is as active in the destiny of great powerful nations as in the destiny of poor insignificant men.

387

In a rough kind of way, and after sufficient periods of time have matured, a man's outward conditions will keep in some sort of step with his inward development.

388

The people one meets, the events one confronts, and the places one visits may be highly important but they are, in the end, less important than one's thought about them.

389

A lesson which the multitude has to learn is that acquiescence in brutality and aggressiveness does not pay in the end any more than the perpetration of such crimes themselves. Nevertheless, although a people which acquiesces in the deeds of its rulers has to share the karma of those deeds, it need not necessarily share all the karma.

390

Providence has made great men of unattractive or undersized physical appearance, or made them crippled, hunchbacked, lame, and so on, apparently in order to give the mob a striking lesson that men are not to be judged by outer appearance alone but much more by inner worth.

391

Because the Mind at the back of the Universe's life is infinitely wise, there is always a reason for what happens to us. It is better therefore not to rail at adverse events but to try to find out why they are there. It may be consoling to blame others for them, but it will not be helpful. If we look within ourselves for the causes, we take the first step toward bringing adversity to an end; if we look outside, we may unnecessarily prolong it.

392

We come normally into higher-class surroundings if our tendencies pull us to them, or if our actions (karma) justify them. But in an age of transition such as ours, where social ranks are thrown into confusion, where democratic levelling of all alike creates ethical and social chaos, where religion is losing its meaning and materialism prevails, no one is to be judged by the old rule of appropriate birth, of being in the station to which God has called him. In any case, neither lower nor higher class escapes the alternations of suffering and joy, misery and happiness in some way. That is the human lot.

393

A choice which is thrust upon a man by circumstances is no choice at all.

394

Our economic condition and our personal history, our physiological situation and our astrological horoscope all contribute to making us what we are. There is a spurious peace which is really nothing more than stagnation and which will be pushed aside or even destroyed with the first waves of change—whether the change be economic, physiological, or psychological.

395

Karma is not merely applicable to the individual alone but also to groups, such as communities, towns, countries, and even continents. One cannot get away in some particular or other from the rest of humanity. All are interconnected. One may delude himself, as nearly all people do, into thinking that he can live his own life and let others go hang, but sooner or later experience reveals his error. All are ultimately *one* big family. This is what reflection on experience teaches. When one reflects on Truth, he shall eventually learn that, as the Overself, all are one entity—like the arms and legs of a single body. The upshot of this is that he has to consider the welfare of others equally with his own, not merely because karma is at work to teach the individual, but also because it is at work to teach humanity *en masse* the final and highest lesson of its unity. When this idea is applied to the recent war, one sees that the latter was partly (only partly) the result of the indifference of richer peoples to poorer ones, of well-governed nations to badly governed ones, of the isolationist feeling that one's country is all right and if others are not, then that is unfortunate but their own affair. In short, there is no true prosperity and happiness for any country whilst one of its neighbours is poor and miserable; each one is his brother's keeper.

396

Great catastrophes, such as earthquakes and floods sweep hundreds to their doom, but individuals here and there escape, for their destiny is different. Such escapes often occur miraculously; they are called away suddenly to another place or protected by seemingly accidental occurrence. Thus individual destiny, where it conflicts with collective or national destiny, may save one's life where others are struck down.

397

If Alexander is to be praised for spreading Greek civilization as far east as India by the simple process of invading other countries, then the generals Flaminius, Sulla, and Mummius are to be praised for spreading Roman civilization by the simple process of invading Greece. There is a karmic connection between the two.

398

What tradition, family, society, and surroundings have bequeathed to him, consisting of beliefs, ideas, customs, culture, and manners, may need revision, examination, sifting, and sometimes even scrapping.

399

There are so many still latent possibilities for good and evil in most men that only the turns of circumstance's wheel can develop them.

400

Man changes the world, and the world changes him.

401

Philosophy does not reject the belief in the power of environments over man. They are important. But, it adds, even more important is the power of man himself.

402

The study of recompense (karma) reveals that mankind have to pay not only for what they have wrongly done but also for what they have failed to do. Such neglect is largely due to this, that man's intensely personal outlook makes him estimate the character of events primarily by the way in which they affect his own existence and only secondarily by the way in which they affect the larger human family to which he belongs. We are all workers in a common task. This is the inevitable conclusion which shares itself as soon as the truth of humanity as an organic unity is understood.

403

If you study history and think it over for yourself, instead of accepting the book-built theories of blind historians, you will find that the rise of great upheavals among men—whether spiritual or social, military or intellectual—always synchronized with the birth and activity of great personalities.

404

History vividly shows us that at certain psychological periods unusual men arise to inspire or to instruct the age. They are men of destiny.

405

Every successful man feels this sense of power supporting him, although the time comes when it also deserts him. Why? Because the map of his destiny has already indicated this change. Napoleon on St. Helena felt this loss, this difference from his former state. Disraeli, in his late sixties, said, "There were days when, on waking, I felt I could move dynasties and governments; but that has passed away."

406

One of the most impressive biographical facts about most of these men is the mixture of fate and free will in their lives.

407

It is a fundamental lesson of my world-wide observation that Heraclitus was completely right when he wrote: "Man's character is his fate."

408

Character is the root of destiny. An evil character must lead to an evil destiny.

409

A creative and original mind can undertake work for his own profit or benefit. If he undertakes it in addition for the benefit of others, he gains karmic merit. One refers, of course, to worthwhile work.

410

Wherever man goes he still takes his own mind, his own heart, his own character with him. They are the real authors of his troubles. Nothing outside will change these troubles so long as he does not begin to change his psychic life, that is, himself.

411

Fate gives them unbounded faith in their own future; it forms their character and shapes their capacity to enable them to carry out an historic task in human evolution.

412

Although it is true that the strong or the prudent man rules his stars and conquers his circumstances, it is equally true and often overlooked that the strength and the prudence to do so come from within, are born in the man much more than acquired by him.

413

Most of the great figures of history—be they great in war or thought, art or industry—have felt that some higher power than their own was largely responsible for the upward arc of their career. Napoleon felt it and said: "I feel myself driven toward an end that I do not know. As soon as I shall have reached it, as soon as I shall have become unnecessary, an atom will suffice to shatter me."

414

Responsibilities tend to gravitate to the shoulders of those who can bear them best.

415

His character was already in existence at birth, but it is now somewhat modified by environment and experience, by karmic happenings.

416

Destiny uses certain men to work out its large public aims yet lets them work at their little personal ones all at the same time.

417

Men like Lenin and Lincoln—strange as the conjunction may seem—are the instruments of destiny.

418

It is nonsensical to say that a single man *makes* a historical epoch. He is the embodied reaction called to play his part by the destiny of his times and by the thoughts of those among whom he is thrown.

419

Destiny uses such a man to fulfil her ends, to bring about the changes for better or worse. Hence destiny makes or breaks him.

420

History teaches us that the hour produces the man, yet if we are too addicted to the things of earth, if we have forgotten the diviner principles of righteousness, truth, and justice, then the man arises to our doom. The awful chaos of the French Revolution spawned forth after awhile its predestined figure of Napoleon. He brought the beginning of the end of the old feudal age in every European country wherein he fought but he brought it through a holocaust of misery, war, suffering, and bloodshed.

421

To accomplish a notable historic event, two elements are required—the man and the destiny.

422

Karma may use a person as the unwilling agent for its decrees.

423

Destiny usually fits its man. What he is tends to shape what he experiences.

424

Hitler was a vain and violent man who had absolutely no conscience, no sense of good or evil other than the barbarous rule that his own success was the sole good, his own failure the sole evil. In the vast contours of this century's history, this would-be world dictator will be seen for what he was and it will then find no other words with which to conclude its judgement than that Hitler was a criminal lunatic, a pathological and paranoic creature whose own insanity showed up the general craziness of his people and of his own groups who followed him in other lands. This is a true judgement of Hitler the man, but there was also Hitler, the instrument of destiny.

We can read the cryptic signs of these historic events aright when we read in him the half-conscious karmic agent who broke the decaying foundations of an ageing structure, who hastened the final dissolution of a shallow period which was governed by refined hypocrisies and self-deceptions and materialistic jealousies. Hitler had his part to play in the universal drama, albeit a very wicked one. But this does not for one moment mean, however, that we are to welcome Hitler's birth or to regard him as other than he was—the wickedest of all human beings, the most sinful of all sinners, the most vindictive of his contemporaries, the most barbarous of human creatures, the most devilish of all the enemies of truth and culture. Let there be no misunderstanding about this man who made murder a method of propaganda and oppression a method of government. If history has a place for Hitler, it can be only in her annals of brutality without parallel, falsehood on a gargantuan scale, and aggressiveness raised to the degree of utter bestiality. He has amply illustrated Emerson's saying that all history resolves itself easily into the biography of a few stout and earnest persons, even though his stoutness was devoted to an evil cause and his earnestness to an aggressive aim. This said, we must finish by curling our lips in disgust.

425

The modification of a man's destiny calls for the modification of his moral character and personality trends as essential prerequisites.

426

Although it is quite true that much of the vaunted free will of man is quite illusory, it is equally true that most of the events in his life, which consequently seem so predetermined, grow inescapably out of the kind of moral character and mental capacity which he possesses. They are neither merely accidental nor wholly arbitrary. Choice and reaction, attitude and decision depend ultimately on his psychological make-up and influence the course of events in a certain way. "Character is fate"—this is the simplest statement of the greatest truth. Where is freedom for man when heredity and the history and state of his family and race prearrange so many physical factors for him?

Astrology, fate, and free will

427

Philosophy teaches us a wiser course than mere fatalism, a truer one than mere faith in free will. It teaches us that even when the stars in the firmament appear to work against us, the stars of worthy ideals will always work for us. It liberates us from anxieties about our horoscope because it gives us certitudes that the right causes we set going must have right effects. It gives our life's ship sails and rudder, port and map; we need not drift.

428

The present comes to us out of the past and the future is being made in the present. All three are linked together and a horoscope is simply their map. This is one of the oldest ideas to be found in human culture, this idea that man's life is subject to a higher power, that he is personally responsible to a higher law for his actions and that he cannot escape its retribution for wrong-doing or its reward for righteousness. The Stoics of ancient Rome had this idea and called it Fate. The Platonists of ancient Greece had it and called it Destiny. And the Indians, mostly Buddhists and Hindus, had it and have it and call it Karma.

429

The planets do not control your individual destiny, but their movements determine the times when the latent karma which you have earned shall become active and operative. Hence the sky is like a gigantic clock whose hands point to the fateful hours of human life but it is not a storehouse of forces influencing or dominating that life.

430

I am not sure but that our modern reformers have swept away some sound doctrines in their efforts to purge astrology of its "superstitions." They lose sight of the fact that astrology could never have been formulated by the thinking brain of man but was essentially a revelation. This wonderful knowledge could only have been discovered by great seers, whose lucid clairvoyance compelled the star-gemmed skies to deliver up their secrets. It is a great pity that the Oriental system is so little known in the West, for without its aid we shall never come nearer to an impeccable science.

431

The horoscope is a map not only of the present reincarnation, but also of the relation existing between the ego and the soul. It indicates what particular lessons have to be learned.

432

The question of astrology comes up afresh too often these days to let us forget it. If it were wholly true, this predictive reference to the planets, it could easily be tested and established in the company of all the respected sciences. If it were wholly false, it could just as easily be tested and discarded once and for all. But because the correct appraisal lies at some undetermined point between these two extremes, the question can only receive a tantalizing and confused answer. Those who reject astrology totally prove thereby that either they have never or insufficiently investigated it. Those who accept it totally are in grave danger of denying to man his gift of limited free will in mind and action as well as of losing their way in a silly fatalism. Since it is man himself who has made the larger part of the destiny which he must undergo, it is he who can unmake it. Thus there is no room for extreme fatalism. Nevertheless, because his individual will is governed by a higher will, some part of his destiny remains so strong that it is beyond his capacity to change it. The Overself must surely be granted the simple power to know, before each reincarnation on earth, the potentialities for virtue and sin, for spiritual rise and fall, that lie innate within its progeny, the ego. But this no more commits man to a hopeless fatalism than does the knowledge that he will eat a couple of meals tomorrow. Let him ask his own reason and past experience whether these shining points of light in the sky are more baleful influences on his life than his own weaknesses, shortcomings, egoism, and lack of self-control. What can they do to him worse than what he can do to himself?

433

Lodovico, the Italian medieval prince, fell into one trouble after another despite his faithful following of advice given by a personal astrologer. For there are several different ways of interpreting a starry relationship—be it square or trine, conjunction or opposition. Astrology can point more easily and more certainly to its nature, as whether it be good or bad. But it cannot point to the precise meaning of a configuration in such detail that all astrologers would agree among themselves. Hence astrology is not a science so much as an art. The perfect astrologer would have to be omniscient and dwell far above the common human scene.

434

Astrology was given by the primeval sages as a revelation to early mankind. No human being on earth could have created out of his own head this mysterious science of astrology. It was given to help human beings who still were far from spiritual attainment, as a concession to their human nature. But when man has come by spiritual advancement, under the grace of God, directly, or through a teacher, it is not possible to construct a horoscope that will perfectly fit him because his testimony will always be liable to modification and alteration.(P)

435

The ancient Roman belief that books are born under some kind of horoscopical destiny, just like human beings, seems, in my experience, to have a basis of truth.

436

Overstress of such beliefs as astrology may cause him to understress or even forget entirely his creative possibilities. They are both extreme swings of the pendulum. Astrology rests on the ground of karma in tendencies and deeds. Freedom of decision rests on the evolutionary need to let man express the creativeness he gets from the Overself. He must put both factors together to find truth.

437

While lesser lights of the modern literary world are content to dismiss the subject of astrology with a contemptuous sneer, England's greatest dramatist treated it with the respect grown of proper understanding. This is proved by abundant quotations from Shakespeare's plays that could be made. But advanced astrologers ought to realize the incomplete and fragmentary nature of their present knowledge.

438

We may defy the karmic law for many years in matters of the body's health and not have to pay for it until middle or old age. We may defy it in matters of conduct towards others and not have to pay until a later birth. But the law is always enforced in the end, always registered in the horoscopal chart imprinted on the very form of the body and nature of the personality.

439

Whatever happens to a man is in some way the consequence of what he did in the past, including the far-gone past of former births. But it may also be in part the imposition of the World-Idea's pattern upon his own karmic pattern. If it comes, such imposition is irresistible for then the planetary rhythms are involved.

440

Were those Romans wrong or superstitious who returned home if the day's start was unfortunate or marred? Was there nothing but chance in such accidents? Or were they, as astrologers believe, ill-omens to be heeded?

441

An Indian astrologer: "The planets do not compel anyone to be a villain and proclaim from the house tops 'Evil be thou my Good.' Unique in the history of [the] world's astrological adventure, the Indian systems have carefully explained that the planets just indicate a rough outline of future events. Individuals and nations must realize not merely their potentialities for good and evil, but their limitations as well, as indicated by planetary configurational patterns, if life is to be lived in peace and harmony."

442

Man's inner life is fulfilled by rhythms which are under laws as much as tides and dawns are under laws.

443

Whoever will take the trouble to investigate the subject can discover that the events of life concur with the changes indicated in the skies.

444

All we may rightly say is that there is a fated element in every human life. But how large that element is in each particular life is generally unknown; what shape it will take is often unpredictable. We certainly ought not to say that such an element is the sole one. Therefore the wise man will take no horoscope, however expertly cast, as absolutely inevitable and no clairvoyant, however reputed, as absolutely infallible.

445

When astrology uses the stars and planets to explain the events which happen to us as pointers to the good and evil, the wisdom and ignorance *within ourselves*, as the prime causes of these events, it serves a purpose. If, however, it uses *them* as the real causes, then it renders us a disservice.

446

Have astrologers ever answered the criticism of Saint Augustine, that twins born under identical aspects do not have identical fortunes in life?

447

Do the sparkling planets which circle around our sun put the thoughts in our heads, the tendencies in our hearts, the words in our mouths, and the events in our lives? Do they throw roses in one man's path and rocks in another man's?

448

The first science ever created by the brain of man was astronomy.

449

The warning prophecies of these clairvoyants are useful in that they are to some degree what the oracle of Delphi was to Socrates. Those old Greeks had a wisdom all their own. They were not far wrong when they saw in unusual good fortune the forewarning of dread calamity; to them the gods did not desire mortals to remain happy too long.

450

It was a common act for the instructed persons among the earlier races of man, whether Egyptian or Greek, Roman or Indian, Chinese or Sumerian, to undertake no important enterprise and no long voyage without first consulting the will of the gods. And this they learnt within the secret walls of the temple, or from the lips of some revered holy man, or by studying the omens given by certain objects or circumstances. Men as gifted and as astute as Macedonian Alexander did not disdain to make the unpleasant journey to a corner of the Egyptian desert solely to consult the oracle at the temple of Ammon. It was here that Alexander, after dismounting from his horse at the door of this mystic shrine, was told that victory would follow his flag and that the world would be put into the hollow of his hand. Let us not think so slightingly of the people who lived before us, but remember that they too had culture, civilization, and religion.

451

Why is it that a man's own dreams have sometimes made a correct forecast of coming events?

452

Do the planets work sometimes for and sometimes against him or are they quite neutral?

453

Astrologers might be called "Interpreters of Over-Ruling Justice." It is not generally known that in India (although not in the West) astrology admits that in the horoscopes of advanced persons there appears what is called the *Gurukula*. When this is present, the astrologer takes it for a sign that at any moment Grace may change the character of the picture thereby presented. It is true that this doesn't appear in the horoscopes of ordinary persons. This point should be investigated by individuals who are particularly interested in the subject since it could have an important bearing on one's thinking.

454

In the horoscopes of ordinary people, in which a concatenation of several planets called the Gurukula does not appear, the expert can with reasonable accuracy plot the course of their future life because their characters are not likely to change very much. But, in the horoscopes of those few people in which the Gurukula does appear, it is not possible to prognosticate the future. Usually such persons have a great mission to perform, whether public or hidden. The individual karma from past lifetimes, even of the present one, may be changed during the fulfilment of such a mission. Ramana Maharshi had the Gurukula in his chart, as did Gandhi, and all Masters have it.

Philosophy agrees that karma can be changed, modified or counteracted for the most part, but there are certain limits beyond which one cannot go.

455

Although astrology cannot be regarded as an exact science, in the sense that astronomy is, it does offer some useful, informative clues and probabilities. A man's capacities and talents, the forces in his character, even some major happenings may be indicated by a horoscope. But interpreting this chart offers scope for human error.

456

This is not to go back to medieval superstition, but to go forward to modern, carefully investigated discovery.

457

Scholars and priests of the earliest known antiquity have drawn on the traditions of astrology to link our human fortunes with the starry firmament.

458

It is ridiculous for any sceptic to assert that it is impossible to foretell the future when science itself is doing it successfully every day of every year. Astronomical science foretells the time of eclipses of the sun and moon long in advance to the very minute of their happening. Chemical science foretells what will happen to litmus paper when it is applied to alkaline or to acid.

459

The horoscope indicates the future only for ordinary people and can never become a fixed certainty for the spiritually awakened. For wherever an individual has come under Divine Grace, he directly or indirectly through a teacher can be rendered independent of his past karma at any moment that the Divine wills it to be so. The will is free because Man is Divine and the Divine Self is free.

460

In its practice, astrology is resorted to by its believers too frequently and for too trivial matters. In its Western popularization through newspapers, periodicals, and pamphlets, it is presented so deceptively as to be half-falsified. In its theory only the most honest and most expert of its practitioners will admit the truth that it is not a precise science and that its interpretation trembles under the human frailty of its interpreters.

461

One important use of an astrological horoscope is principally to detect the presence of new opportunity, and to warn against the presence of dangerous tests, snares, and pitfalls. It is often hard to make a decision, when an important crossroad presents itself, if one of the roads leads to disaster and the other to good fortune. At such a time a correct horoscope will be helpful in arriving at a right decision.(P)

462

Whoever succeeds in discovering his deeper identity by penetrating through the personal ego's surface and sub-surface life will thenceforth cease the efforts to discover his worldly destiny. The oracles which others seek so eagerly, the turns of the wheel of fortune which they hope to learn in advance, are left alone that he may enjoy serenity.

463

The receipt of a proposition or the beginning of a new undertaking or the making of a momentous decision, the founding of an enterprise or the occurrence of a grave crisis may offer signs which show the future destiny of the affair or advice as to the course to be taken. Such signs could be given by a particular phenomenon in Nature or the character of a particular event. These signals omens auguries and auspices need interpretation or divination; they may be favourable or unfavourable. It is as if Nature herself or Karma itself cast a kind of horary horoscope to direct those who are uncertain about the future or undecided about the present.

464

Those who use the *I-Ching* or astrological ephemerides and horoscopes as predictive instruments which are infallible tend to over-use them in the end and thus become complete fatalists devoid of self-reliance. Moreover, even apart from the question of infallibility, human interpretation enters into them, which is certainly not infallible.

465

All our Western education, training, mentality, and instinct has refused to accept this distasteful fatalism of the Orient, and so has rejected it utterly in the past. But since the war a wide belief in astrology has been spreading through Euramerica. Is not its inevitable consequence summed up in the Muhammedan's exclamation: "Inshallah"?

466

It is a mixture of wish and desire, fear and anxiety, which brings them repeatedly to the door of the fortune-teller, the predictive astrologer, and the like.

467

In most of the future-reading methods which have come down by tradition, such as Tarot, palmistry, and so on, the left side represents the past and the right side represents the future. The left eye, for example, represents receptivity and the right eye represents positivity. The same symbolism is carried through into ceremonial forms.

468

Does anyone really possess the power of predicting events weeks or even months before they happen? Accuracy about the past or present could alone give one some confidence in predictions about the future.

469

Some who cannot succeed in any other profession or who are unfit for honourable work, take to fortune-telling and quickly learn the art of deceiving those who consult them. Sometimes their predictions happen to come true but in ninety percent of cases they do not.

470

Critics insist that character-readers and fortune tellers appeal only to the grossest superstitions. One can understand the attitude of those who are so antagonized by exaggerated claims as to dismiss the whole subject of destiny and its foretelling with irritated impatience. The old Brahmin astrologers of India rigidly refrained from allowing their astrological knowledge to percolate down to the masses, for fear that it would be misunderstood or misused. This is precisely what has happened today. The popularization of knowledge in these democratic days is not altogether a good thing.

471

There are some enthusiastic exponents who, not content with claiming that every event in a man's life can be predetermined with the utmost precision, even turn these arts into a creed. I am a believer in the stellar science, with certain reserves—for I perceive its incomplete and fragmentary nature—but I have never found that astrology could provide the spiritual solace for which one looks to religion or philosophy.

472

The situation in the world with its anxiety, stress, and strain has produced a remarkable phenomena of recrudescence of fortune-telling and notably of astrology. A whole army has encamped in the midst of the metropolis which professes to provide its patrons with glimpses of the events of their future life. I do not regard astrology as nonsense. I believe there is some basis for the doctrines, but I regard the whole trade of fortune-telling as having been riddled through and through with quackery. Those who place their faith in the predictions of these gentry will, in the vast majority of cases, be sadly disillusioned. The prosperity, fortunate marriage, and fame which form so common a feature in their venial prophesies prove to be hollow bubbles that are pricked by the spears of time. The mentality which accepts every prediction as authentic is as primitive and as moronic as the mentality which utters it, as in the days of the decline of ancient Rome. Superstition battens on unsettled minds and fearful hearts, on all those who feel the need of some assertions about their personal future during the disturbed epoch. The wise man will refuse to follow the mass of slander, but will derive his assertions from the study of philosophy and practice of meditation.

473

However much we pry into the future we do not come a bit nearer real peace, whereas faithfully seeking and abiding in Overself gradually brings undying light and life.

474

Predictions were not only unfulfilled but actually their very reverse happened; this was because they were based on the false theory of materialism on the one hand and the cynical estimate of human nature resulting from it on the other.

475

All talismanic precautions, gem influences, and so on, either amplify or modify the other influences (karmic, environmental, and personal) which may be at work; they do not stand by themselves. More may be done in this way by changing the kind of prevailing thoughts, and especially by keeping out negative harmful and destructive thoughts, together with prayer for guidance.

476

Given a certain set of characteristics in a man, it is often possible for the psychologist to foretell in advance how he is likely to act in a given situation.

477

Some possess an instinctive belief in astrology. They look constantly to the planets for advice about the right timing of their moves.

478

He may intuitively know—not reason out—that certain events will happen even before they do arrive.

479

There is a danger that negative predictions may also act as suggestions and, by influencing mental or emotional causes, bring about physical effects which fulfil the predictions.

480

Although the ancients were much addicted to divination, Socrates counseled the use of one's own reason and judgement in solving problems, and only when these failed should one resort to divination.

481

There are no lucky house-numbers and no unlucky ones. If a man has had a series of misfortunes in a certain house, it is not the fault of its number but the fault of his karma. His evil karma fell due during that period and would have ripened into sorrowful experiences even if he had occupied a totally different house with a totally different number. Now karma arises ultimately out of character for the better and thus ultimately changes his karma to some extent. Then let him move back into the same house which once brought him sorrow. He will find that this time it will not do so. Its so-called unlucky number will no longer harm him.

482

I am a believer in portents. This is one weak little superstition I allow myself, that the beginning of an event carries quite an auspicious significance for me.

483

That at times it is possible to foretell the future, to know beforehand what is going to happen, is a matter of personal experience with the sensitive man.

484

The "lucky gem" which can thwart the power of karma and bring a man to the high position which he does not deserve has not been found; the "unlucky stone" which can deprive a man of the fruits of his endeavour has not been formed.

485

A warning must be given about astrological predictions. The readings must be taken with the greatest reserve. Every astrologer makes mistakes—and, frequently, tremendous mistakes—because the full knowledge of this science is lost in the modern age and there is only a partial knowledge nowadays.

486

"He resisted the temptation to introduce himself [to the woman who later became his wife]; he felt it was not the right moment either for him or for me—But now, six months later, he knew that the right time had come." It proved so! Thus the importance of timing in relation to events is once again illustrated by this short story, and constantly illustrated daily by the work of astrologers.

487

We may freely leave the future to our stars, if we know that we can be true to ourselves.

488

It is more important to face the future equipped with right principles and strong character than with predictions concerning its details. If we establish good attitudes toward it, we cannot get bad results.

489

Uncritical and imaginative believers will mold, press, and distort the history of their life and the pattern of their character to fit the fortune-teller's reading or an astrologer's horoscope. In this task they mostly succeed, for there are usually some points in any reading or horoscope which are correct for any person.

490

The astrologically inclined may think they can sidestep the blows ordained by the stars.

491

If we consider the wide range of possibilities which the future holds for us, we will make predictions hesitantly.

492

When I was in the teen-age group, I studied astrology and looked anxiously or expectantly at my horoscope several times each month. Now I have not seen it for years, and care little what is in it. Why?

493

The accurate prediction of future events is not something that can be as rigidly scientific as mathematics, for instance. There are incalculable and elusive factors always at work. Nevertheless, the broad trend and general ways of events can be forecast with some soundness.

494

Shall we delay our journeys in deference to the planets?

495

If I have lost interest in having my fortune told, it is because I have found my real fortune *in myself.*

496

In dealing with the adverse statements of fortune-telling, Alan Leo, who was years ago the greatest of British astrologers, pointed out that these predictions were the consequence of what would happen if no precautions were taken against them. This attitude of a modern, Western, European astrologer is interesting when compared with the predictions made by an Indian or other Oriental astrologer, for their view is far more fatalistic.

497

Where a horoscope shows that any physical relationship with women—much more any promiscuous one—is adversely aspected by the planets, to ignore this warning would simply bring trouble after trouble in a man's life. However hard, an unmarried chaste state must be accepted.

Karma, free will, and the Overself

498

What man really dominates his destiny? The great person may succeed in modifying it, but the psychological and physical factors with which the ordinary person starts the course of life are already in his genes and predicate both character and fortune. He is at the mercy of events until he learns this secret of modifying and influencing them.(P)

499

We all have to bear the consequences of our past deeds. This cannot be helped. But of course there are good deeds and bad deeds. We can, to a certain extent, offset those consequences by bringing in counter-forces through new deeds; but how far this will be true will necessarily vary from person to person. The one who has knowledge and power, who is able to practise deep meditation and to control his character, will necessarily affect those consequences much more strongly than the one who lacks these.

500

Karma gives a man what he has largely made himself; it does not give him what he prefers: but it is quite possible at times that the two coincide. If he is partially the author of his own troubles, he is also drawing to himself by mental power his good fortune.

501

Some measure of fate, prudence, destiny, must exist in the world of human affairs if they are to be part of a divine order, and not of a mere fortuitous chaos.

502

Sufficient unto the day is the evil thereof say the apathetic, the sluggish, the inert, and they refuse to look forward. They experience the evil alright.

If time is simultaneous and the future already exists, what is the use of making any effort? This despairing but plausible objection overlooks the parallel fact that the future is not fixed for all eternity; it is always fluctuating because it is always liable to modification by the intrusion of new factors, such as an intense effort to alter it or an intense interference by another person. The future exists, but the future changes at the same time.(P)

503

Both the benign and the malefic are already concealed in destiny's decrees for the child at its birth. To the extent that outer fortunes are directly traceable to inner tendencies, to that extent they are controllable and alterable. How large or how small a part of its life is quite beyond its free choice and direction is itself a matter of fate.(P)

504

He may feel powerless in the presence of fate, too diminutive against the vast cosmic power that shapes men's lives, and overwhelmed by it into apathy or impotence.

505

Resignation to circumstance, adaptation to environment, coming to terms with the inevitable, and acceptance of the unavoidable, however reluctant—these have their place as much as the use of free aggressive will.

506

If it were true that every act of man and every event which happened to him was predestined in every point, the destruction of his moral responsibility which would necessarily follow would be as disastrous to society as to himself.

507

If certain evils are written in our destiny and may not be avoided by effort, it is still sometimes possible to minimize them by prudence.

508

Just as threads are crossed and laced to make textiles on a loom, so destiny and free will are interwoven to make a man's life.

509

If he had not done this, life would still have arranged for it to happen; but in that case it would then not be quite the same nor happen just at the same time.

510

Fate must have its way and impose its will, for that is its work and power. But man may interfere with what it does by introducing his own doings, or equally help it in its course.

511

In the somewhat mysterious way whereby fated decree meshes its gear in with willed free choice, the final result appears.

512

To say that everything depends on fate is an exaggeration; to say that it depends on one's effort is misleading.

513

With most persons whom one encounters, destiny has withheld something they ardently desired and persistently looked for.

514

We are not so tightly bound by fate as we think.

515

What man has more than partial freedom? All men have to receive the come-back of past activities, although the wise and disciplined ones may counter it to some extent by new actions.

516

The karma is a part of himself and he cannot get away from it. But just as he may bring some changes about in himself, so there may be a corresponding echo in the karma.

517

Philosophy never encourages a passive attitude towards the law of recompense, but it does not fall into the error of these misleading schools of thought which hold out false hopes.

518

No one transgresses against these higher laws without self-injury, quite apart from the punishment which the transgression itself invokes.

519

Karma brings us the results of our own doing, but these are fitted in the World-Idea, which is the supreme law and shapes the course of things.

520

There are occasions when it is either prudent or wise to practise Stoic submission. But there are other occasions when it is needful to do battle with the event or the environment.

521

The old arguments about fate and free will are in the end quite useless. It is possible to show that man has the full freedom to improve himself and his surroundings, but it is also possible to show that he is helpless. This is so because *both* sides of the matter are present and must be included in any account of the human situation. The World-Idea renders certain events and circumstances inevitable.

522

To strive hard for a worthwhile aim but to resign oneself to its abandonment if destiny is adverse to its realization, is not the same as to do nothing for it at all but to leave that aim entirely to fate. To eliminate within oneself the avoidable causes of misfortune and trouble but to endure understandingly those which are the unavoidable lot of man is not the same as to let those causes remain untouched whilst blindly accepting their effects as fate.

523

Only so far as personal planning obtains destiny's sanction will it be able to achieve its goals.

524

Socrates: "Uncouth, uncivilized, unkind—destiny decreed all those things for me, but I, through perseverance, managed to change a little."

525

Trying in the wrong way hinders us and trying in the right way helps us. Rebellion against fate does not help; acceptance and correction of fate does.

526

It is not easy to know when to follow destiny's lead or when to fight it.

527

When we find inward peace, we cease to struggle with the fates.

528

The ordination of the universal life includes the ordination of man's life.

529

We have only to look back and sum up the events of a whole lifetime to read in them the one sure meaning of it all. The future is pre-existent in us from the very beginning. Although it is not so hard-set that a change in ourselves will not modify it by reflected reaction.

530

He may do all he can to circumvent his destiny but although he can succeed in some particulars he cannot in others. For instance, a person cannot change the colour of his skin. But the kind of experiences which fall to his lot in consequence of that colour are to some extent subject to his influence and character, while his own emotional reaction to them is to the fullest extent certainly subject to them.

531

Karma does not wholly cancel freedom but limits it. If the present results of old causes set walls around him, through a better character and an improved intelligence new causes may be initiated and other results be attained.

532

There is no complete freedom but, on the other hand, there is no complete necessity. There is a confined free will, a freedom within bounds. Philosophy makes, as the basis of this freedom in man, both the intelligence it finds in him and the Divine Spirit from which that intelligence is derived.

533

Those who object to the doctrine of self-determined fate, who put forward an absolute freedom of will, have to show how free will can change the results of a murder. Can it restore life to the corpse or save the criminal from death? Can it remove the unhappiness of the murdered man's wife? Can it even eliminate the sense of guilt from the conscience of his murderer? No—these results inevitably flow from the act.

534

When we uphold the existence of free will, we uphold implicitly the existence of fate. For enquiry into the way the thought of freedom arises in the mind reveals that it always comes coupled with the thought of fate. If one is denied, then the other is thereby denied also.

535

What is the use of fooling oneself with stirring phrases about our freedom to mold life or with resounding sentences about our capacity to create fortune? The fact remains that karma holds us in its grip, that the past hems us in all around, and that the older we grow the smaller becomes the area of what little freedom is left. Let us certainly do all we can to shape the future and amend the past, but let us also be resigned to reflective endurance of so much that will come to us or remain with us, do what we may.

536

Whoever imagines that all his actions are entirely the result of his own personal choice, whoever suffers from the illusion of possessing complete free will, is blinded and infatuated with his ego. He does not see that at certain times it was impossible for him to act in any other way because there was no alternative. And such impossibility arose because there is a law which arranges circumstances or introduces a momentum according to an intelligible pattern. Karma, evolution, and the individual's trend of thought are the principal features of this pattern.

537

The human will's freedom has its limits. It must in the end conform to the evolutionary purposes of the World-Idea. If, by a certain time, it fails to do so voluntarily, then these purposes invoke the forces of suffering and force the human entity to conform.

538

What will happen to each one of us in the future is not wholly inevitable and fixed, even though it is the logical sequence of our known and unknown past. It is still unset and uncrystallized—therefore changeable to a degree. That degree can be measured partly by the extent of our fore-knowledge of what is likely to happen and the steps taken to circumvent it. The ability to evade these events is not a complete one, however, for it is always subject to being overruled by the will of the Overself.

539

Why not preordain events by using a hard will?

540

When the belief in destiny is allowed to paralyse all energy and over-whelm all courage, it should be re-examined. When the belief in free will is allowed to lead men into egoistic arrogance and materialistic ignorance, it also should be re-examined.

541

Had his choice between roads been made differently, his life would certainly have been very different, too. But was his power of choice really as free as it seemed to be?

542

Is it possible to distinguish between a calamitous destiny which we all-too-obviously fashioned for ourselves and a calamitous fate for which we seem utterly unresponsible?

543

Until a certain time the course of a man's destiny is within his area of influence, and even of control; but beyond that time it is not.

544

That which delays the expression of a man's dynamic thought in modi-fications of his environment or alterations of his character is the weight of his own past karma. But it only delays; if he keeps up the pressure of concentration and purpose, his efforts must eventually show their fruit.

545

The law of consequences is immutable and not whimsical but its effects may at times be modified or even neutralized by introducing new causes in the form of opposing thoughts and deeds. This of course involves in turn a sharp change in the direction of life-course. Such a change we call repen-tance.

546

If fate is absolute, then is prayer useless? Ought men, like the medieval Sufi, Abdullah ibn Mubarak, never ask God for anything?

547

Many men unwittingly break the higher laws of life. Others, either knowing of them or believing in them, fail to understand them well enough to apply them personally.

548

While men are not yet ready for the conscious and deliberate development of their spiritual life, they must submit to its unconscious and compulsive development by the forces of Nature.

549

Is it believable that situations which are themselves the product of man's will and thought should not be alterable by that same will and thought? No!—let him accept his responsibility at this stage of their history as he admitted it at the beginning stage.

550

Which of us has the power to change the consequences of his former actions? We may make amends, we may be penitent and perform penances. We may counter them by the opposite kinds of good deeds. But it is the business of karma to make us feel responsible for what we do and that responsibility cannot be evaded. In a certain sense, however, there is a measure of freedom, a power of creativity, both of which belong to the godlike Higher Self which each of us has.

551

What has happened has happened and there is nothing we can do about it. We cannot rewrite the past, we cannot repair our wrong actions, we cannot put right the wrongs we have done, the hurts we have given, or the miseries we have caused both to others and to ourselves. But if the past records cannot be changed, our present attitudes towards them can be changed. We can learn lessons from the past, we can apply wisdom to it, we can try to improve ourselves and our acts, we can create new and better karma. Best of all, having done all these things, we can let go of the past entirely and learn to live in the eternal now by escaping into true Being, the I am consciousness, not the I was.

552

He submits himself to karma as mutely and as will-less-ly as a sheep to the slaughterer's knife.

553

Are some faults of conduct, weaknesses of character, quite incorrigible? Give the man enough time, that is to say, enough lifetimes, and he will be unable to resist change and reform, that is to say, unable to resist the World-Idea. God is will in religious parlance.

554

Does he really choose to do these acts or are they already preordained by fate? Is his activity genuinely free and what he wanted to do or is his liberty a mere illusion and his desire mere reflection?

555

A man may conquer a continent but himself be conquered by a power before which he is as helpless as a babe—the power of divine retribution. The harvest of his aggressive war will then be gathered in.

556

If the currents of life are running adversely, if you suffer an irreparable calamity, why not submit and save your energies and your tears, says the fatalist.

557

In the end, and whether by his own surrender or by outside compulsion, his own personal purposes have to be subordinated to the World-Idea's lines of force.

558

Must fate (karma) always take its course? Are we helpless automatons? It seems a chilling thought.

559

If, after exhausting all our efforts, nothing comes of them, then we shall have to accept that as Destiny.

560

Greek tragic drama shows how event after event may turn against a man at the bidding of a higher power—destiny. It shows how little human will can do to avert catastrophe or avoid disaster when the universal will is set in an opposite direction.

561

The law of recompense is not the only one to compel man to right thought, feeling, and conduct. On a higher plane, there is the Overself. Were there no rewards for goodness and no punishment for wickedness, either here on earth or somewhere in a death-world, it would still be a part of man's highest happiness to express the compassion that is, through the Overself, his purest attribute.

562

This deadly doctrine of karma seems to leave us no loophole. It catches us like animals in the iron trap of fate.

563

A higher power than human will rules human lives. Yet it does not rule them arbitrarily. Even though man does not control its decisions, he does contribute toward them.

564

There is a certain amount of destiny in each life as the result of past karma, but there is also an amount of free will if it is exercised. Every happening in our lives is not karmic, for it may be created by our present actions.

565

We need not dally idly in the stream of happenings because we believe in destiny. The Overself is deeper than destiny. The Overself is omnipotent; the related links of the chain of Fate fall to the ground at its bidding; it is worse to disbelieve in the Overself and its supremacy than to believe in destiny and its power—not that the Overself can outwit destiny, it merely dissolves it.

566

In the final chapter of *A Search in Secret India*, I provided some hints of the cyclic nature of life, writing of how "every life has its aphelion and perihelion" (paraphrase). Now the time has come to particularize this statement and cast some light on the great mystery of fate and fortune. The knowledge of this truth renders a man better able to meet all situations in life, both pleasant and unpleasant, in the right way. "With an understanding of the auspicious and inauspicious issues of events, the accomplishment of great Life-tasks becomes possible," taught a Chinese sage. According to the Chinese wisdom, Tao, in its secondary meaning, is the divinely fixed order of things; under this there are four cycles of history. The first two are "yang" and the last two are "yin." This law of periodicity refers to individual lives no less than to cosmic existence. Every human life is therefore subject to periodical changes of destiny whose inner significance needs to be comprehended before one can rightly act. Hence the method of grappling with destiny must necessarily vary in accord with the particular rhythm which has come into the calendar of one's life. Every situation in human existence must find its appropriate treatment, and the right treatment can only be consciously adopted by the sage who has established inner harmony with the law of periodicity.

The sage seeks to do the right thing at the right moment, for automatic adjustment to these varying fortunes. This is called, in the Chinese Mystery School teaching, "mounting the dragon at the proper time and driving through the sky." Hence I have written in *The Quest of the Overself* that the wise man knows when to resist fate and when to yield to it. Knowing the truth above of the ebb and flow of destiny, he acts always in conformity with this inner understanding. Sometimes he will be fiercely active, other times completely quiescent, sometimes fighting tragedy to the utmost, but at other times resigned and surrendered. Everything has its special time and he does not follow any course of action at the wrong time. He is a free agent, yes, but he must express that freedom rightly, because he must work, as all must work, within the framework of cosmic law. To initiate the correct change in his activities at the incorrect time and amid wrong environing circumstances would be rash and lead to failure; to start a new and necessary enterprise at the wrong moment and amid the wrong situation of life, would also lead to failure. The same changes, however, if begun at another time and amid other conditions, will lead to success. The sage consults his innermost prompting, which, being in harmony with truth, guides him to correct action in particular situations accordingly. We can neither dictate to him as to what he should do, nor prescribe principles for his guidance, nor even predict how he is going to respond to any set of circumstances.

The proper course of action which anyone should adopt depends ultimately upon his time and place both materially and spiritually. In short, human wisdom must always be related to the cosmic currents of destiny and the divine goal. Man must be adaptable to circumstances, flexible to destiny, if his life is to be both wise and content. Unfortunately, the ordinary man does not perceive this, and creates much of his own unhappiness, works much of his own ruin. It is only the sage who, having surrendered the personal Ego, can create his own harmony with Nature and fate and thus remain spiritually undisturbed and at peace. As Kung-Fu-Tze (Confucius, in Western parlance) pithily says: "The superior man can find himself in no situation in which he is not himself." The wise man defers action and waits if necessary for the opportune and auspicious moment; he will not indulge in senseless struggles or untimely efforts. He knows how and when to wait and by his waiting render success certain. No matter how talented he be, if his circumstances are unfavourable and the time inopportune to express them, he will resign himself for the while and devote his time to self-preparation and self-cultivation and thus be ready for the opportunity which he knows the turn of time's wheel must bring him. He puts himself into alignment with the hidden principle which runs through man and matter, striking effectively when the iron is hot, refraining cautiously when it is cold. He knows the proper limits of his activity even in success and does not go beyond them. He knows when to advance and when to retreat, when to be incessantly active and when to lie as still as a sleeping mouse. Thus he escapes from committing serious errors.(P)

567

Your karma led you into this horror but your cleared sight can now lead you out of it. This will act as a healing. The conjunction of your character, temperament, and qualities with the time, surroundings, and history being what they were, the result was what it was. Now the more you can displace the so-called freedom of the ego, submit to the call of Overself, the more you will share the greater possibility which it hides.

568

The yearning to free himself from the limitations of personal destiny and the compulsions of outward circumstance can be gratified only by losing the sense of time.

569

Karma comes into play only if the karmic impression is strong enough to survive. In the case of the sage, because he treats life like a dream, because he sees through it as appearance, all his experiences are on the surface only. His deep inner mind remains untouched by them. Therefore he makes no karma from them, therefore he is able when passing out of the body at death to be finished with the round of birth and death forever.

570

The view that karma operates like an automatic machine is not a wholly true one; this is because it is not a wholly complete one. The missing element is grace.

571

The privileges of enlightenment can only be justified on the basis of karma— "My own, my own, shall come to me," as the poet intuited.

572

He will be content to leave the mutations of his future in the disposal of the higher power. He knows that it is rendered secure by his obedience to, and conformity with, the higher laws.

573

Man may attempt to defy his destiny, but unless he has emancipated his spirit, it will get him.

574

It is sometimes asked, why should the Overself, through its grace, interfere with the workings of its own law of consequences? Why should it be able to set the karma of a man at naught? If the recurrence of karma is an eternal law, how can any power ever break it or interfere with its working? The answer is that the Overself does not violate the law of consequences at any time. If, through a man's own efforts he modifies its effects upon him in a particular instance, or if the same is brought about by the manifestation of Grace, everything is still done within that law—for it must not be forgotten that the allotment selected for a particular incarnation does not exhaust the whole store of karma existing in a man's record. There is always very much more than a single earth-life's allotment. What happens is that a piece of good karma is brought into manifestation alongside of the bad karma, and of such a nature and at such a time as completely to neutralize it, if its eradication is to be the result, or partially to neutralize it, if its modification is to be the ended result. Thus the same law still continues to operate, but there is a change in the result of its operation.

575

There is no other judge of your deeds than the law of recompense, whose agent is your own Overself.

576

Even if human karma were rigidly implacable and against it human will sadly impotent, divine Grace is still available and divine Mercy is yet accessible.

577

Do your best to mend matters, the best you can, then leave the results to destiny and the Overself. You can't do more anyway. You can modify your destiny, but certain events are unchangeable because the world is not yours but God's. You may not know at first what events these are, therefore you must act intelligently and intuitively: later you can find out and accept. Whatever happens, the Overself is still there and will bring you through and out of your troubles. Whatever happens to your material affairs happens to your body, not the real YOU. The hardest part is when you have others dependent on you. Even then you must learn how to commend them to the kindly care of the Overself, and not try to carry all the burden on your own shoulders. If it can take care of you, it can take care of them, too.

578

The working of a man's karma would never come to an end if his egoism never came to an end. It would be a vicious circle from which there would be no escape. But when the sense of personal selfhood, which is its cause and core, is abandoned, the unfulfilled karma is abandoned too.

579

The law of recompense has no jurisdiction over the eternal and undivided Overself, the real being, only over the body and mind, the transitory ego.

580

On this question of fate and free will, Ramana Maharshi was the supreme fatalist. He once said, "Make no effort to be active or to renounce activity for your effort is your present. What is predestined to arrive will arrive. Leave things to the Supreme Power, you cannot choose to renounce or to keep."

581

If a man comes into alignment with the Overself-consciousness, he is compelled to give up his earlier position of free will and free choice—for he no longer exists to please the ego alone. The regulating factor is now the Overself itself.

582

How wonderful it would be if a man could fall asleep one night and wake up in the morning finding himself fully enlightened, that is, someone else!

583

What we have yet to learn is that destiny makes its chesslike moves according to our thinking and doing. Whoever will offer himself unto the Overself, and will be blessed by its benediction so that he becomes as one inspired, may then perceive this strange figure at his side working for the good of man.

FREE WILL, RESPONSIBILITY, AND THE WORLD-IDEA

The limitations of free will

The events of our future remain in a fluid state until a certain time. We have the free will to modify them during that period, although it is never an absolute freedom.

2

Inevitably and ultimately, will *must* prove stronger than fate because it is our own past will which created our present fate.

3

The awareness that they are weak and faulty makes some persons regard free will, not as the boon it is generally supposed to be, but as a danger. Saint Therese of Lisieux even asked God to take it away because it frightened her.

4

He who asserts that he is free to do what he wishes to do would more correctly state his situation by confessing that he is enslaved by his ego and goes up or down as its emotional see-saw moves.

5

It is not only the karma of a man which may oppose itself to his free choice and free will; there are also the possibilities of opposition by human institutions and organizations, natural calamities and catastrophes, genetic heredity and racial predisposition.

6

If a man's will were really free, he would have to think of using it before he actually did so, and then again to think of thinking of using it, and so on in an endless series. Since this situation never occurs, are we to believe that his will is never free? This is a question that no man can answer for it ought never to be put.

7

Even the man who believes that he possesses the attribute of free will finds himself forced to accept certain events just like others who do not believe they possess it.

8

Too many persons claim a freedom to choose and to will who in reality have only the very opposite—a captivity to their desires. These desires respond like a machine to the conditions which surround them and delude them into the belief that they are deliberately choosing from among those conditions. The moods and emotions of these persons are changed by every change of outer circumstance, provoked favourably or unfavourably by the nature of each change. Where is the freedom in this? Does it not rather show dependence?

9

Most human beings are so automatic and predictable in their habitual reactions that they are like machines. And where is the freedom of a machine? They are really helpless creatures, devoid of free will. Despite this, they do possess a latent freedom, even though they are not evolved enough to claim it.

10

A man imprisoned in the circle of his own ego still imagines he has free will!

11

Where is the freedom for the immense masses of men who are ego-bound? They are held hand and foot: it is only their illusion that they move freely. Where is the free choice for those who merely, unwittingly, blindly, express the tendencies with which they were born?

12

Even while he believes that he is making a free choice between two or three alternatives, a man is really obeying the strongest tendency of those which constitute his character. His "I" does what his tendency tells him to do; its freedom is only an apparent one.

13

A mistake in my published writing has been the emphasis on man's possession of free will. I did this deliberately to counteract the common impression that Oriental mystical teaching is associated with a paralysing fatalism and a futile inertia. Unfortunately, I overdid it. Consequently, I gave the impression that the quantity of free will we possess is about equal to or even more than the quantity of fate allotted to us. But, in their combination, the effects of our past, the pattern of our particular nature, and the influence of our environment govern our immediate actions very largely whilst the divine laws govern our ultimate direction within the universe quite fully. In such a situation, personal freedom must actually be less than we usually believe it to be. Again I have taught that no experience could come to us which we had not earned by our karma, which in turn was entirely the product of our free will. But I have since discovered that some experiences can come to us solely because we need them, not at all because we earn them. This is an important difference. It increases the sphere of personal fate and diminishes the sphere of personal freedom. However, in self-justification I ought to point out three things here about the kind of fatalism now put forward. First it is *not* paralysing but, on the contrary, inspiring. For it tells us that there *is* a divine plan for us all and that true freedom lies in willingly accepting that infinitely wise and ultimately benevolent plan. Second, it emphatically offers no grounds for inertia for it bids us *work with* the plan—not only to secure our own individual happiness but also to help secure the common welfare of all. Third, it does not introduce anything arbitrary or despotic into God's will for us but retains the rule of intelligent purpose and restores evolutionary meaning to the general picture of our individual lives. If quite often the free will we imagine we are exercising does not exist outside such imagination, this need make no difference to our practical attitude towards life. It does not stop us from getting the best (in the philosophic sense) out of life. And it only reassures us that in deserting the herd and taking to the spiritual path we are putting whatever freedom we do possess to the most sensible use. Although I must henceforth correct the balance of my personal work and stress the inevitability of things, I know that in urging aspirants in the past to liberate themselves from the lower nature through exercising the consciousness of their higher self and its knowledge, I pointed to the only real freedom worth having and within reach. The mass of humanity exists in the deepest slavery, often unconsciously. All talk of exercising free will whilst chains clank round its thought and feeling and action, is unreal if not self-deceptive.

14

Life comes from a source beyond man's knowledge and outside his control. Only the expression is within it.

15

Whether we are in bondage to the body or to the intellect, we are still prisoners.

16

The life to which we are predestined from birth—which means the major events of the life we actually experience—is like a house. We are free to move about within its walls but not outside them.

17

The delusion of deliberate choice is easy to fall into, hard to escape from.

18

Out of his own nature and in conformity with the universal plan, a stream of influences flows over him out of the past and forces his acts and thoughts to take a certain direction. He may believe that he is following this direction quite independently and freely. In this incapacity to see how limited is his present freedom lies his subtlest illusion.

19

There are enough enforced limitations to each life that whoever claims he possesses complete freedom of will and choice is neither stupid nor wise—merely mad.

20

Deserting the ultimate level where all universes have vanished into the great Void, and coming back to the immediate level where they are actively existent, one finds there is no full freedom anywhere in the world. All are bound in some way and to some extent.

21

"I am the master of my fate, I am the captain of my soul," affirmed W.E. Henley's brave lines written on a hospital bed. But the measure of truth contained in them is only a limited one: they need the counterbalance, "I am the creature of my environment."

22

It is only a wrong sense of values which could glorify such mechanical sense-reactions as expressive of a free will.

23

It is often not easy—but the sooner he does so, the sooner his mind will become less resentful and more tranquil—to recognize that this happening, this position or this person is part of his fate, that his only freedom in such a case is a moral one. He can select his mental attitude.

24

His moral response to a happening, as also his mental attitude toward it and emotional bearing under it, are largely free. It is in this realm, moreover, that important possibilities of further spiritual growth or else materialistic hardening are available. He may renew inner strength or fall back into sensual weakness.

25

"In *The Spiritual Crisis of Man* you say that everyone has a choice of action in life's situations. I do not understand this because, for instance, if I find a wallet on the street with identification and one hundred dollars in cash, it seems to me that the action I will take under these circumstances will be the result of my total experience (thinking) up to this point. I may feel that I make a choice between finding the owner and keeping the money because I am aware in my mind of the two possibilities but I feel that my life (or lives) up to this time would determine what I would do and so I do not really have a choice. I can see that as a person gains experience and grows towards a spiritual being that his idea tomorrow will not be what it was yesterday but the decision he makes is the *only one* he *can* make at the time.

"The idea of free will has always been hard for me to understand. What I have said above does not depress me because I feel that as we learn more our actions will be wiser but I would like to know what there is that I do not realize when you speak of man's free will." This is the text of a reader's letter. Here is my answer.

Many Orientals put all happenings under the iron rule of karma. There is no free will, no individual control over them. One has to accept them fatalistically and, if dismayed by their evil, turn to the Spiritual Source for the only real happiness. In mental attitude, in personal inward response to events, lies one's chief freedom of will.

It might, however, be questioned how far such freedom is illusory, since the response, the attitude, are themselves conditioned by the past and many other things. It is quite correct to state that the past inclines us to think and act in a certain way. But it is also admitted that we can grow, can improve our lives and change in the course of time. So this is an admission that we are free to choose to grow or to remain exactly as we were. A man who commits robbery with violence may say that he is fated to act violently. With each offense, he is arrested and suffers imprisonment. After this has happened several times he begins to change his course. Eventually he fears imprisonment so much so that he resists temptation and ceases to be a criminal. This change of mental attitude was an act of free will. His past inclined him to the old direction but it did not compel him.

The reader claims that "the decision he makes is the only one he can make at the time." But the real situation is that it is the only decision he was *willing* to make. A man may not be conscious at first of conflict between two impulses inside himself. It is the presence of the Overself behind the ego which sets up the conflict. At first it remains in the subconscious, then in a dim vague way it becomes conscious. He may dismiss the alternative choice, but it was there all the time. Jesus said: "What you sow, you shall reap." The criminal chooses not to believe it, because he does not want to believe it. Inclinations from the past do not compel a man, but he unconsciously uses them as an excuse and claims he can do nothing else. The will is being expressed even when the man thinks he is, and seems to be, compelled to act in a certain way. It is expressed in the mental attitude adopted towards the situations in which he finds himself. Whenever he accepts the ordinary materialistic, negative, egoistic view of a situation, he is actually choosing that view. He *is* choosing even though he believes the contrary is true.

Where there is no choice, where circumstances make the decision, one must bow one's head to them. Fatalism is acceptable only in the sense of recognizing what is inevitable and what is not. But fatalism is unacceptable as a blind, unquestioning, helpless submission to every happening.

26

The Oriental way of putting responsibility for untoward happenings always on fate enables the individual to escape feeling any guilt for what he has himself done to bring them about.

27

Such is the power of suggestion, tradition, and environment that the average European and American does have a feeling of being free to make his own decisions and of being able to act in the world as he wishes, whereas the average Indian has no such feeling; the latter believes that he acts according to some unknown preordained pattern. Although these two feelings are so contradictory, there is a solid basis of fact beneath each of them. The contradiction arises because they are not sufficiently understood. In the Westerner's case, it is from the Overself's freedom that his feeling is originally derived. In the Indian's, it is from the Overself's allotment of karma that his own is derived.

28

Hemmed in as he is by inheritances not only from his personal past history but also from society's, it would be futile to talk of having complete freedom of choice. But it would be an error in thought and conduct to behave as if he had no freedom at all. Some measure of it does exist, since in most of his situations, if not in all, he is always faced with at least two possible lines of choice—a higher and a lower one.

29

A single decision may entirely shape the next fifty years of a young man's future.

30

The circumstances in which he finds himself and the events which happen to him are not more to a man than what he thinks and does about them. For his reaction, his attitude are more often within his control than they may be.

31

What happens to us today is a necessary consequence of what happened in the past—not only to us but also to the others who are now concerned along with us. The amount of active free choice and free will that we can slip into this situation today is, however, not non-existent but of limited existence.

32

We Westerners have made and kept such a strong mental habit of thinking our will and choice to be free that the Eastern belief in its opposite seems most unconvincing.

33

Men usually do not have the freedom to choose between two highly desirable things but only between two imperfect things.

34

Most of our decisions are what they are by necessity; only in a minority of them are they free choices in any real sense.

35

You are free to turn this page over if you wish, the choice is entirely your own; but what you do not see so clearly is that the choice was predetermined by all that has made you what you are and your environment what it is. Apply enough reason and you will see that freedom is fettered.

36

There are times when a man may boldly go forward and take his chance, when fortune's wheel will turn in his favour. But such times do not fill the whole of a lifetime and during the negative periods he should lie low and risk nothing.

37

When fate, or seeming chance, brings an opportunity that seems worthwhile or much needed, it is an error to put off its acceptance for a later time. By this very postponement it may be lost altogether; and anyway, the circumstances later will be different and may modify the opportunity itself.

38

If it is to happen at all it will happen at the opportune moment—not a day too soon, or too late.

39

No situation in which we find ourself will ever repeat itself in precisely the same way. As a consequence of the changes brought about by time, the likelihood of the factors concerned reappearing in an identical combination is practically nil.

40

When he is presented by circumstances with two alternatives, the choice he makes will usually be the outcome of the collective tendencies of his nature. From the eventual results of that choice, whether pleasurable or painful, he will have the opportunity to learn how right or how wrong those tendencies may be.

41

If our independent choice is to play no part on the stage of events, then life becomes a mere travesty.

42

The claims of physicists, like Jeans, that the new physics with its theory of indeterminism endorses the doctrine of free will, is not valid. For the idea of free will is a psychological or theological one and cannot be brought into a realm like physics with which it has nothing to do at all.

43

Introduce new factors at the proper time and you may influence the flow of events. The course destined for them is not rigidly destined.

44

The right timing of our actions is not less important than the right thinking which should precede them.

45

Life offers us only a single favourable chance of the same kind. If we throw it away, through bad judgement or blind handling, no one is to blame except ourselves when it never recurs again. The same chance never repeats itself. If it is not used when it comes, it is lost *in that form* for this lifetime.

46

Right timing and fit circumstance are necessary to right action, otherwise the latter may be premature and may even lead to failure instead of success.

47

In the hour of opportunity, we act according to the balance struck by our temperament and character, our nature and capacity, our knowledge and desire.

48

The materialistic scientist believes that man acts according to the chemical constitution of his physical body and that therefore he has no real freedom to choose which way he shall act.

49

There are even those among Orientals who consider any kind of self-help to be an endeavour to force the divine will, and therefore a blasphemy!

50

"There would be no utility in any particular commandment if the individual were not free to obey or disobey."   —Maimonides.

51

The optimist sees large freedom of decision in man's possession whereas the pessimist sees little.

52

It is open to him to see each situation in two alternative and opposing ways, to take what is known in metaphysics as the immediate or the ultimate view. He can see it on the one hand physically and materially or on the other mentally and spiritually.

53

It is utterly beyond the power of man to perform an act of completely free will. In all situations he is presented with a limited series of choices and he must accept one of them, reject the others.

54

When good luck follows on good judgement, the result is sure.

55

Shakespeare: "There is a tide in the affairs of men, Which, taken at the flood, leads on to fortune. Omitted, all the voyage of their life is bound in shallows and in miseries. We must take the current when it serves, Or lose our ventures."

56

It is not enough to have ability. It must meet with opportunity too or it will waste itself in a vacuum. Nor is this couple enough. There must be judgement to recognize the opportunity as such.

The freedom we have to evolve

57

At a time when his destiny balances itself upon his decision, wisdom may be sorely absent if he has never sought it.

58

No man has free will if he is enslaved by things or affected by events outside of himself. He has it only when he is inwardly detached from them.

59

There is much talk by those who always want their own way, but who forget that self-discipline is not less necessary than self-expression.

60

"We ought to exert our efforts in all (things) as though they were absolutely free, and God will do as he sees fit."   —Maimonides (P)

61

Where is there freedom of choice for the man who, because his five senses rule him, reacts mechanically to his environment? Only where the man has attained objectivity towards his body, instead of being totally immersed in it, can we say such choice exists.

62

He may regard what happens to him as unalterable destiny or as usable opportunity. The future is not wholly beyond his control but it may be if he fails to use his will upon, or sometimes against, the instinctive and automatic tendencies inside himself.

63

In the very *fact* of time's illusoriness, in the actuality of the eternal present, there is our best hope, our finest opportunity. For it means that the future *can* be shaped, within due limits. We can help to make tomorrow, can contribute something to it, at least by bringing it into today. But all this remains only a mere possibility if we do not take advantage of the paradoxical and astounding truth. We must begin by clearing away some of the debris with which past habit, thought, feeling, and attitude have cluttered up our insides.

64

If freedom of will is utter illusion we have to ask ourselves why the Buddha, greatest of all advocates of the truth of inexorable karma, and whose enlightenment is incontestable, gave as his dying legacy to disciples the words, "Work out your own salvation." If this is not a call to the use of will, of a free will, what is? It is hard for Westerners to accept a doctrine of complete fatalism, and the difficulty is not wholly due to their ignorance of spiritual facts which are elementary to Indians. It is also due to their instinctive refusal to be robbed of their initiative, and to their insistence on moral responsibility for ethical decisions and actions.

65

Only those people are entitled to freedom who understand and accept the responsibilities involved in it. And even such people are entitled only to so much of it as accords with the extent to which they possess this understanding and yield this acceptance. Outer discipline may go only if, and only so far as, inner discipline replaces it.

66

The man whose weakness when confronted by temptation is so great that his yielding is plainly predictable, can not be said to have the same freedom of choice that the man of strong self-mastery has.

67

Most people experience events brought about by a mixture of heredity, environment, other people's influence, and karma; not many exert their will determinedly, use their thinking power correctly, and control their energy and time to create chosen results.

68

Freedom is not in itself a good or bad thing; the way it is used, whether wisely or recklessly, will determine its value.

69

An indiscriminate granting of freedom would, in the present condition of human nature, mean at least as much evil as good. Without going to the extreme of regimentation, some limitation upon it is absolutely needed.

70

What kind of choice, what different option, has the poor benighted victim of a criminal or lunatic heritage, set in the lowest of sleazy ugly slums?

71

We need a measure of outer freedom if we are to search after and find the inner freedom.

72

If you demand freedom you must accept the responsibility which accompanies it. This is not only a human and social law but also a divine and karmic law.

73

The disunited man will suffer from inner conflict as he feels the risk and the responsibility which come from his power of choice.

74

Because man surrenders his own will to God's will, this does not mean he should sit back and do nothing.

75

He who thinks freedom leaves him free to be undisciplined is a fool.

76

The reality of a man's freedom is measured by his acceptance of responsibility.

77

To say that environment, being the expression of thought, can be changed only by changing thoughts is correct only as the ultimate truth of the situation. And then to say that one feels too weak to change one's thoughts sets up a vicious circle from which there seems no escape. The immediate truth must be brought in as a counterbalance. And that is, that an outer change will make easier the inner one.

78

It is a narrow view which holds that acceptance of the doctrine of grace necessarily leads to rejection of the doctrine of free will. Christians like Luther and Augustine have held it, but not Christ himself. It dooms the sinner to his sin, predestines frail humanity to error and wrong-doing. The belief which wrongly denies human free will because it rightly affirms divine absoluteness, denies human responsibility for wrong-doing and affronts human dignity. Its moral results in feeling and conduct can only be deplorable when anyone feels that he cannot act freely or choose independently, when he believes that he is a mere puppet led about by forces outside his control, when he all-too-easily puts the blame for his own sinfulness where it does not belong or, admitting it, passes it on to God. He thinks he can do whatever he pleases and not be personally responsible for its harmful consequences upon others.

79

A real free will would not be the merely random upsurges of an irresponsible irrational being. It must be developed out of self-mastery.

80

The notions of some sects that inward spirituality confers immunity from outward trouble or bodily death need correction. Freedom, whether of choice or from limitation, is mental. The consequences of belonging to the human species include sharing human conditions. The body is born, grows, and dies. The people among whom a man has to live react to him according to their own character, affect him adversely or beneficially.

81

The really determined spiritual man has more powers of free will than others—powers to mold his life and to offset his karma and to create good karma to wipe out threatening or existing bad karma.

82

If the past is out of his hands, the future has fallen into them.

83

The possession and power of will are only assumptions, yet they are not altogether false assumptions. He who holds the reins still has a limited power of free choice left after the immense impulsions of temperament and environment, of character and society, of mental capacity and hereditary race have done with him.

84

In life we do not find man is entirely free to work his own way and will, nor do we find him entirely blown about by exterior forces and circumstances; both are present side by side though not necessarily equal in extent. Human existence is the resultant from their combination.

85

The ring of circumstances sometimes holds us too tightly to be slipped off the finger of existence by determined will.

86

Man is forced in the end by life itself to undertake disciplines he resents or resists. The neophyte in philosophy, for the sake of his own personal development, anticipates them, accepts them, and co-operates with them.

87

To the extent—which is often very large—that the future arises out of man's own character and capacities, it is both controllable and alterable, and yet at the same time bound to happen as if it inexorably had to conform to fate. What he is inhibits his freedom, yet if it were not there he would have remained as he was throughout all the reincarnations. But the changes of environment, the events of his personal history, draw out this freedom.

88

Who possesses complete independence? Who has all the freedom he wants? Who is able to make his choices freely, unaffected by his circumstances, by social pressure, by events, or by heredity? The answer, of course, is no one. But, to the extent that anyone learns to control his thoughts, to become master of himself, he begins to control his fate.

89

If in the larger sense free choice is illusory—or cosmos would become chaos—in the narrower sense it is real enough in reference to mental attitude, to spiritual standpoint, to the thought we have about a situation. The World-Idea must be fulfilled, but within that limit there is some amount of personal freedom.

90

The destiny of an entire lifetime may be set by a single mistake, itself the consequence of ungoverned emotion or passion.

91

As Fortune's wheel turns up or down, man himself contributes to its movements. Without ambition, for instance, the poor youth would remain hopelessly immured in the miserable monotonous existence of the slum where he happens to be born.

92

Fate hands him the opportunities and the difficulties: what he does with them is his choice, for which *he* is responsible.

93

In what manner are men free who, in some way, to some extent, are enslaved by sex, society, ambition, swelling desires, possessions, neighbours, associates, and family?

94

Coaxed by pleasure in some incarnations and driven by pain in others, man slowly learns to use his faculties and powers aright.

95

Can we wonder that some men have rebelled against the passive suffering which a misguided religious instruction bids them endure? Why they become impatient with their guides and begin to look elsewhere for teaching?

96

The saying that "experience is the best teacher" is one I often thought should be altered to "experience is most often the only teacher." It is surely better to be taught by reflection and intuition.

97

The method of disposing of personal difficulties by trial and error is risky and faulty, whereas the method of disposing of them by calm, impersonal, and dispassionate reflection is safer and surer.

98

There is a shorter and better way to practical wisdom. What the ordinary man arrives at only after the several events of long years, the wiser one will arrive at earlier by intuition and reflection.

99

Because men have been given some freedom to choose between alternatives, they have been given the chance to evolve capacity and develop character through trial and error, thought and action.

100

Even the most obscure and insignificant person, who feels that he can do little or nothing to change his destiny in the future, because it is the consequence both of his life in the past and his surroundings in the present, is not quite correct. He may be powerless to move away from its major trend, but there is within him a creative force and an untapped knowledge, only it must be sought for and found.

101

It is the ego that lives in time and experiences these different abstractions of past, present, and future; but the real being behind the ego is on a different plane altogether. Now if mentalism throws light on the problems of time, of the real and the illusory, it also throws light on the question of free will and determinism. Since all is within the mind, to the extent that we learn to control mind we are able to exercise free will. But there it stops.

102

The principle of indeterminacy which governs the deep centre of each atom in the universe assures man of freedom of will in his own centre. But just as the atom's behaviour is unpredictable only within certain limits, so man's freedom is operative only within certain limits. In neither the case of the atom nor of man is there absolute freedom.

103

Nothing in life is so rigidly ordained that man cannot influence, modify, or even divert it in some way. This is because the preordaining factor is not wholly outside himself: it exists in his own past, which through the law has been brought into his present. If he will really make the present a fresh experience, and not merely a copy of the past, he works creatively upon his inheritance. For instance, a man who is destined to die at an early middle age because he neglects his body, is careless about his health, toils so over-ambitiously to increase possessions or improve position that he fails to rest as well, will certainly die then. But a man in a similar case who awakens to his danger, takes life more easily and learns to relax, does not try to do too much for his strength or time or dissipate his energies in other ways, will lengthen the number of his years.

104

There are two things in life before which a man must bow in helplessness. One is the Irretrievable; the other is the Inevitable.

105

The belief that man can do nothing to improve his lot is unworthy of man!

106

The whole debate of fate versus free will, which has continued since centuries and is just as active in our own, would be dropped if the debaters knew and understood where both forces had their *habitat*. They are *in* time, relative to it: what they bring about lies in the past, present, or future, whereas they take their rise out of an eternal NOW. Time is in the mind and to assume its complete and ultimate reality is to falsify the experiences and the happenings in it.

107

In itself the will is free but in its activity it is not. This is because the effects of past acts and the necessities of evolution incline it toward a certain course.

108

A man may move to a given point by crawling or walking, running or swimming, driving or diving; it is largely his free choice in the matter. But karma dictates where the point shall be and here his freedom ends.

109

As to how far a man may direct the course of his life, and how it is directed for him by overriding destiny, the answer has been given variously by the wise.

110

The movement of personal destiny is beyond man's control so far as it is part of the World-Idea, but it is not totally beyond his control. To some extent, varying with his own development, with his own knowledge of and obedience to the higher laws, his own intelligent or intuitive foresight, it is possible to control this movement.

111

He is free to identify his own purposes with the pattern of the World-Idea, or to disregard it. In both cases he must take the consequences. In the one case he will have again and again, voluntarily if reluctantly, to subordinate his ego. In the other, he will seek to satisfy it and may at times succeed in doing so. But then he will meet those consequences because the law of karma has to give him back his own.

112

Law rules the universe: the latter could not have been conceived as it is, so mathematically, so orderly in numerical values, unless all things were in conformity with and obedient to the World-Idea. Functioning as part of this cosmic necessity is karma. But within this condition there is some freedom to choose and to act—very limited but there.

113

We are part of a process whose course and outcome are alike determined by the will of Heaven. In that sense the vaunted freedom of man is a mere chimera. But within those limits there are always two or more possibilities open to him and there lies his free choice. The philosopher and the fool have been flung upon this star; both must walk the same course and arrive at the same goal. Yet each may do so in his own individual way, may proceed more circuitously or more slowly or more swiftly as his inclinations decide.

114

Where is man's free will? He is free to choose whether he will conform to the pattern of the World-Idea, whether he will obey or not obey the higher laws.

115

The larger pattern of destiny is already traced for us but the smaller patterns which fit into it are left for our own tracing.

116

The structure of the physical brain contributes largely to the way a man acts. This leaves him less room for free will than he thinks he has. But the brain (and the whole body) structure is itself the product of past self-made karma now functioning.

117

The activities of the present life necessarily make their contribution towards the results now being experienced as destiny from previous lives. They may even go farther than this and may influence, modify, or altogether offset a destined experience which is reserved for the future and has still to materialize. Thus, there is no room for a hopeless fatalism in this teaching. Destiny is alterable. It is made more pleasurable by our good deeds, more bearable by our wise decisions, more painful by our bad deeds, and more unbearable by our foolish decisions.

118

If circumstances cannot be changed, they may be modified. If they cannot be modified, they may be viewed with a changed attitude of mind.

119

The man who wins is the man whose dice are loaded with invincible optimism, with unfailing effort, and with creative thought.

120

True freedom must include freedom from what has come into being previously.

121

Since the gift of creativity belongs to all of us and is usable in all spheres of a man's life, he can do much to mold that life if he exerts strength and holds to determination.

122

The planet's future is written in the divine World-Idea and this necessarily includes the future of all dwellers upon it. But within this general preordained pattern there is some latitude for human dwellers.

123

He acts out of his own free choice yet at the same time that very choice was part of the universal pattern, the World-Idea. His personal freedom does not stand alone, isolated, absolute. It is inseparable from a helpless determinism. Such is the paradox of the human situation.

124

Those who talk of human freedom to alter the course of things should beware of their words. They are constrained not only as adults but as children and still more as embryos. Only the measure of their freedom and the extent of this constraint varies. Inwardly there is more freedom for thoughts to create attitudes, but outwardly there is more constraint. Basically all situations are subject to the World-Idea, that is to say in popular religious language, The Divine Will.

125

Each is limited by what is possible for his own particular personality, but as against this each has untapped inner resources.

126

If anyone believes in complete fatalism, if he feels that he is being carried on to the fulfilment of a preordained destiny in every particular point, then it may be so. But it means that he denies the creative power in the deeper level of his being. It means that he has drugged himself by misconceptions about himself and about the purposes for which he has been put on earth.

127

No human creature dare claim to be free: such an attribute—if a descriptive term dare be used at all—can only be assigned to infinite and transcendent incomprehensible Mind.

128

The truth is that both are present in life, the destiny ordained by karma and the freedom towards which we are struggling. Both are present in each human existence, but it is only the advanced soul who has created that fine equilibrium between them which unites them both in harmony.

129

The power of karma is matched by the power of personal effort, and out of the balancing of the two supported by wisdom a better result will always be obtained.

130

Fate, necessity, destiny, determinism—these are inexorable, compulsive, and inescapable in reference to the broad general evolution of the whole race. But within that larger circle the small circle of an individual is relatively free to rotate in its own course. This is the great secret, the final solution of the enigma of man's freedom.

Human will in the World-Idea

131

If men were really free to choose and decide, to will and to act, then God would be limited to the very extent that they were free! In other words, God would not be God at all! This is the final argument which reason can propound on the subject.

132

A man's ignorance and helplessness is in proportion to what he feels about the Universal Mind. If he denies its very existence, if he is an utter materialist, then he has set himself at cross-purposes to Nature and will one day discover that his power and knowledge are as nothing. If he believes in the existence of a Universal Mind, but regards it as something utterly apart and separate from himself, then his position is much safer. If he recognizes that he is rooted in the Universal Mind, and seeks to develop his awareness of it, then he will become strong and wise in proportion to this development. In the first case, the man's attitude will constitute a permanent danger to him; in the third case, it will constitute a deliverance for him.

133

We find life in this world thrust upon us. Thus the very beginning mocks at arrogant men who claim that human will is free.

134

Life is presented to each individual in a pattern that is given by a higher power—call it karma or God, destiny or divinity. He may be able to put in the smaller details, but the larger outlines are preordained. The freedom he thinks he has is illusory. But where he does not suspect it, he does have freedom, and that is his higher self, his Overself.

135

If one's previous ill-marked history cannot now be rewritten, and if one's future history is to be affected by it, then his best recourse, and indeed his only true one, is to turn to the Eternal NOW. But to do so he must take the middle way.

136

Oriental fatalism, which makes God's power and will the only power and will, leaves man's power useless and renders his will superfluous. This is somewhat disheartening to the Occidental's mind and enervating to his hand. But he need not accept it; it is also the unbalanced half-dangerous fatalism of half-knowledge. Man is intended to grow up into consciousness of his Godlike essence, and through that into joyful co-operation with God and deliberate participation with God's World-Idea.

137

No man is really and fully free since all men are carrying out the World-Idea. The feeling which he usually possesses that he is acting under his own power and making his own choices is due to his ignorance.

138

If the earth which carries us through space has no freedom of choice but must fulfil its role in the World-Idea, that is, has no free-will to wander in and out of its prescribed orbit even for one second, how unlikely is it that we, the tiny creatures on its back, have been allowed what has been denied it!

139

If the man in you is held down by his body, his surroundings, his karma, the godlike in you is not: it is free. But through this freedom it chooses to be in harmony with God.

140

A man's attitude toward the question of free will changes after he has surrendered to the Overself. It has to change. For henceforth he is to be loyal not to the ego's desires but to the Overself's injunctions. If the two coincide, it is well and pleasant for him. If not, and he obeys his higher self as he must, then it can no longer be said that he has full freedom of will. But neither can it be said that he has not. For the Overself *is in him*, not outside, not something alien and apart; it is indeed himself at his best and highest level. Because the Overself is under no other law than that of its own being, which it always obeys, both freedom and fate are harmoniously united in it. Hence, the truly wise man will reconcile and unite the tenet of karma and the tenet of free will. He knows that only a limited vision will range them against each other.

141

The sun, planets, and stars must move in their regular orbits. They are not free to change their course each day. Can this little creature, man—a mere speck on one of them—claim a larger freedom than theirs without being insane?

142

In the end the only freedom we have is to conform to the order of the universe and *be* what we have the possibility of being, and that is to move upward, transcend the little ego, and discover the hidden greatness of Overself.

143

Man's free will and God's preordained will are simultaneously coinciding, acting together. It does not matter what man's freedom leads him to do: in the end it will be turned to the accomplishment of God's evolutionary purpose. His evil will even be turned, by God's laws of karma, to good. He will be forced to evolve ultimately.

144

As I emerge from a trance of self-realization, the white sun sets in golden bars across the Thames. My body is seated in the half-Buddha posture on a grassy bank of the river. I find the solution of the problem which has weighed on my mind all day. I, hapless victim of a hard fate, I have communicated with myself! But now, I am conscious of the truth, for I have been lifted like a babe out of all anxiety for the future, all regret for the past. In the spiritual self, I feel a timeless life: I breathe the calm air of the Eternal. I feel safe and I could not worry even if I wanted to. To live in the true Self is to be released from all cares concerning what the morrow may bring. This is real *freedom*. Even if fate is all-powerful, even if an unpleasant fate be in store for me, yet, if I cannot change it, I can change myself. I can enter into my inner self and therein take refuge from my fate.

145

If perfect freedom of the will is impossible, at least that man is nearest to it who acts entirely from his innermost being, not from passional drive, emotional pressure, or physical necessity, who is guided by wisdom, not enslaved by the ego's desires or the animal's ignorance.

146

Those who have vaunted man over fate should remember his powerlessness over recent world events. Only with his attainment of life in the Overself will the solution be reversed; only with his achievement of power over himself will his history become more amenable to his will.

147

Jesus had a passion to urge every man to live up to his higher possibilities. The man who is living a lower level than his best is not performing his proper function in life. This attitude of Jesus was in direct contrast to the widespread fatalism of the Orientals.

148

What he wills in his highest moments is both a free act and a necessary act. In these moments the conflict vanishes, the paradox appears. In them alone the ego attains its fullest power yet falls also into complete powerlessness.

149

When troubles descend or desires are frustrated, it is easy to lose faith in the higher power, to doubt its very existence, or to question its goodness. This is because we want our own will to be done, even though God's will may be better for us in the end.

150

The peasant who plants corn does so only because he expects to profit by his work in the form of a harvest. He relies on Nature's law. He knows it is implacable, that if he will not sow, he will not be able to reap.

151

The Overself's foreknowing of the ego's line of action is not the same as the forcing of it. The limited element of human freedom remains intact, the divine element of grace still remains possible.

152

The infinite wisdom of the World-Mind is behind the world and rules its course, which is not left to the accidents of chance.

153

Although I have emphasized the belief in free will in my writings, I have done so only to refute the prevalent criticism that mystical philosophy inevitably leads to inertia and lethargy. However, from the standpoint that all existence—including our own—must ultimately conform to this plan, I am able to give only very limited room to free will. In this sense, I am more of a determinist than a libertarian—but please note that this should not be confused with the materialistic interpretation of determinism.

154

People are not so far apart in their thinking as sometimes appears. A man may think of himself as a spiritual determinist while maintaining a flexible, rather than a rigid form of determinism. Such flexibility must allow for the introduction of Grace, which, to the advanced mystic, is a very real thing. This idea, of course, might not yet find its place in the thinking of one who has made a purely intellectual analysis.

155

Thoughts come to a man without his trying to bring them on, without his willing them into existence: they are there as a part of his human conditioning. The same applies to feelings. Where then is his freedom of choice, and what then is the use of preaching to him that he should be good or aspirational? What is the use of teachings which lull him into the belief that he is free to create his own mental states, both good and evil, when moods, emotions, and ideas happen of themselves or come to him by themselves? Is it not better for him to understand his limitations and not deceive himself, to know what he can and cannot do and thus not fall into illusions about his spiritual progress or spiritual failure? Moreover, if all is happening by the will of the World-Mind and all is comprised in the World-Idea, he himself is really doing nothing, thinking nothing, for all is being accomplished irrespective of his ego. To understand this situation and to accept it and to free himself from the idea that *he* is thinking, *he* is feeling, and *he* is doing, is to free himself from the illusions of personal agency, doership, and egohood as being the ultimate truth about his own experiences.

156

The World-Idea will work itself out in any case, or as people say, Nature will take its course. The World-Idea has been operative through all past centuries, is operating now, and will operate through foreseeable time. Whatever man does, he cannot obliterate it nor alter it and whenever he thinks he is doing so he is merely carrying out unwittingly the World-Idea.

157

With reference to your second point, fate and free will, what I meant was that ordinarily man is subject to fate simultaneously with the fact that he is also operating his will. The two factors are ever present. But as the same fate was made by him in former lives, and he had the freedom to make it as he wished, ultimately there is freedom. You ask why "the dilemma is self-created and does not exist in Nature?" I plead guilty to having been deliberately obscure. I could not explain the problem without going at length into the esoteric philosophy, the study of which proves that where everything is ONE the individual will and fate fall out of consideration from the standpoint of the ONE, or Nature. The Sage is the man who has realized this oneness and hence for him such questions do not arise.

158

There are some actions a man does not for a moment include in his planning, yet when the time comes he does them. Why? Is he driven by a higher power? Is it in fulfilment of the World-Idea?

159

The truth is that we are both free and not free. The one is illusion because the hidden factors, the karma in the situation, shape its history. The other is actuality because knowing that, you demean yourself unnecessarily. The ego is surrounded by truth and goodness. Why not reach out and up to the Overself?

160

To claim that because he did not ask to be brought into the world, he is not responsible for himself or for his behaviour to parents is a short-sighted assertion. It is the consequence of ignoring or rejecting the idea (itself a part of the World-Idea) of reincarnation.

161

K.S. Guthrie, *Plotinus' Philosophy*: "His position on free will is almost exactly that of Kant. Virtue and the motion of the soul in the intelligible realm are free; but the soul's deeds in the world are part of the law of continuity. Plotinus has no taste for the crude predestination of fatalism, and like immoral doctrines. . . . The soul is, in respect to her three lowest faculties, which belong to the World Order, rigidly conditioned: yet in the higher self is as free as self-existence can make it; and the soul will therefore be free exactly according as to whether she identifies herself with her higher or lower faculties. Man is therefore a slave of fortune when his reason has identified itself with his sense world, but free when his reason has identified itself with his individual Nous, turning all things to intellect."

162

The power which operates the World-Idea is the same power which operates the processes of what the Asiatics call karma. The law of karma, or come-back of consequences, of causes and effects, is inseparable from the World-Idea. Behind the World-Idea is the World-Mind. Behind karma is God.

163

Are we mere figures in a dream and therefore deceiving ourselves, or are we mere puppets on a stage and therefore playing ourselves? If either of these be true then it would seem that the value of choosing right over wrong seems discredited and the freedom to choose good over evil becomes lost. If so, where is the need to carry out the moral precepts of religion and philosophy? Why submit to the disagreeable conditions which the Quest imposes upon us if the very end of the Quest is worth no more than its beginning? The answer is that these are half-truths which, taken alone, dangerously falsify the whole truth. The human being is not the victim of his own illusory living in a world of utter make-believe; he is ultimately and in his true selfhood a ray of the Divine Mind. It is his thoughts about himself that live in their own illusory world of make-believe, but he himself lives in a world of truth and reality.

Index for Part 1

Entries are listed by chapter number followed by "para" number. For example, 1.56 means chapter 1, para 56, and 1.104, 80 means chapter 1, paras 104 and 80. Chapter listings are separated by a semicolon. Please note also that, for the reader's convenience, the first number in the right-hand running heads throughout the text indicates chapter number.

Index for Part 2

Entries are listed by chapter number followed by "para" number. For example, 2.154 means chapter 2, para 54, and 1.49, 58, 67–68 means chapter 2, paras 49, 58, and 67–68. Chapter listings are separated by a semicolon. Please note also that, for the reader's convenience, the first number in the right-hand running heads throughout the text indicates chapter number.

The 28 Categories from the Notebooks

This outline of categories in *The Notebooks* is the most recent one Paul Brunton developed for sorting, ordering, and filing his written work. The listings he put after each title were not meant to be all-inclusive. They merely suggest something of the range of topics included in each category.

1 THE QUEST

  Its choice —Independent path —Organized groups — Self-development —Student/teacher

2 PRACTICES FOR THE QUEST

  Ant's long path —Work on oneself

3 RELAX AND RETREAT

  Intermittent pauses —Tension and pressures —Relax body, breath, and mind —Retreat centres —Solitude — Nature appreciation —Sunset contemplation

4 ELEMENTARY MEDITATION

  Place and conditions —Wandering thoughts —Practise concentrated attention —Meditative thinking — Visualized images —Mantrams —Symbols —Affirmations and suggestions

5 THE BODY

  Hygiene and cleansings —Food —Exercises and postures —Breathings —Sex: importance, influence, effects

6 EMOTIONS AND ETHICS

  Uplift character —Re-educate feelings —Discipline emotions — Purify passions —Refinement and courtesy —Avoid fanaticism

7 THE INTELLECT

  Nature —Services —Development —Semantic training — Science —Metaphysics —Abstract thinking

8 THE EGO

  What am I? —The I-thought —The psyche